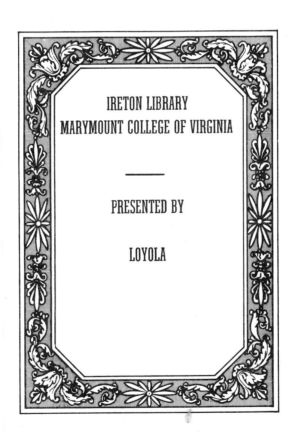

PARTICIPATION
IN
ORGANIZATIONAL CHANGE

Participation in Organizational Change

The TVA Experiment

Aaron J. Nurick

PRAEGER

PRAEGER SPECIAL STUDIES • PRAEGER SCIENTIFIC

New York • Philadelphia • Eastbourne, UK
Toronto • Hong Kong • Tokyo • Sydney

Library of Congress Cataloging in Publication Data

Nurick, Aaron J.
  Participation in organizational change.

  Bibliography: p.
  Includes index.
  1. Industrial management–United States–Employee
participation–Case studies. 2. Quality of work life–
United States–Case studies. 3. Tennessee Valley
Authority. I. Title.
HD5660.U5N87   1985   658.3'152   84-26652
ISBN 0-03-002749-7

Published in 1985 by Praeger Publishers
CBS Educational and Professional Publishing, a Division of CBS Inc.
521 Fifth Avenue, New York, NY 10175 USA

© 1985 by Praeger Publishers

56789 052 987654321

Printed in the United States of America on acid-free paper

INTERNATIONAL OFFICES

Orders from outside the United States should be sent to the appropriate address listed below. Orders from areas not listed below should be placed through CBS International Publishing, 383 Madison Ave., New York, NY 10175 USA

Australia, New Zealand
Holt Saunders, Pty, Ltd., 9 Waltham St., Artarmon, N.S.W. 2064, Sydney, Australia

Canada
Holt, Rinehart & Winston of Canada, 55 Horner Ave., Toronto, Ontario, Canada M8Z 4X6

Europe, the Middle East, & Africa
Holt Saunders, Ltd., 1 St. Anne's Road, Eastbourne, East Sussex, England BN21 3UN

Japan
Holt Saunders, Ltd., Ichibancho Central Building, 22-1 Ichibancho, 3rd Floor, Chiyodaku, Tokyo, Japan

Hong Kong, Southeast Asia
Holt Saunders Asia, Ltd., 10 Fl, Intercontinental Plaza, 94 Granville Road, Tsim Sha Tsui East, Kowloon, Hong Kong

Manuscript submissions should be sent to the Editorial Director, Praeger Publishers, 521 Fifth Avenue, New York, NY 10175 USA

TO DIANE

FOREWORD

Managers have long been concerned with the planning and conduct of organizational changes. Social and behavioral scientists began serious study and theory formulation during the 1930s, and this work has flowered during recent decades. During the 1960s, an ideological as well as theoretical impetus was provided by the human relations and sensitivity group movements and their associated research. In the 1970s, a broader base of interest emerged from public concerns about the prevailing quality of work life and from managerial recognition of the potential economic, competitive and survival value of organizations that are redesigned to cultivate optimal use of human resources. Organizational change has become a recognized arena for basic research, theoretical exploration, and professional practice.

Much of the accumulating knowledge in this field has come from case studies—that is, from intensive inquiries focused upon single organizations that are undergoing planned changes. The methods used range from historical reconstruction of events, to brief contemporary studies, to extended longtudinal studies that span a significant sequence of change events and their consequences. Only a few studies have attempted experimental designs, or coordinated any comparative studies of multiple organizations. True experiments, and studies of populations of organizations, are formidable in their scale, cost and time demands, but their potential power and efficiency suggests that they will be undertaken more frequently as funding and access to cooperating organizations allow.

The ideal case study of organizational change has not yet been done, and, in any case, many are needed to capture the generalized features associated with success and failure. Some case studies do display admirable features of conception, design and insightful interpretation. A case study, clearly, can be an effective vehicle for the researcher who desires to pursue his or her idiosyncratic ideas, often with a sharp focus upon certain limited aspects of the case, responsiveness to unanticipated opportunity, and interpretations unconstrained by established theory or prescribed concepts. An alternative use of case studies is to form a public pool of information about instances of organizational change, with the information planned to facilitate cross-case comparisons, multiple theoretical interpretations, and the application of meta-analytical procedures.

To serve these latter purposes the cases should have certain properties that are not commonly found, such as comprehensivenss in information coverage, inclusion of measures and observational categories from diverse theoretical schemas, direct measurements and observations over an appropriate long span of time, reference to many of the outcomes of consequence to individuals, organizations and and the public, inclusion in public reports of raw or partially analyzed data in forms that allow their use by others, and a sufficiently detailed account of the change actions and their consequences to invite competing and complementary interpretations of the results.

This book by Aaron Nurick is a contribution of the latter kind. It describes a serious and extended effort to improve further the quality of work life and the performance within an engineering design division of the Tennessee Valley Authority. Mr. Nurick, then associated with the University of Tennessee, joined a small team from the Institute for Social Research to observe, record and measure the actions taken by this organization and to trace their consequences. In this instance, the action program was undertaken jointly by the management and the two unions at the site. Their efforts were observed for about six years. They consented to this independent and public report in the expectation that their experiences, some rewarding and others disappointing, might be helpful to others who seek the same ends through organizational change programs.

This case report is not an isolated one. It is a part of a set, eight in number, from similar inquiries conducted in diverse organizations that have undertaken similar change programs with similar methods for research and reporting. A report summarizing and comparing these eight cases is in preparation.

Stanley E. Seashore
Program Director, Emeritus
Institute for Social Research
Ann Arbor, Michigan

ACKNOWLEDGMENTS

The TVA quality of work life experiment has been a significant part of my professional life for almost nine years. I joined the project in early 1976 as an eager graduate student seeking research experience and dissertation data in an area that I considered important and exciting. I received a plethora of both. Though some of the initial grandeur has mellowed as have I since those early days, I retain my enthusiasm for this project.

Throughout my involvement with the Quality of Work Program and the writing of this book, I have been endowed by the talents of many special people who have contributed immeasurably to this final product. First and foremost, I want to thank Stanley E. Seashore for encouraging me to write this book. He has been a source of inspiration for many years through his contributions to social science, and his grace, dignity, and eloquence as a human being. I also thank Edward E. Lawler for his continued encouragement and support. I extend my admiration and gratitude to all employees and managers at TVA who gave their time and energy to the project and to our measurement effort.

I am grateful to Barry Macy, who as Study Director was responsible for the entire measurement program at TVA. He supervised all of my work, contributed ideas, and was a considerable source of guidance all through my association with the Institute for Social Research. I will always be indebted to Michael E. Gordon, my friend and mentor at the University of Tennessee, who guided me through my dissertation and made my doctoral work a profound learning experience.

More recently, my colleagues and friends at Bentley College have contributed greatly to the completion of this endeavor with their ideas and words of support. I particularly want to express my personal gratitude to Anthony F. Buono, Edward S. Marshall, Judith B. Kamm, Dharmendra T. Verma, and D. Richard Harmer for all of their help and friendship. I thank Dean John Burns for facilitating the time necessary to carry out this effort. I also wish to honor the memory of Arthur H. Walker who greatly enriched my life in an all too brief span of time.

Mary Trimble, word processor supreme, and Ellen Kilcoyne, my work study assistant, worked diligently on the manuscript and tables and made the preparation of the book so much easier. Ruth

Horwitz and her media staff did an excellent job on the artwork. I thank the editors at Praeger for their help in putting the book in final form.

Finally, a work of this nature cannot be done without the emotional support of one's immediate family. I thank my mother for her encouragement on this and all other accomplishments. I am most deeply thankful to (and for) Diane Austin, my wife, partner, collaborator, friend and heart. Her humor, humanity, intelligence, and loveliness speak for themselves.

Boston, Massachusetts
November 1984

CONTENTS

PART III
OUTCOMES

LIST OF TABLES AND FIGURES

1 QUALITY OF WORK LIFE IN PERSPECTIVE

It is abundantly clear that the quality of work life has been a major concern during the past decade. The number of scholarly and popular articles relating to the concept continues to grow, and several centers at the regional, national, and international level have been established to study quality of work life issues and develop experimental projects. Several major experiments have been conducted (e.g., Goodman 1979; Guest 1979; Beer 1979), and most major corporations have some identifiable "quality of work life" program. Some programs, such as those at the General Foods Topeka plant, General Motors' Tarrytown assembly plant, and an automotive mirror company in Bolivar, Tennessee have received extensive media attention.

This book provides an assessment of a three-year organizational change experiment that occurred in one division of the Tennessee Valley Authority. The project was one in a series of experimental sites known collectively as the Michigan Quality of Work Program launched in 1972 by the American Center of Quality of Work Life in affiliation with the Institute for Social Research, University of Michigan. The projects were designed as demonstration experiments, initially funded by the Ford Foundation and the U.S. Department of Commerce, to stimulate thought and action toward system-wide improvements in organizations based on a collaborative strategy between management and employees (Seashore 1983). The Institute for Social Research (ISR) was responsible for a program of assessment of each experiment, applying a broad array of measurement techniques to disseminate knowledge throughout the academic, business, and labor communities about organizational change and the quality of work life.

TVA provided an ideal site for a quality of work life experiment. The organization was born as a grand social experiment, part of

Franklin Roosevelt's New Deal, to develop a region devastated by the Great Depression. As the largest energy producer in the United States, TVA was highly visible during a time of increased concern about the nation's energy needs. TVA was well steeped in democratic ideals of citizen participation, a theme that echoed throughout the entire quality of work life movement. The division within TVA chosen as the experimental site was almost exclusively a white collar organization. Since much of the focus of organizational change strategies had been in traditional blue-collar work sites, the TVA project was an opportunity to explore work improvement techniques in the service sector of the work force. Moreover, TVA since its inception has been a subject of fascination for social scientists as a complex public institution, a symbol of democratic ideals that have more or less persisted over fifty years, and a history replete with ironies and paradoxes as it has carried out its vast mission (Neuse 1983). The TVA quality of work life experiment adds a significant chapter to the legacy.

THE MEANING OF QUALITY OF WORK LIFE

While the amount of activity under the QWL banner is increasing, it remains unclear as to what is meant by the term "quality of work life" (QWL). A recent special report in Business Week (May 11, 1981) used the term to apply to new forms of industrial relations in which cooperation between unions and management is the central theme. More often, QWL is invoked as a euphemism for worker participation, industrial democracy in the European tradition, work redesign, or a myriad of other organizational change techniques. Lawler (1982) provided an internal-external dichotomy for defining QWL. A high QWL is exemplified by either the prevalence of certain organizational conditions and practices or by the impact that such conditions have upon the well-being of individuals. The latter internal definition was preferred by Lawler, although "well-being" is open to a variety of interpretations. Nadler and Lawler (1983) traced the evolution of the term QWL, first as a variable, then as an approach to change, as specific methods, and finally as a movement with ideological underpinnings. Their working definition included two major themes: an emphasis on the impact of work on the individual and organizational effectiveness, and participation in problem solving and decision making. QWL, in their view, represents a way of thinking about these issues. It is unclear from the literature whether or not quality of work life should include productivity or if the two concepts are conceptually linked (Lawler and Ledford 1982).

During the past two decades the lexicon of organizational change has grown to include a host of ambiguous terms such as organization development, management by objectives, and job enrichment. Academicians and practitioners alike tend to refer to the terms as if there are universally accepted definitions accompanied by precise methods for implementation. To attempt to sort out the hairline differences among the many terms is to wander aimlessly through the "semantic wilderness" identified and explored by Mills (1975, p. 128). As he suggests, we are left with a broad but nameless field of inquiry. It is the premise of this study that the "quality of work life" cannot be defined with anything other than the most general of terms, and, therefore, is quite meaningless when viewed as a unitary concept. It is better understood as an interacting set of issues and processes directed at improving life at work. The various meanings attached to the concept seem to cluster within four distinct, yet related domains. In essence, quality of work life has been viewed as:

1. a philosophy with underlying values and assumptions;
2. a set of structures and methods for organizational change;
3. a set of human processes operating as a function of planned change; and
4. a set of outcomes that can be monitored and assessed.

Quality of Work Life as a Philosophy

The quality of work life has been viewed as a "movement" (Guest 1979; Nadler and Lawler 1983) which grew out of the era of general questioning and changing of cultural values of the 1960s. Books such as Toffler's Future Shock (1970) posited that work in its traditional form was causing widespread worker alienation, the so-called "blue collar blues" and "white collar woes." A study conducted by the Department of Health, Education, and Welfare titled Work in America (1973) seemed to support these contentions. Senate hearings and public debate suggested a crisis of national proportions. The quality of work life theme began to be espoused at national conferences by both management and union officials. Guest (1979) credits Irving Bluestone, a vice-president for the United Auto Workers, for initiating the quality of work life movement in a 1972 speech. The subsequent agreement between GM and the UAW in 1973 leading to the Tarrytown experiment is considered to be the cornerstone of the quality of work life ideology.

During the same time period organizational change programs were becoming more eclectic and complex, and the concept of organizational change was expanded to include whole systems over a longer time frame. Underlying many change efforts was a general value system based on the premise of collaboration. Trist (1977) defined collaboration as emergent social processes adaptive to the increasingly turbulent environments of the new postindustrial order. Crucial to this value system was the acceptance of interdependence and a willingness to negotiate rather than coerce. In essence, "win-win" replaces "win-lose" in management-worker relations. Trist's thinking was elaborated by Appley and Winder (1977) who extended the definition of collaboration to include mutual aspirations, interactions based on justice and fairness, a consciousness of one's motives, and caring and commitment in relation to others.

This basic philosophy had been espoused much earlier by Burns and Stalker (1961) as an "organic" management system and generally paralleled the Human Relations School of Organization Theory which included McGregor's (1960) Theory Y, Argyris' (1957) fusion of individual and organization, and Likert's (1967) System 4. The philosophy was further crystallized by Herrick and Maccoby (1975), forming the basis of the Work Improvement Program. These Harvard-based QWL projects were designed to create a "spirit of mutuality" between management and workers based on the principles of security, equity, individuation, and democracy. The Bolivar project, which eventually became part of the Michigan Program, was based on this conceptual foundation (Duckles and Duckles 1977).

In actual practice, such pure ideology often results in different interpretations by managers and union officials. Seashore (1982) recently observed that QWL represents a rather "mixed bag of purposes." There are any number of implicit assumptions that can underlie experimental organizational change programs. Some proponents of QWL believe work should be improved in order to increase intrinsic rewards, i.e., to make work more enjoyable and to reduce the unhealthy effects of stress. Others are motivated by more financial interests such as increased efficiency and productivity, based on the unproven assumption that satisfied workers are more productive. In some cases QWL programs are undertaken either to promote or undermine a more far-reaching political ideology (e.g., industrial democracy or power equalization) that may have little to do with the specific problems of a given workplace. Clearly, not all of these objectives are compatible and the implicit purposes behind improving the workplace may conflict with external appearances. For example, some early QWL efforts were designed either to undermine or avoid unions rather than engage in a collaborative enterprise.

In assessing a change program, it is useful to begin by examining the philosophy implied by the actions undertaken. QWL programs often revolve around a dominant individual who personifies and articulates the underlying assumptions that otherwise remain hidden, such as Sidney Harman at Bolivar and Irving Bluestone at Tarrytown. It seems that programs that gain more widespread support have a central philosophy that is well disseminated by key individuals and accepted by those to be affected by changes.

QWL as Structures and Methods

The assumptions underlying organizational change are manifested by formal structures and interventions representing a unique "program." The collaborative philosophy is usually implemented by a formal committee structure providing representation for employees (or union) and management. The primary task of such a committee is to develop and generally oversee the change program. Although joint committees are certainly not a new device (the steel industry has used them for many years), they took on a new prominence during the QWL era of the 1970s.

The Michigan QWL program used a "multi-tier" committee structure (Drexler and Lawler 1977). A hierarchy of committees is established at each site which parallels the organizational layers of both management and unions. A top level of advisors forms a core committee that manages the program. Depending on the type of organization, several other joint committees are formed at the plant level and sometimes at the departmental or workplace level. Additionally, special task forces may be created to deal with more specific issues. The committees proceed formally with regular meetings and agendas. In most cases, open elections are held to form the committees. Variations of this structure were employed at each experimental site in the QWL program.

The creation of such an elaborate mechanism for improving the quality of work life is designed to confirm that any program will be jointly sponsored and the "client" for change will be a collaborating body rather than management or the union. The committees provide equal representation from management and employees and ensure that any benefits of the program will be shared. The committees usually assume the responsibility for hiring external consultants, setting program goals, and making arrangements to evaluate the results of any interventions.

Intervention strategies in QWL programs cover a broad array of areas such as pay, job design, physical environment, training programs, organizational structure, and many others. Most often the interventions are not of pure form, and sorting out the various changes at a QWL site can be an arduous and sometimes fruitless task. It seems that in most programs of this nature the emphasis is more on how change occurs rather than which particular techniques are applied. The most effective programs employ an integrated mix of methods aimed at mutually established objectives. The changes emanate from within the organization, are more in line with workers' needs, and are less likely to be biased toward the whim of the consultants.

According to Lawler and Ledford (1982) the success of QWL committees lies in the original design. Determining the appropriate number of committees, their location, size and constituency are all critical issues in the eventual functioning of these structures. With multilevel committees, it is also important to provide adequate communication channels among the layers and to extend the lines of communication to the general organizational constituency. This prevents the formal structures from becoming insulated and, thereby, overly concerned with their own preservation as an elite corps. It is also important at the outset to stipulate whether a joint committee has the power to implement changes on its own or if it serves only as a recommending body to management. Clarification of these and other issues requires a considerable amount of time, but the benefits of the slow and delicate initial period can pay off in the form of fewer mistakes. According to Lawler and Ledford (1982) the early mistakes are most often irreversible, leading to the eventual downfall of a project.

QWL as a Process

The formal structures described above result in emergent human processes that operate throughout the change effort. For example, joint committees are designed to promote employee participation in change, a concept that was at the core of the interventions at TVA. The assumption underlying the participation hypothesis is that the more employees become involved, the greater their feelings of ownership of the changes, resulting in reduced resistance to changes and their consequences, and ultimately, positive outcomes in the form of increased motivation, improved attitudes, and the possibility of greater productivity (Coch and French 1948; Marrow, Bowers, and Seashore 1967).

While setting up a hierarchy of collaborative committees provides the opportunity for employees to participate, there is no guarantee that the committees will actually function in a participatory manner. In organizational cultures characterized by top-down decision making, it is doubtful that employees know how to effectively participate or understand where a participatory program fits into the existing system. Well-intentioned organizations often strive to set up the formal structures for participation without considering the crucial interpersonal processes that must operate within them. They are left with a rather fragile "house of cards" that either tumbles down or slowly deteriorates.

The interpersonal aspect of QWL projects is complex and difficult to study objectively. Yet, some of the most important elements of the change process are interpersonal in nature. Since much of the QWL process involves employee participation via committees, the members of such committees are subject to very complex interpersonal, group and intergroup dynamics. The issues of influence, power, conformity, cohesiveness, and decision making become magnified. Individuals may suffer from role conflict when serving the needs of both a QWL committee and their own organizational constituency. Interpersonal and intergroup conflict can arise when a committee develops programs that may be perceived to benefit a particular person or department at the expense of another. The QWL committee may develop a sense of detachment and common purpose which can lead to the suppression of conflicting ideas resulting in ineffective decisions or no decisions at all.

Ultimately, improving the quality of work life results in human processes that can only be facilitated by the formal structures. The interpersonal component of participation has often been neglected or assumed away by both consultants and researchers. Therefore, it is imperative for the assessors of such programs to document the emergent phenomena occurring as a function of the formal change activities. It is at this level that a true understanding of the effects of the organizational change process begins.

QWL as Outcomes

The quality of work life concept is perhaps most commonly perceived as a set of outcomes to be measured as variables (Nadler and Lawler 1983). One may collect data on employee attitudes, attendance, turnover, accidents, and so forth and use these as indicators of the quality of work life within a particular organization. The collection of data, usually in the form of surveys and personnel records, is often a first step in implementing a change program. The information can be used to diagnose problems and provide an agenda for working committees. Survey feedback can be a very powerful intervention in and of itself (Bowditch and Buono 1982).

Since there is little agreement on the meaning of QWL, identifying the important variables to be measured presents a problem. The perennial criterion problem that has always plagued organizational research is nowhere more evident. According to Lawler (1980), it is best to consider QWL projects as "adaptive" experiments. The salience of measures may change depending on the direction the experiment takes. Evaluation becomes more difficult, but it is more likely to capture the significance of events as they occur. It also allows for any unintended consequences of an experimental program. It appears to be most useful to measure as many aspects of an organization as possible since change rarely is limited to single issues in specified areas. Such a broad approach was employed with considerable success by the Institute for Social Research in assessing the series of organizational change projects. The assessment was standardized in order to compare across different sites, yet flexible enough to include unique characteristics of the organizations measured. Significant components of the measurement package were designed especially to fit the nature of interventions that were occurring within each setting (Seashore 1983).

Adaptive experimentation has had a developmental impact on organizational assessment in several ways. The concern with improving QWL has increased the desire to conduct experiments within live organizations. The rise in the number of field studies has encouraged researchers to use more quasi-experimental designs such as the nonequivalent control group design (Campbell and Stanley 1966). This type of experimentation comes closer to studying actual organizational phenomena and reduces the sterility often found in laboratory studies. The use of longitudinal designs requires the assessors to develop a greater rapport with the organization and potentially provides a richer source of data. The assessors are more likely to know why particular measures changed over time because of a greater awareness of how the changes evolved.

This heightened relationship with the organization, however, raises important ethical issues, especially in the delineation of proper roles for the researchers, participants, and stakeholders (Mirvis and Seashore 1979). The issues of voluntary consent, confidentiality, and privacy are magnified in field research. Researchers often find themselves occupying conflicting roles when trying to meet expectations of the parties involved in a planned change program. Mirvis and Seashore (1979) suggest defining and clarifying the researchers' role prior to experimentation.

As a positive side benefit, field experiments have served as a catalyst to increase the level of sophistication in the measurement and methodology used in organizational assessment. Major breakthroughs in this area have taken the form of identifying different kinds of change (Golembiewski, Billingsley, and Yeager 1976) and developing more accurate statistical methods for measuring changes occurring over time in specified variables (Bedeian, Armenakis, and Gibson 1980). There has also been a revival of applying qualitative field methods to change projects (Van Maanen 1979). The emergent processes are difficult to document quantifiably and require careful observation over time. A phenomenological approach employing elaborate case histories can provide more accurate depictions of the evolution of change in addition to surveys, particularly when studying interpersonal processes and organizational culture. The use of such complementary methods has increased our knowledge of the richness not only of organizational change, but also of organizational life in general.

A FRAMEWORK FOR EXAMINING THE TVA EXPERIMENT

The foregoing discussion has been an attempt to sort out the complex issues that arise when examining the quality of work life. If we are serious in our intentions to improve life in U.S. workplaces, a more thorough understanding of organizational change is necessary. The four domains specified and discussed above provide a useful point of departure. Any effort to initiate or examine a QWL program should consider all four domains. However, this typology still represents a static approach to organizational change issues.

The development of a comprehensive organizational change program actually results in the creation of a new organizational subsystem in which the four QWL domains interact. Figure 1.1 is a depiction of these dynamic interdependencies. The philosophy and implied assumptions about an ideal work life are derived from the larger organization and environment, and provide the inputs to the change system. These values are then formalized as a program of action consisting of new organizational structures and interventions (i.e., joint-committees, changes in jobs, pay systems, work schedules). From the philosophy

FIGURE 1.1. QWL as a Change System

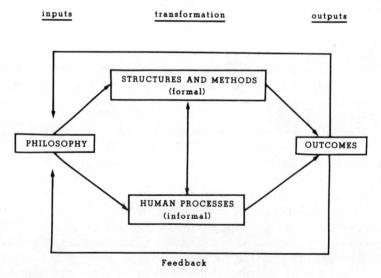

and structures, an informal system emerges characterized by human processes such as interpersonal interactions, mutual influence, and group dynamics. Organizational outcomes such as attitudes and effectiveness, however measured, logically follow in the sequence, impact the larger organization, and provide feedback which can affect the philosophy, structures and processes in the future.

PLAN OF THE BOOK

This study assesses the TVA project as a participatory change experiment. The major research objective is to present a comprehensive and integrated analysis that explores the philosophy, structures, processes, and outcomes of the experiment. The first part of the book describes the organizations and unions that participated in the study. Chapter 2 presents a brief history of the Tennessee Valley Authority and describes the organization, structure, and employees of both the experimental and comparison sites for the study. The unions involved in the experiment and the historical development of the cooperative labor-management relationship in TVA are described in Chapter 3. The two chapters provide the foundation and context for the experiment with particular emphasis on the underlying democratic ideology that pervaded the organization.

The history of the experiment itself is presented in Part II, focusing on the structures and methods of the change program. Chapter 4 is a rather straightforward historical account of the initial period of the project, including the decision to participate in the experiment, start-up activities, the establishment of the Quality of Work Committee, the selection of external consultants, and the events of the first 18 months of the experiment. In Chapter 5 the events of the second period of experimentation are recounted, featuring the implementation of new programs and the changes occurring in the wake of the departure of the external consultants. The final phase of the experiment is documented in Chapter 6, a period that culminated in the fusion of the experimental program into the permanent cooperative structure of the division and TVA.

Part III provides the assessment of the experiment, beginning with design issues in Chapter 7. The Michigan assessment model is explained and adapted to the TVA site. The analytical models, hypotheses, and variables are described in this chapter along with the natural constraints imposed by a field study of this magnitude. The quantitative results, comparisons of the experimental and comparison sites, the particular effects of participation in change, and reactions from employees and managers appear in Chapter 8. The ninth chapter explores qualitative results, delving into process issues with particular emphasis on the power and politics of the program. The interpretations of events stem from the analysis of observation and interview data. A case study of the Quality of Work Committee is presented as an analytical tool. The results are summarized and explored more fully in Chapter 10. Here the learnings and implications of participatory organizational change are explored. Participation is seen as a series of paradoxical issues which have implications for both research and practice. An assessment of current thinking about the quality of work life and future trends is included in this final chapter.

A NOTE ON THE APPROACH

Throughout this study, there is the recurring theme of the interweaving of structure and process, the blending of rational models, and intuitive interpretations of events. Empirical methods are employed to gain knowledge about what happened as a result of the various interventions, i.e., which measured variables changed over time. Concurrently, qualitative methods are used to discover the underlying meaning of the events—the whys of the experiment. The purpose here is to capture themes that make up the political fabric of the program. While the quantitative results shed light on the amounts of change in influence patterns and individual attitudes, the process analysis focuses on the power issues that arose and the network of relationships occurring within the formal structures of the experiment. Both forms of analysis are complementary and, when viewed together, provide a more meaningful interpretation of the multitude of events constituting the TVA experiment.

PART ONE
THE SETTING

The following two chapters set the stage for the TVA Quality of Work Experiment by presenting an overview of the organizational setting of the project and the institutions that were involved.

The experiment occurred within a unique organization—a publicly-owned utility that over the course of forty years had become one of the major influences in the entire southeastern region of the United States. Chapter 2 describes the history, organization and characteristics of TVA along with sketches of the two divisions that were the focal points of the experiment. The third chapter provides the background of union management relations in TVA, including the formation of the structure for collaboration that foreshadowed the Quality of Work Program. The two unions participating in the experiment are also described.

2 THE ORGANIZATION

At the time of the Quality of Work Life Project, the Tennessee Valley Authority was the largest power generating utility in the free world, employing over 24,000 people. It continues to be one of the most significant sources of energy production in the United States, producing and transmitting electric power to seven southeastern states through its combination of hydroelectric, fossil fuel, and nuclear generating plants. This chapter provides the context for the experiment by tracing the historical development of TVA, examining its structure, and presenting a description and demographic profile of the experimental and comparison divisions involved in the Quality of Work Life project.

A BRIEF HISTORY OF TVA

The Tennessee Valley Authority was established by an act of Congress signed by President Franklin D. Roosevelt on May 18, 1933 as an independent, corporate agency of the federal government. The original incorporators were Arthur E. Morgan, an engineer and president of Antioch College who was appointed as the first Chairman of the Board; Harcourt A. Morgan, President of the University of Tennessee; and David E. Lilienthal, a lawyer and member of the Public Service Commission of Wisconsin (Owen 1973). This "great experiment" culminated nearly a century of thought and development concerning the efficient use and conservation of the abundant natural resources of the Tennessee Valley region. Since the first Congressional appropriation for improvement of the Tennessee River in 1852, various government agencies had attempted separate development programs

15

with the aim of improving the river for navigation. Examples of such efforts include Hales Bar Dam, completed by a private power company in 1913 with navigation locks provided by the federal government, and Wilson Dam, completed in 1925 by the Army Corps of Engineers. However, these early navigational improvements had only begun to tap the river's potential for electric power, and by the time TVA was initiated, had yet to provide any means for flood control.

Although the technical rationale for further development of the Tennessee River basin seemed quite well enunciated by the early 1930s, there were yet more basic and far-reaching considerations involved in developing the area. In 1933 the average income of the region was less than half the national average. The primarily agrarian economy had begun to erode as machines reduced the need for hand labor on the farm. There was a dire need for industrial growth to provide jobs and spur the economy of an area stricken by the Depression. The rich natural resources of the river basin provided a sound base for raising the standard of living. Thus, TVA was launched as the first comprehensive and unified federal program to develop resources and provide jobs for people desperately in need of economic relief.

The early years of TVA were marked by the continued harnessing of the Tennessee River, efforts to restore the soil, and the proliferation of electric power throughout the Tennessee Valley. The 1940s brought a shift in direction as the Authority applied its resource development expertise to support the national defense. This was done by providing crucial electrical power to industries in the valley. By 1942, TVA was in the process of constructing 12 new dams as well as a steam plant, and employment reached an all time high of 42,000. It was during this wartime era when power production of the Authority burgeoned. In 1939, TVA had produced less than 2 billion kilowatt hours of electricity. By fiscal year 1945, power generation approached 12 billion kilowatt hours. In addition, the wartime construction had not only expanded power production capability, but also had furthered the completion of the navigation and flood control facilities of TVA.

The 1950s witnessed the proliferation of low cost electricity and the movement into river transportation, flood control, agriculture, and forestry. By the end of the 1960s the Tennessee Valley region had undergone a major shift away from an employment pattern dominated by agriculture, as the percentage of manufacturing workers in the region was now larger than the national average. Per capita personal income had grown to 70 percent of the national level bringing into reality some of the ideals of TVA's founders. Emphasis at this time was placed more on local needs through a program known as Tributary Area Development. There was also an increased concentration on such areas as recreation and water quality. Throughout this expansion, demand for electricity continued to increase at an exponential rate.

TVA began construction of the world's largest thermal nuclear plant in Brown's Ferry, Alabama in 1967 to meet this continuing demand for electrical power. Coupled with the drive to increase power production through nuclear and coal facilities was a rigorous program to protect the environment. Research was begun on such areas as air and water pollution, reclamation of strip mines, and disposal of solid waste. In 1973-74 TVA budgeted $170 million for pollution control facilities, research, and monitoring.

The evolution of TVA over a half century demonstrates an integrated program of resource development. In addition to its primary function as an energy producer, TVA has greatly influenced the economic and social life of a region through flood control, navigation, as well as agricultural and industrial development.

TVA AS AN ORGANIZATION

Although TVA is a corporate agency of the federal government, it is not part of any federal executive department and, therefore, operates autonomously much like any private corporation. The powers of the corporation reside in a three-member Board of Directors. Members of the board are appointed by the President of the United States, with Senate approval, to serve nine-year overlapping terms. One member of the Board is designated by the President as Chairman. The Board appoints the General Manager who serves as TVA's principal administrative officer.

The organization of the various offices and divisions in TVA as they existed in 1974 is depicted in Figure 2.1. It is clear that in its design TVA fit the pattern of a decentralized[1] bureaucracy with a well defined division of labor and hierarchical chain of command. The major offices were subdivided into divisions that were further divided into branches and sections. Each division was headed by a director who reported to the manager of the larger office. Although there were some variations, this pattern of organization was quite consistent throughout the Authority and, according to Owen (1973), had changed very little since its original design in 1938.

The functioning of TVA as a government-established, independently operated organization has been the subject of considerable research (Pritchett 1943; Selznick 1949; Lilenthal 1953; Owen 1973).

---

[1]Lilienthal's (1953) concept of decentralization stipulated that administration of the Authority would be enacted in the field and not by "remote control" from Washington (p. 148).

FIGURE 2.1. Organization of the Tennessee Valley Authority*

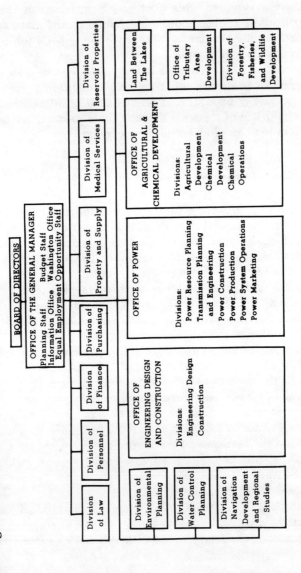

*As of 1974.

18

The Authority has been heralded as a prime contributor to the concept of democratic planning. David Lilienthal, one of TVA's founders and an articulate proponent of the democratic ideals underlying the Authority's operation, stated the raison d'être of TVA as follows:

> to accept an obligation to harmonize the private interest in earning a return from natural resources, with the dominant public interest in their unified and fruitful development. The method—and this is the distinctive part of the experiment—is to try to bring to bear at the grass roots the skills of public experts and administrators not for negative regulation but to make affirmative action in the public interest both feasible and appealing to private industry (Lilienthal 1953, p. 109).

Through its "grass roots" administration, TVA was characterized by its close relationship to local institutions. The essence of the grass roots philosophy of administration was a unified working partnership composed of TVA, local communities, voluntary private organizations, as well as state and federal agencies, with the primary concern of developing the region's resources. This concept of management grew out of a general feeling that an imposed federal program would alienate the people of the area and accomplish very little.

Selznick (1949) cited the uniqueness of TVA not only as a government-owned power producer but as an entity having some responsibility for developing the resources of an entire region. His intention was to examine the grass roots method of carrying out responsibilities with attention given to the problems involved in the organization adjusting itself to the local centers of interest and power.

Selznick stated his overriding hypothesis as follows:

> . . . the Authority's grass roots policy as doctrine and as action must be understood as related to the need of the organization to come to terms with certain local and national interests; and that in actual practice this procedure resulted in commitments which had restrictive consequences for the policy and behavior of the Authority itself. (p. 12)

The concept underlying this hypothesis was defined by Selznick as cooptation or "the process of absorbing new elements into the leadership or policy-determining structure of an organization as a means of averting threats to its stability and existence" (p. 13). Cooptation was conceived of as a process by which power, the burdens of power, or both, are shared.

Data for Selznick's research were obtained primarily from TVA files and through interviews with key organizational members. Since the investigator's reliance on interviews, company documents, and gossip channels ran the risk of factual error, he made an effort to minimize these through various consistency checks.

Although the primary outcome of the research was a set of sociological directives that provided a frame of reference for organization theory, especially the study of informal organizational structures, Selznick made some interesting conclusions concerning the administrative process of TVA during the early 1940s.

1. The grass roots concept was essentially a "protective ideology" (p. 262). The adoption of the grass roots doctrine enabled TVA to become a champion of local institutions and at the same time justify its managerial autonomy within the federal system. However, in so doing, TVA created conflicts with other federal governmental branches such as the Department of Agriculture and the Department of the Interior.
2. Potential sources of local power in the Valley were in some cases covertly absorbed into the policy-determining structure of the Authority. This informal cooptation process was exemplified by the agricultural program.

Selznick demonstrated through his analysis the problems and forces that impinged upon the democratic process even to the point of altering it. He concluded that TVA was a "morally strong and fundamentally honest" organization that had quite effectively achieved some of its major goals "including the mobilization of a staff of very high quality" (p. 265). The fact that covert cooptation was evident in such a paragon of democratic administration made Selznick's findings even more noteworthy in the study of organizations.

THE EXPERIMENTAL SITE

The site chosen for the experiment in TVA was the Division of Transmission and Engineering. At the start of the project in 1974, Transmission Planning and Engineering (TPE), located in Chattanooga, Tennessee was one of 27 divisions of TVA. Functionally situated in the larger Office of Power (see Figure 2.2), TPE had as its mission the planning and designing of TVA's extensive transmission and communication systems which were required to produce and deliver electric power to consumers. This vast network consisted of 17,000 miles of transmission lines and 640 substations including interconnections with neighboring power systems. Although TPE operated primarily as

FIGURE 2.2. Office of Power

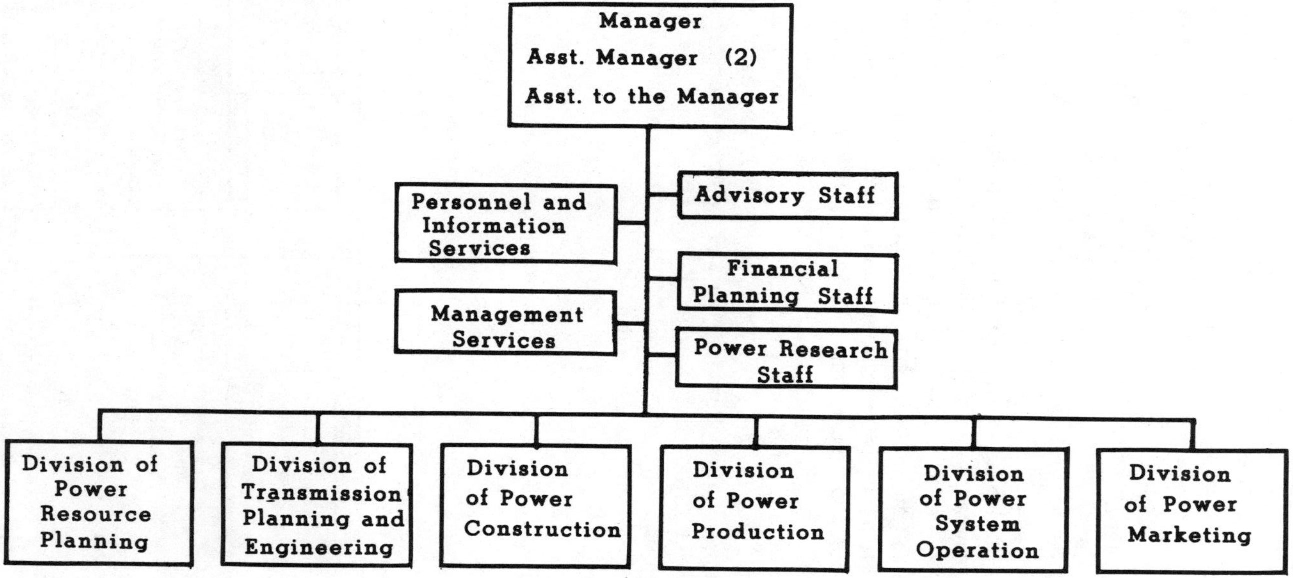

Manager
Asst. Manager (2)
Asst. to the Manager

Advisory Staff

Financial Planning Staff

Power Research Staff

Personnel and Information Services

Management Services

Division of Power Resource Planning

Division of Transmission Planning and Engineering

Division of Power Construction

Division of Power Production

Division of Power System Operation

Division of Power Marketing

an engineering division, it also was responsible for forecasting future
transmission needs a decade or more in advance, making much of the
work accomplished in the division uncertain. There was often a ten-
year lag between inception of a design in TPE and its eventual construction by another division in TVA. Despite a considerable element
of uncertainty in TPE's function, the work itself and the methods and
structure employed in the division were remarkably stable. In fact,
many of the same engineering practices had remained unchanged for
over a decade. This combination of interdependence, uncertainty, and
stability within TPE made it an ideal site for a quality of work life
project. Obviously, any gain in effectiveness in TPE could have potential repercussions elsewhere in TVA over the long term.

At the start of the QWL project in 1974 the division consisted
of about 380 employees: approximately 40 management and supervisory
personnel, about 150 engineers and similar professional staff, 150
technical support personnel, and about 40 clerical and administrative
personnel. Functionally, TPE was arranged in a rather straightforward hierarchy with four branches: Transmission System Planning,
Electrical Engineering and Design, Civil Engineering and Design,
and Communication Engineering and Design. Each branch was headed
by a Branch Chief reporting to the Director (see Figure 2.3). A description of each major unit of TPE at the beginning of the project
(1974-75) appears in Appendix A.

FIGURE 2.3. Division of Transmission Planning and Engineering

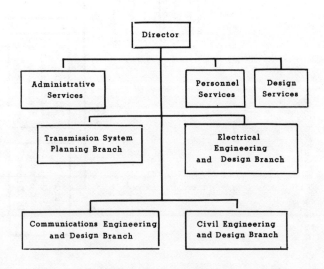

The Employees of TPE

Appendix B provides demographic characteristics of TPE employees (N = 382) at the beginning of the experiment. Of the 382 employees in the TPE division responding to the initial survey by ISR, the majority were male (77%). About three-quarters of the sample population (74%) were married. There was a reasonably broad age distribution in the division, however, the heaviest concentrations were in the 26-30 (18%) and 46-55 (24.1%) age brackets. About one-third of the sample (33.2%) were between the ages of 26 and 35. About 6% of the sample were older than 56 years. A majority of TPE employees (61.3%) had either attended or graduated from college. About 4% had received graduate degrees. The proportion of minority employees in the division was small, including 4.5% Black, 0.5% Oriental, and 0.5% American Indian. Most TPE employees (78%) were the primary income earners of their household and almost half of the sample had worked for TVA 11 years or more.

The Branch breakdown of TPE employees was as follows: Transmission System Planning (13.4%), Electrical Engineering and Design (25.9%), Civil Engineering and Design (27.2%), Communication Engineering and Design (13.4%) and Director's Office (11.5%).[2]

Growth of TPE

Table 2.1 represents the growth pattern of the TPE Division up until the beginning of the experiment, indicated by total yearly manpower statistics and total yearly production expenditures for the four engineering branches. As can be seen from the table, average yearly employment remained relatively stable with a slight drop-off during the last several years prior to the experiment in 1974. The rising production expenditures reflected increasing costs of facilities and cost of living allowances. The energy "crunch" of 1973 and the subsequent increased power rates resulted in a decrease in employees in TPE that was being held constant in 1974. Productivity remained relatively stable during this period. Average yearly employment in TPE for 1975 was 384 employees. The total 1975 expenditure for production was $7.978 million.

---

[2]Data were obtained from employees responding to a baseline questionnaire administered by ISR in September 1974 to all division employees.

TABLE 2.1. Growth of TPE

Average Yearly Employment		Dollar Value of Production (millions)[a]	
1967	383	1967	$4.394
1968	371	1968	4.523
1969	366	1969	5.760
1970	374	1970	5.444
1971	383	1971	5.895
1972	399	1972	6.474
1973	396	1973	7.071
1974	387	1974	7.414
1975	384	1975	7.978

[a]Costs directly charged to immediate projects. This measure does not include costs charged to long-range projects, which usually ran about one half million dollars per year. Costs also reflected cost of living increases which ranged from 4-1/2—8% yearly.

THE COMPARISON SITE

As a field experiment, the TVA quality of work life project required an organization by which to compare any changes occurring over time in the experimental site. Such a site was to be highly similar to the experimental unit, preferably in the same organization and region, and performing comparable tasks. ISR selected sections of the Division of Engineering Design (DED) to serve as the comparison sample for analyzing the effects of the various changes implemented in the experimental organization (TPE). Controlled experimentation is rare in research dealing with planned change in ongoing organizations, yet it remains essential to determine change over and above that which occurs through the natural passage of time. The numerous attitudinal and behavioral indicators were examined in both organizations in order to make direct comparisons. By selecting a similar organization in which no planned change was occurring, there was a greater possibility of holding constant many extraneous effects (e.g., passage of time, characteristics of the organization, and employees being measured) that could have influenced the outcomes of the change program. Through such a comparative analysis, it was possible to a considerable extent to isolate organizational outcomes that are directly attributable to the Quality of Work Program in TPE.

Description of DED[3]

The Division of Engineering Design, within the general scope
of approved planning reports and project authorizations, prepared or
obtained complete technical designs and specifications for structures
and engineering works coming under the responsibilities of the Office
of Engineering Design and Construction, including site development,
architectural treatment, landscape design, materials, machinery,
and equipment and their quality assurance inspection and testing. The
division also made technical evaluations of all procurements it sponsored. It investigated and evaluated environmental, architectural,
and engineering feasibility factors, including regulatory factors, involving design features in the location of proposed projects to be con-
structed in the TVA program.

The entire DED division in 1974 was composed of 12 separate
and distinctive branches plus the Division Director's Office. The total
size of the division was approximately 2,000 people. Two of the
branches, Civil Engineering and Design and Electrical Engineering
and Design, along with the Director's Office within DED were chosen
as the comparison sample for the TVA Quality of Work Project. The
sample consisted of approximately 327 employees, the majority of
whom were professional engineers. Figure 2.4 provides the location
of the comparison branches in DED along with their respective subunits. A functional description of the major activities of the comparison sample units at the beginning of the project is provided in Appendix C.

The Employees of DED

Appendix D provides the demographic characteristics of DED
employees chosen as the comparison sample. Of the 327 DED employees included in the comparison sample, the majority (92%) were male.
Over 80% of DED employees were married. About two-thirds of the
comparison employees were younger than age 35. The heaviest age
concentration (27%) fell between the ages of 26 and 30. About 4% were
older than age 56. Most DED employees were college educated. Thirty-
six percent of the sample had attended some college; an additional 33%
had received a bachelor's degree. Nineteen percent had attended some
graduate school and almost 7% had graduate degrees.

The race distribution of the DED sample was composed mainly

---

[3]Adapted from a TVA internal report, dated August 22, 1975.

FIGURE 2.4. Division of Engineering Design

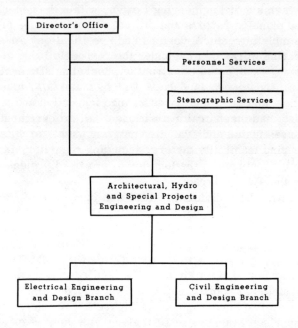

of Whites (92%); 6% were Black and less than 1% were Oriental. Most DED employees (90%) were the primary income earners of their household. About one-third of the DED sample had worked for TVA for 1 to 3 years. Twenty-four percent had worked longer than 11 years for the TVA.

A little over 8% of the sample was located in the Director's Office, 42% in the Civil Engineering and Design Branch, and 46% in the Electrical Engineering and Design Branch. Less than 1% was located elsewhere in the division. [4]

Growth of DED

Table 2.2 reflects a growth pattern for DED's 12 divisions characterized by significant increases in both manpower and production. In the decades prior to the experiment, DED's total employment

---

[4]Data were obtained from a baseline questionnaire administered by ISR to DED employees in April 1975.

had increased fourfold. At the end of 1975 there were 2,077 employees working for DED compared with 507 ten years previous. Production for this period was reflected in two ways: total man-years devoted to production and total dollar expenditures charged to production. Both indicators along with the employment figures give witness to a constantly increasing expansion of the DED division during this time period. Production expenditures must be interpreted with a degree of caution since they reflected increases resulting from inflation as well. Yet, inflation notwithstanding, total in-house expenditures increased by $10 million in the last year and had doubled in the last three years prior to the QWL experiment.

TABLE 2.2. Growth of DED

Fiscal Years	Total Production[a] Expenditures	End of Year Employees	Total Production[b] Man-Years	Total Income[c] Expenditures (millions)
1965	$ 5.494	507	533	
1966	6.110	549	512	
1967	7.684	621	575	
1968	9.015	682	695	
1969	11.166	742	772	
1970	13.624	900	860	14.747
1971	17.182	1133	1072	19.428
1972	20.568	1320	1265	23.375
1973	24.644	1432	1401	26.918
1974	35.550	1833	1690	34.127
1975	54.509	2077	2125	44.184

[a]Includes work subcontracted to other firms; excludes sub-orders funded by other TVA divisions.
[b]1 man-year = 1800 man-hours.
[c]Reflects production done exclusively by DED, including work for other divisions. This record was not recorded prior to 1970.

SIMILARITIES AND DIFFERENCES BETWEEN EXPERIMENTAL AND COMPARISON ORGANIZATIONS

TPE and DED were quite similar along several dimensions. Both the experimental and comparison organizations were functionally located in the power and electrical operations component within TVA.

This functional similarity as well as geographic proximity of the two divisions exposed them to many of the same organizational and environmental constraints. TPE and DED were also demographically compatible. The demographic profiles reflect very similar patterns of employee characteristics. Most TVA employees were born and educated in the Tennessee Valley Region and, therefore, shared many cultural norms and traditions. Among these norms were outward friendliness and receptivity to outsiders (i.e., hospitality) and loyalty to institutions. It was not uncommon for one to join TVA upon graduation from high school or college and remain there for one's entire career. Another important similarity was in the actual work performed in both organizations. The selected branches within DED (i.e., Civil Engineering and Design, Electrical Engineering and Design, Director's Office) overlapped considerably with TPE which contained identical subunits.

The differences between the two organizations were associated with structural and growth characteristics. The total DED division was a much larger organization composed of 12 main branches as opposed to the 4 branches of TPE. This means that the various interdependencies within DED were much more complex than in TPE. Most branches in DED were structured along the lines of project or matrix units, whereas TPE was structured in more of a hierarchical fashion. Additionally, DED had been undergoing a rapid expansion in both manpower and production whereas TPE remained relatively stable during the decade prior to the experiment.

Some of these differences were reflected by the physical facilities of both organizations. TPE was located in an old (circa 1920) twelve-story bank building in downtown Chattanooga. The building had changed very little and had retained many of its original characteristics including brass elevators, tile floors and steam heat. Some conference rooms and offices had been renovated. By contrast, DED was located in the newly completed TVA headquarters in Knoxville. The twin towers were very modern in design, and most staff engineers worked in open office spaces with partitions. Private office space was reserved for administrators. The physical facilities reveal a striking contrast between the stability and tradition of TPE and the dynamic complexity of DED.

SUMMARY

This chapter has provided an overview of the organizational context of the TVA QWL experiment and a comparative description of the focal units in the study. The TVA project could be viewed as an experiment within a larger social experiment. What began during the Depression as a manifestation of the New Deal had by the early 1970s evolved into a vast stable bureaucracy with a vital relationship to its surroundings. It is apparent from viewing TVA's history and development that its growth was heavily influenced by a pervasive philosophy of democracy and grass roots involvement through participation in decision making, a theme that will be echoed throughout the remainder of this study.

3 UNION-MANAGEMENT RELATIONS

As part of the stipulated goals of the American Center for Quality of Work Life, the TVA experiment was a collaborative project between management and labor. TVA provided an ideal setting to carry out this objective because of its long history of labor-management cooperation formally established in TVA's early years. This chapter will document this unique labor-management history. The two unions directly involved in the experiment will also be described.

LABOR-MANAGEMENT HISTORY

Since its inception, the Tennessee Valley Authority encouraged and supported labor-management cooperation. It was organized labor's approval that influenced Congress to establish an area development project of such magnitude. TVA planners also recognized the importance of organized labor in converting the Tennessee Valley Region into a major industrial area (National Center for Productivity and Quality of Working Life 1976). This original mutuality of purpose extended well into the 1970s in the form of TVA's vast network of cooperative conferences. The following is a brief summary of events that led to the establishment of the rather unique union-management relationship within TVA.

Very soon after TVA was established in the early 1930s several groups of salaried employees organized. These groups remained rather informal in structure, lacking explicit jurisdictions and boundaries. Their consultations with management representatives prior to the formal establishment of a labor relations policy did not take on the actual quality of bargaining, although issues of concern to employees were raised and discussed.

The Employee Relationship Policy was published by TVA in August of 1935. Developed over a two-year period, this document was the earliest official pronouncement by TVA management of its collaborative stance. The Policy applied to all employees of TVA and set the stage for forthcoming union-management developments. With this document, management recognized the right of employees to organize and bargain collectively. In addition, the Policy established a grievance system, emphasized that promotions and the like should be based on merit, and endorsed the development of a cooperative program between employees and management (Brookshire 1975).

Following the release of the Employee Relationship Policy, the Tennessee Valley Trades and Labor Council was formed on February 17, 1937. This body was composed of representatives of 14 international craft unions affiliated with the American Federation of Labor and represented TVA blue collar workers. The Council was recognized by TVA as the principal bargaining agent for trades and labor employees. The Council served as a precedent for the later bargaining relationship between TVA and white collar employees (Brookshire 1975).

By 1943 there were seven mutually exclusive bargaining units providing representation to virtually all employees in TVA. Two independent associations, the TVA Engineers Association and the Association of Professional Chemists and Chemical Engineers, represented most professional employees while the Council of Office, Technical, and Service Employees Unions covered the remaining nonprofessional employees. These organizations were able to engage in formal collective bargaining on matters affecting salaried employees.

On November 16, 1943, the three organizations (The Council of Office, Technical, and Service Employees, the TVA Engineers Association, and the Association of Professional Chemists and Chemical Engineers) combined into the Salary Policy Employee Panel which was recognized immediately by TVA. This alliance assumed a unique position in the history of white collar unionism since it had been induced by management and had brought together three diverse white collar organizations. It has been stated that the development of the Panel was a necessary but not sufficient condition for meaningful collective bargaining concerning a wide range of issues within TVA (Brookshire 1975).

TVA's encouragement of union-management cooperation remained consistent over a forty-year period. Expressions of the value of a cooperative union-management relationship could be found during the period of the quality of work program:

> The success of TVA's program depends on a large degree
> of mutual understanding and unity of purpose among em-
> ployees and between employees and management. Respon-

sible unions recognized by TVA as exclusive representatives of employees in defined bargaining units, and working together through the Salary Policy Employee Panel and
the Tennessee Valley Trades and Labor Council, provide
an orderly and effective means through which mutual understanding and unity of purpose can be achieved. Through
them, employees participate in forming and administering
the personnel policies and rules under which they work
and in increasing interest, initiative, and cooperative effort
on behalf of the TVA program. For these reasons TVA
encourages employees represented by these unions to
become and remain members of such unions; and TVA
negotiates agreements with the Salary Policy Employee
Panel and the Tennessee Valley Trades and Labor Council and otherwise deals with them and their constituent
unions in a manner which recognizes their contribution,
and the contribution of the employees they represent, to
the TVA program (TVA, 1976, p. 13).

Brookshire (1975) concluded that the bargaining relationship between
the unions and management in TVA was characterized by "an unusually
high degree of mutual respect and a reasonable degree of mutual trust"
(p. 305). Yet, he maintained that the attitudinal climate for bargaining
had significantly changed over the years, drifting more in an adversary
direction as the unions became stronger and more aggressive vis-à-
vis management that held a harder line in negotiations and contract
administration. This conclusion is particularly pertinent in light of
a dramatic shift in labor-management relations in the years following
the Quality of Work Project (see Epilogue).

THE COOPERATIVE CONFERENCE

An aspect of considerable significance for TVA as a Quality of
Work Program site was the existence of the Cooperative Conference
program as a mechanism for labor-management collaboration. The
conferences were inaugurated early in TVA's history as part of the
basic labor-management relations structure (TVA, 1976). The Employee Relationship Policy of 1935 contained a passage in which the
TVA Board of Directors formalized its position regarding cooperation.

As a further development of this policy the Board of Directors looks forward to the establishment of joint conferences between the duly authorized representatives of
the supervised employees and the supervisory and man-

agement staff for the purpose of systematic employee-
management cooperation. . . . It is suggested that such
joint conferences might well devote themselves to further-
ing the objectives for which the Tennessee Valley Authority
was created (National Center for Productivity and Quality
of Working Life 1976, p. 32).

The cooperative program began formally in 1942 with an agreement between TVA and the Public Safety Service Employees' Union
(PSSEU) to establish a union-management cooperative program to be
operated at the local level. The cooperative program was given formal
status in the 1950 Articles of Agreement (Brookshire 1975). It is important to recognize that the cooperative program was not intended to
supersede collective bargaining activity in TVA. It was conceived,
rather, as a supplementary device to strengthen collective bargaining
by improving the underlying union-management relationship (Rogers
1973). It was agreed to from the beginning that the conferences could
not discuss any issues regarding work, compensation, organization,
or other matters deemed negotiable through collective bargaining. It
was suggested in the original employee relations policy that the conferences take up issues such as elimination of waste in production,
conservation of material, health and safety, and the correction of
grievances and misunderstandings.

During the quality of work experiment, there were 90 conferences operating within TVA representing almost every workplace.
Labor and management cochairmen of a conference were appointed
or elected for a given term (usually one year). Four management and
four "grass roots" members were similarly chosen. The conferences
met regularly on a monthly basis during working hours. Most meetings were about two hours in length involving as many as 10 to 20
members (Brookshire 1975). The major objective was to improve
efficiency and morale by providing a harmonious atmosphere for employees and management (Rogers 1973). In addition to the local conferences was the Central Joint Cooperative Conference which was
charged with coordinating local conferences and administering an
annual valley-wide conference (Brookshire 1975).

Culminating the activities of the conferences throughout the year
was the annual valley-wide meeting. Attending these meetings were
members from the various local conferences, members of the Central
Joint Cooperative Conference, and often TVA top management. Perhaps the major benefit of this formal meeting was the opportunity for
top management to speak directly to a large number of employee representatives (Rogers 1973). Thus, the entire cooperative program in
TVA served to facilitate both upward and downward communication,
thereby operationalizing some of the original principles of employee

participation and union-management cooperation envisioned by TVA's founders. Because of its participatory structure, the conference concept highly resembled European work councils as vehicles to promote industrial democracy. As was often true for its European counterparts, the cooperative conference was subjected to criticism for being an inconsequential arrangement that only went through the motions of meaningful participation. The major limitation was the inability of a conference to deal with issues of substance, i.e., those that were considered negotiable. The cooperative conference was criticized for involving itself in such worthwhile but nonsubstantive areas as blood drives and picnics.

The official invitation to the American Center for Quality of Work Life to begin an experiment in TPE was made by the cooperative conference representing the division. As part of the experiment, the division waived the prohibition against discussion of negotiable issues to enable the joint Quality of Work Committee, which was formed as part of the experiment, to exercise free rein in considering a wide range of problems. Consequently, in October 1975, midway through the experiment, TVA management and unions formally agreed to remove the prohibition as part of the union contract.

THE UNIONS IN THE QWL PROJECT

Two unions representing the employees in TPE were involved in the TVA experiment, the Tennessee Valley Authority Engineers Association (TVAEA) and the Office and Professional Workers International Union (OPEIU). The former organization was the local association representing about 4,000 scientific and technical employees in TVA and OPEIU was an international union affiliated with the AFL-CIO. Both unions represented nearly all nonmanagement employees in TPE.

While both unions engaged in traditional collective bargaining for wages and benefits and other negotiable issues, TVAEA was considered more a professional association than an adversary union. OPEIU remained more traditional in its bargaining approach. TVAEA members were actively involved, initiating the events leading to the establishment of the quality of work life experiment within TPE.

Table 3.1 presents the distribution of union and management affiliation for both TPE and DED at the beginning of the experiment. The experimental and comparison samples are characterized by highly similar patterns of affiliation and membership. TPE was 65% unionized while 70% of DED employees were members of either union. There was one top union leader in TPE and 3% were middle leaders. The pattern in DED was very similar (Table 3.2). It is clear that most

TABLE 3.1. TPE Union–Management Distribution (N = 382)

Union/Management Affiliation	N	Percent
TVAEA	219	57.3
OPEIU	33	8.6
Management Schedule	42	11.0
None of the above	53	13.9
Missing	35	

Level in Management/Union	N	Percent
Member	240	62.8
Top Leader	1	0.3
Middle Leader	11	2.9
Top Management	8	2.1
Middle Management	34	8.9
None of the above	53	13.9
Missing	35	

TABLE 3.2. DED Union–Management Distribution (N = 327)

Union/Management Affiliation	N	Percent
TVAEA	205	62.7
OPEIU	24	7.3
Management Schedule	53	16.2
None of the above	45	13.7
Missing	0	

Level in Management/Union	N	Percent
Member	221	67.6
Top Leader	0	0.0
Middle Leader	8	2.4
Top Management	4	1.2
Middle Management	49	15.0
None of the above	45	13.8
Missing	0	

union employees in both divisions were represented by TVAEA (57%, TPE and 62%, DED) with less than 10% belonging to OPEIU. The relatively small degree of representation of OPEIU limited its influence in the quality of work life experiment.

SUMMARY

The TVA experiment was unique among QWL sites because of the existence of the cooperative conference. The project was seen as a means to strengthen this structure for union-management collaboration. Such a philosophy of labor relations was embedded in TVA's founding mission, and harmony was clearly a way of life. The underpinnings for a collaborative organizational change venture were already in place as both unions recognized that the QWL project could enhance their organizations, and they were willing participants in the experiment. From the beginning, the project was a truly cooperative endeavor.

PART TWO
THE TVA EXPERIMENT

      The history of the TVA Quality of Work Program is presented in the following chapters. Correspondingly, the events of the project are roughly divided into three major time periods. Chapter 4 describes the first period, beginning in Fall 1973 and extending throughout the summer of 1975. This period encompasses the events leading up to the experiment and the initial work of the external consultants. In Chapter 5, the second period is covered in detail, spanning the period September 1975 through June 1977. During this time, the experiment focused on larger issues such as organizational structure and workflow. Chapter 6 concludes the trilogy, picking up the sequence of events in July 1977, continuing through December 1977 when the experiment formally ended, and projecting into early 1978, when the change process became a permanent part of the organization.

4 INITIAL ACTIVITIES
AND
THE CHANGE PROGRAM

This chapter traces the historical development of the TVA project. The initial time period spans from mid-1973 through the summer of 1975, when the first consultant contract ended. The events described include: the decision by TVA to participate in an organizational change experiment, start-up activities at the experimental site, the selection and arrival of the external consultants, the forming and functioning of the Quality of Work Committee, and the conditions and early critical events of the change program. Emphasis is placed on the participatory nature of the change process.

THE DECISION TO PARTICIPATE[1]

The idea for an organizational change experiment within TVA grew out of conversations in mid-1973 between the Director of Personnel at TVA, the head of the Employee Development Staff of the Division of Personnel, and Ted Mills, soon to become Director of the American Center for the Quality of Work Life.[2] As a member of the

---

[1]Historical information has been adapted from a TVA public relations document titled The Quality of Work Program and the TVA Experiment, vol. 1, released in 1976. The original draft manuscript of this document was prepared by B. A. Macy, the ISR study director.

[2]The American Center for Quality of Work Life was originally the National Quality of Work Center (NQWC). The name was changed in 1976 to avoid confusion with other similarly labelled national centers. The two names are used interchangeably in this chapter.

National Commission on Productivity and an articulate advocate of the quality of work life movement in the United States, Mills was searching for potential sites for experimental programs. Because of its national prominence and visibility as a public utility, TVA seemed an ideal location for a site. After a series of discussions among these key officials, the idea of an experiment within the Power Production Division of TVA arose. This was a central division within TVA since it ran the Authority's power stations.

In pursuit of an eventual experiment, a meeting was arranged with all line and staff personnel of the Power Production Division in which the undertaking of a project was approved. An additional meeting was held with the Trades and Labor Council and Salary Policy Employee Panel, a consortium of TVA's unions, in order to garner union support of the proposed project. The Trades and Labor Council, which provided the representation for TVA's blue collar workers, refused to participate in the project as a result of labor-management problems concerning the combining of jobs. Since the quality of work program required active union support, the project in the Power Production Division was scrapped. The white collar unions in TVA remained very interested in developing an experiment, and representatives from TVAEA and OPIEU suggested the Transmission Planning and Engineering Division (TPE) in Chattanooga as another proposed site.

The senior officials in the Personnel Division suggested that the Director of TPE, the Division Personnel Officer, and a TVAEA representative attend a Quality of Work Life Conference which was to be held in Chicago on December 9, 1973. At the conference, the three TPE representatives learned of the national quality of work program and the general philosophy pervading the conference. They discussed the possibility of a project in TPE with Ted Mills, who agreed to visit Chattanooga to meet with management and union leaders as well as the division's cooperative conference. Upon returning from the Chicago conference, the Director of TPE held meetings with the Manager of the Office of Power, the Director of Personnel, and the division staff during January 1974 to discuss the possibility of the project in TPE.

Mills came to Chattanooga in late February 1974 and held separate meetings with management and union representatives. Each party agreed to participate in the experiment as long as the other party agreed. Each party separately agreed to waive the prohibition of a cooperative conference examining issues considered to be negotiable through collective bargaining. Such a waiver would enable the division to consider issues crucial to both labor and management for the duration of the project. On March 1, the cooperative conference agreed by consensus to participate in the project if funding for external consultants could be obtained. The conference also agreed to form a six-person committee that would determine if the union-management committee to be formed to oversee the project would be the conference itself or some other body to be established separately. On the same day the Office of Power gave its endorsement of the project.

In mid-March, Mills and the Director met with the General Manager of TVA in Knoxville to update him on the nature of the experiment and to inform him that it would require some funding from TVA, could have an impact outside of the division, and that the results would be assessed and subsequently published by an outside agency (i.e., the Institute for Social Research, University of Michigan). The General Manager was supportive of the project and indicated that he would follow it with interest.

Start-up

A series of meetings was held in TPE during March and April 1974 to determine the characteristics of the union-management committee and to inform the division about the project. The selection committee of the cooperative conference reported to the conference at its March 20 meeting that a separate Quality of Work Committee would be formed and that TPE would name the committee as recommended. During the last week in March, the Division Director and an employee representative dealt with issues of representation on the Quality of Work Committee, as it was to be called. Originally, it was recommended that the committee be comprised of ten members (five each from employees and management). It appeared, however, that this number would limit unnecessarily the representation of employees on the committee. It was then decided that the committee would have fourteen members, allowing for seven employee representatives. The Division Director and employee representative arrived at a tentative list of names of members and alternates which they presented to the cooperative conference on March 29. The membership list was accepted and approved by the conference. The conference also suggested that a meeting of the entire TPE Division be held in order to inform employees of the impending experimental program.

The Division-wide meeting was held a week later during which employees heard remarks from the Director and the Business Agent and past president of the TVAEA on the nature and scope of the quality of work program. During the ensuing question-and-answer period, it became apparent that a number of employees believed that they should have had more input into the naming of members of the Quality of Work Committee. The expression of these concerns led to the consideration by the Director and top officials in TVAEA of having elections to fill positions on the committee. These concerns were also discussed with Ted Mills. Timetables and procedures for elections were subsequently established jointly between the Division Director and the past TVAEA president.

The Quality of Work Committee

It was finally decided that the composition of the Quality of Work Committee (QWC) would be fourteen members evenly divided between management and unions. Based on the earlier concerns about representation, the TVAEA held elections in May on a branch basis to fill their union positions on the committee. The five members represented the System Planning, Electrical Engineering, Civil Engineering, and Communications Engineering and Design Branches in addition to the Director's Office. To provide continuity and to represent TVAEA's central role in the program, the TVAEA past president placed himself on the committee. The other union, OPEIU, elected a secretary from the Civil Engineering Branch as its representative. Because of personnel transfers occurring soon after the formation of the QWC, two of these original members were replaced by their respective branches.

The management positions on the QWC were appointed by the Director who also placed himself on the committee. These positions consisted of three Assistant Branch Chiefs (Electrical, Civil, System Planning), one section supervisor (Communications), and one union employee from TVAEA. The latter appointment, a Black woman, was in direct response to expressions of concern from Black employees that no minorities were represented on the QWC. The seventh management position remained open until a later time. The Division Personnel Officer (DPO) was to sit in on the QWC meetings as a nonvoting observer and resource person.

The QWC held its first weekly meeting on June 6, 1974 with ten members present. During this initial meeting, the goals of the Quality of Work Program were discussed along with major complaints about the division. The primary task of the QWC during the summer of 1974 was the selection of external consultants for the project. Most of the early meetings were devoted to considering materials presented by various consultant candidates and establishing interview guidelines. The committee decided at its second meeting to rotate the position of chair on a weekly basis. Decisions were made by consensus, except on rare occasions when a formal vote was taken. The QWC established the criterion that 80 percent of all members (present or not) must cast an affirmative vote in order for a motion to carry.

Selection of Consultants

Three consulting groups were interviewed by the QWC during June and July resulting in the selection of a team of consultants from a large nationally prominent consulting firm. The QWC favored this group because of their applied orientation. Their major competition was academically based and perceived as possibly having more difficulty coordinating travel schedules. The principal consultant had fifteen years experience as an organization development consultant, had experience working with unions, and had a considerable background in industry including the position of Corporate Director of Training and Development for a Fortune 500 company. His academic background included a Master's Degree in Social and Behavioral Science and Labor Relations from MIT.

The remaining members of the consulting team included a Ph.D. labor economist with over twenty years consulting experience and a young engineering Ph.D. with some consulting experience. Two other consultants who had lesser roles, entered the project a year later. The choice of the external consultants was communicated to the National Quality of Work Center. The project would start as soon as funding was available from a grant from the Economic Development Administration, and funds were provided by both TVA and the unions.

Funding and Conditions of the Project

Across each of its experimental sites the National Quality of Work Center articulated a set of entry agreements stipulating the conditions for the experiments. These agreements were fully in keeping with the Center's philosophy of collaboration, and provided guidelines for funding, ownership, and assessment of a project. The conditions established at TVA are outlined as follows:[3]

1. Consultant Funding Only
   Funding was to be provided only for the purpose of retaining an external consultant team acceptable to TVA participants. No funds would be provided to the participants. The consultants originally requested a contract for $128,000, for eighteen months; however,

---

[3]Adapted from National Quality of Work Center, Statement of Intent, July 1974.

this was reduced to twelve months at $85,000. A second contract (see Chapter 5) was initiated for an additional six months at a cost of $39,000.

2. Separate Assessment

Assessment of the project would be carried out independently of the consultants' activities by a team of organizational assessment experts from the Institute for Social Research (ISR), University of Michigan. Assessment would occur throughout the official lifetime of the experiment at no cost to the management or the unions in TVA. Moreover, participants were to be aware of the assessment. ISR's role in assessing each project was to be one of complete neutrality. The Institute was concerned only with measurement and the scientific use of data, and necessarily, would not affect the planning and action parts of the program beyond documenting what happened and the impact of these events. To ensure its role as a third party, representatives of ISR visited TVA and formally communicated its policies to the Quality of Work Committee prior to the experimental period. (A further description of the assessment role is provided in Chapter 7.)

3. Labor-Management Committee

The Quality of Work Committee (QWC) would serve as the focal point of all change activity in the division. Its form and its functions and authority were to be determined solely by TVA participants. The committee, if it so desired, could develop joint subcommittees or task forces.

4. Joint Project Ownership

Considered the most crucial of all entry agreements, the spirit of the TVA Quality of Work project was to be fully collaborative between unions and management. In this sense, changes would be jointly determined and outcomes shared by both parties in order to assure equitable allocation of any gains attributable to the project.

5. Instant Termination Rights

Either management or unions in TVA had the right to terminate the project on a moment's notice, returning immediately to status quo ante with respect to any matter affected by the change effort.

6. Full Job Security

No union or management member was to be terminated because of any changes brought on by the experiment. In the event that any jobs were eliminated because of a structural or other form of change, the individuals affected would be retrained by management for work at comparable pay with no loss in seniority or other perquisites. The unions would also cooperate in any recategorization or retraining of employees affected by the project.

7. "Shelter" Agreement

Collective bargaining would remain separate and in no way be affected during the experimental period. The TVA participants decided to waive management work rules and union contractual stipulations during the official lifetime of the project. As a consequence, the QWC and various task forces were free to examine any aspect of the division in developing experimental programs. This waiver became a permanent part of the union contract in October 1975. Valley-wide salary negotiations and the grievance procedure were not to be waived under any circumstances.

8. Matching Funds

The partial funding for the consultants by the grantors (i.e., Department of Commerce, via NQWC) would terminate after approximately eighteen months of official experimentation. In keeping with NQWC requirements, TVA labor and management would provide half of the funding (i.e., $42,500 for the first twelve months). Failing such a contribution, the project would terminate.

9. Project Lifetime

The official lifetime of all experiments was eighteen months, after which all funding would cease. Any continuation of the experiment beyond this point was at the discretion of the participants in TVA. Assessment, however, would continue for an additional eighteen months. In the event of premature termination of the project, all unused funds would be returned to the grantor.

10. Disclosure of Data

The underlying purpose of each quality of work life experiment was to measure, record, and assess the impact of changes, and to disseminate this information to the labor and management communities of the United States. Participants in the TVA experiment, though assured of anonymity with regard to disclosure of assessment data, agreed to the dissemination and use of the data in whatever ways ISR and NQWC considered appropriate.

These ten entry agreements provided the formal collaborative foundation for the TVA project, ensuring management and labor of the clarity of their respective roles, safeguards to protect the interests and rights of both parties, and knowledge about the roles of the grantors and assessors of the experiment. With these agreements as a backdrop, the first part of the change program in TPE will be described in the following sections.

THE CHANGE PROGRAM IN TPE[4]

The change program implemented by the consultants in TPE extended over approximately eighteen months, encompassing the period September 1974 through March 1976. The program was broken down into two formal contract periods. The first period consisted of three phases and covered the period from September 1974 through August 1975. The second contract period began in September 1975 and formally extended through March 15, 1976. The events of the first contract period are documented in the remainder of this chapter; the second contract period is covered in Chapter 5. It should be noted that the various phases involving the formulation and subsequent implementation of changes overlapped to a considerable extent.

Objectives and Philosophy of the Consultants

The consultants first met with their new "client," the Quality of Work Committee in TPE, on September 24, 1974 and stated that their basic objectives were as follows:

[The consultants] will work collaboratively with the Quality of Work Committee of TPE over an eighteen-month period to help them identify, formulate, plan, organize and implement improvements in the total work environment of TPE that are perceived as beneficial to the employees, management and unions involved. These improvements may affect: organizational structure, processes and arrangements; management style; design and configuration of work assignments; systems of communication, information and rewards; and the manner in which work is accomplished.[5]

With the above objectives as a base, the consultants outlined eight basic assumptions they would follow in designing a program linking the particular conditions with TPE and TVA to an action plan

---

[4]Information for this section was obtained from a series of six status reports from the consultants to Ted Mills, Director of NQWC, October 1974, through January 1976, and a public document titled The Quality of Work Program and the TVA Experiment, vol. 1. TVA, 1976.

[5]Revised proposal from the consultants to Ted Mills, Director NQWC, dated August 23, 1976, (p. 3).

directed at improving the quality of working life and productivity in the division. The assumptions were listed as follows:

1. Quality of work and productivity are systemic phenomena—organizational achievements made up of an inseparable mix of interdependent contributions, within a framework of shared social and economic values.
2. Significant and sustained enhancement of the quality of work and of productivity cannot be had by command or even by simple purchase; it requires consent, cooperation, and group problem solving.
3. Conflict management, behavior change and equitable sharing of benefits are necessary aspects of quality of work and productivity improvement, if the parties seek substantial and sustained gains.
4. Successful management of an improvement program requires both skillful preparation by management and skillful bilateral negotiation and collaboration. Either one without the other is insufficient.
5. Employees at all levels of a business have relevant feelings and valuable knowledge pertaining to the quality of work. Their knowledge needs to be evoked by careful problem formulation in a climate of fairness. It must then be combined and refined in a management directed process of quality of work and productivity analysis.
6. If employee morale and motivation are to be permanently raised, there must be a simple, explicit, trustworthy, adaptable way to measure mutual benefits, with knowledge of results at reasonably short intervals.
7. Whatever the capital or labor intensity of an operation, or the mix of skills, the key to improvement is the human element; and the human response depends on dignity, equity and self-interest.
8. Programs to improve the quality of work and productivity require continuous attention and periodic evaluation and revision if they are to remain relevant in the face of changes which they themselves help to bring about.[6]

The Change Program: September 1974–August 1975

The consultants outlined what was termed a "bilateral, total organizational approach" for this contract period, consisting of three distinct phases. The first phase, labeled Reconnaissance, was a pre-

---

[6]Revised proposal, consultants to Ted Mills, August 23, 1973, (pp. 3–4).

liminary survey of TPE aimed at developing an understanding of the division's operations, organization, and environmental context as well as its readiness for an innovative improvement program. Phase 2, Feedback, was designed to integrate the findings from the reconnaissance and identify the issues and subsequent strategies for the improvement program. The major vehicle for this phase was a workshop to be held for the Quality of Work Committee (QWC) and other key management and union personnel. In the third phase, Implementation, the consultants planned to accomplish several objectives: (1) develop corporate and union executive committee sponsorship of the program, (2) explore how the cooperative conference might eventually become a vehicle for replicating other potential Quality of Work Programs in TVA, and (3) launch the activities formulated in the workshop and provide assistance and guidance to the Quality of Work Committee (QWC) and its task forces.

Parallel to the work of the consultants during this period, ISR representatives met with the QWC several times to plan the administration of the Time 1 or "baseline" questionnaire. The attitude questionnaire was administered to all TPE employees on September 18, 1974.

Phase 1: Reconnaissance—September 24, 1974–October 31, 1974

This phase was directed toward familiarizing consultants with TPE and TVA. This was accomplished through a large number of individual and group interviews (usually involving five to seven division members) conducted by the consultants. The interviews, 228 in all, were selected and scheduled by the Quality of Work Committee. These interviews involved 211 TPE employees, 14 managers from other TVA divisions, and 3 union officials. In addition to the interviews, the consultants observed and participated in several Quality of Work Committee meetings, observed a Director's staff meeting, and reviewed a large number of documents dealing with issues perceived as pertinent to the program.

Phase 2: Feedback, Integration, and Summarization of Consultants' Findings and Responses from ISR's Initial Questionnaire

From the above described interviews and an analysis of responses to selected items from the ISR Time 1 questionnaire, the consultants gleaned 170 separate statements that taken together constituted their most salient findings regarding TPE and the organizational and socioeconomic environment within which it operated. Each statement was put on an index card so that the observations could be examined separately and grouped together to form themes. The following are some examples of their observations:

In performing its functions and fulfilling its mission and commitments for TVA, TPE interacts with a number of other TVA divisions, for example, getting key inputs from Power Marketing (forecasting of power requirements) and Power Resources Planning (generating capacity plans), outputting its "products" to Power Construction and Power Systems Operations, and making use of such services as Data Processing, Purchasing, Environmental Planning, and Land Purchasing.

Originally a dynamic, innovative and controversial social experiment, TVA, while successful, has become a bureaucratic organization in which traditions and precedent strongly influence current actions.

Most important decisions in TPE are made by the Branch Chiefs.

Resolution of conflicts or differences among TPE Branches, or between TPE and other TVA functions depends more on relative personal power than on the merits of the conflicting viewpoints.

Most engineers and engineering associates feel that their jobs demand less than their full technical capabilities.

Much of the work done is considered repetitious, specialized and fragmented while 93% of TPE employees indicated that they desire variety in their work.

Many supervisors are viewed as biased with regard to work assignments, job classifications, service reviews, promotions, work rules, and benefits.

There are widespread feelings by TPE employees about inequities in compensation, particularly between engineering and technical (SD) and engineering associate and technical support (SE) employees who performed similar work.

The feedback of such information was presented by the consultants in the form of a week-long workshop in December 1974, involving the 14 QWC members and 8 other participants from inside the division, outside the division, and outside TVA.

A fourth consultant, a female Ph.D., joined in this workshop as part of the group. The first day and a half of the workshop, which became known as "Ramada I" because of its setting, was devoted to the feeding back of the 170 observations, validation and modification of this information, and the identification of "master causes" so that the QWC could select issues to be addressed in the forthcoming agenda for 1975. In the middle portion of the workshop, the participants examined several options for dealing with the issues identified earlier.

In the final phase of the workshop, two parallel tasks were accomplished. The QWC developed its initial agenda for 1975 along with the assignment of responsibilities and a description of the planned process for designing, gaining support for, and implementing the Quality of Work Program in the division. Commensurately, the non-QWC participants identified probable barriers to the program existing outside of the division. In addition, an inventory was developed by these non-QWC participants of possible TVA resources external to TPE that could eventually be used by the QWC in carrying out its plans. The last morning of the workshop involved the sharing of information by both attending groups, and a commitment was made by the QWC concerning some immediate action steps.

Ramada I generated considerable momentum for the change program. The following quote describes a reaction from one of the non-QWC members who attended the workshop:

> The workshop was my first real glimpse of the QWC in
> action. I can truthfully say that I am one of those who
> came away on Friday a slightly different person from
> the "x" person who embarked on Monday morning. As
> I mentioned to one member of the QWC, my emotions
> seemed to be primarily pride, admiration, and humility.
> Pride—to be associated with people of such character
> and obvious dedication and ability; admiration—for the
> manner in which the entire group conducted its business,
> and for the spirit of positive accomplishment which it
> engendered; humility—because the functioning of this
> committee reminds me that the true worth of a person
> is not always explicitly defined by the artificial bench-
> marks of seniority, salary schedules, union or manage-
> ment status, and education attainment which our system
> has created.

The consultants noted a number of objectives that were accomplished in the workshop. The QWC became committed to addressing key issues they identified for improving the quality of work life in the division. The major issues or themes identified by the QWC that were to be incorporated into the 1975 agenda for the change program were:

1. Quality of work life decision-making procedure
2. Division mission and goals
3. Management style and practice
4. Organization structure (staffing, workflow, and communication)
5. Career development
6. Reward-recognition systems

7. Union-management relations
8. Field survey section problems (Field survey crews were a subunit of the Civil Engineering Branch)

According to the consultants, this list of issues reflected the full complexity and interdependency of elements that had an impact on the quality of work life in TPE.

The consultants noted that the members of the QWC developed a more comprehensive understanding of the problems of their division. They became more adept at debating issues openly and in developing consensus more readily. The QWC also developed more confidence in their ability to make a significant contribution to TVA. Managers in TPE who were not on the QWC recognized the committee as a resource as a result of the workshop. Moreover, the QWC developed new perceptions concerning other external forces. The union leadership was now seen more as a resource than a barrier. The QWC developed similar perceptions about the Personnel Division in Knoxville, once seen as having an agenda counter to that of the QWC. It is clear that as a result of the first workshop, several important links were established between the QWC as the central agent of change and its surrounding resources.

The Formal Change Process

A major outcome of the workshop was the development of a formal process for investigation, validation, and the eventual implementation of change within the division. With the assistance of the consultants, the QWC established the following cyclical procedure for change:

1. Identify problem
2. Validate problem
3. Appoint subcommittee of QWC
4. Form and charge task force
5. Consider task force report
6. Recycle as needed
7. Develop action plan(s)
8. Market and/or modify
9. Begin to implement
10. Monitor and evaluate
11. Feedback

This procedure was significant in that it formalized the change process and provided new structures in the division around specific issues. The QWC was clearly at the center of this process, appointing subcommittees of its members to address particular issues, and spawning task forces of other division members. The task forces would meet separately and develop recommendations, and report back to the QWC at assigned times. Eventually a program would be implemented after refinements were made. This process allowed for considerable participation of division members in making changes and was at the core of the interventions in TPE.

Phase 3: Implementation

During January and February 1975, nine task forces or subcommittees were formed by the QWC that investigated and studied the problem areas identified in the workshop. At this point, there were 53 TPE employees actively involved in the Quality of Work Project. Each subcommittee appointed task forces that would make recommendations for change to the QWC for implementation. The following is a brief description of each group in order of their formation:[7]

Division Mission: Switchyard Design—(Subcommittee appointed 12/19/74; task force appointed 1/2/75). The purpose of this group was to assess the feasibility of transferring the switchyard design activity from the Office of Engineering Design & Construction to TPE.

Service Reviews—(Subcommittee appointed 12/19/74; task force appointed 1/10/75). This group was charged with studying current problems in the service review (performance appraisal) process and recommending improvements.

Field Survey—(Subcommittee appointed 12/19/74; task force appointed 2/6/75). Charged with improving the quality of worklife for the entire Field Survey organization of about 45 employees who performed surveys for transmission lines, the subcommittee, along with a six-person task force, met with one of the consultants and the Personnel Officer in a two-day workshop to develop improvements for this group.

Single Line Diagram—(Subcommittee appointed 12/27/74). The group was to explore ways to reduce redundancy of work performed between TPE and the Power System Operations Division (PSO) in producing single line diagrams.

---

[7]Taken from a progress report from the consultants to Ted Mills, March 5, 1975.

Environmental Problems—(Subcommittee appointed 12/27/74; task force appointed 1/30/75). This group was appointed to study the entire process of gaining environmental clearance for projects in order to shorten and smooth out the process.

Division Guidelines—(Subcommittee appointed 12/27/74; task force appointed 1/23/75). This group was charged with instituting technical or other decision-making guidelines within Branches and the entire division to enable decisions to be delegated downward to those doing the work.

Rewards and Recognition—(Subcommittee appointed 1/9/75; task force appointed 1/22/75). The purpose here was to explore a wide range of means by which nonmonetary rewards and recognition could be provided to TPE employees.

Organization Change—(Subcommittee appointed 1/9/75). This group considered structural and workflow changes in TPE. During this time the Systems Planning Branch Chief and his assistant (a QWC member) began to formulate a proposal for restructuring their Branch to be more of a project form of organization.

Employee Utilization—(Advisory Group appointed 2/28/75). This group, appointed by the QWC, was to analyze the 170 observations from the utilization perspective and to make recommendations. The group also reviewed all work that was currently underway by the task forces.

The Issue of Decision Making

Perhaps the most significant and potentially vexing issue that had evolved as of March 1975, when the program was getting under way, was the decision-making process within the QWL program. A question arose about whether the QWC was a policy and decision-making entity or simply an extension of the Division Director's office. It had also become apparent to the consultants at this time that the four Branch Chiefs, one of whom was a QWC member, maintained divergent opinions concerning the efficacy of the Quality of Work Program in TPE. These views ranged from supportive to highly resistant. There were also differences in perceptions of the QWC and Branch Chiefs regarding the problems of the division. The consultants noted that two of the four chiefs were rather threatened by any pressure for change by the QWC. Indeed, one Branch Chief labeled the entire program "communism." This early tension between the QWC and the Branch Chiefs was exacerbated by the Division Director's absence from several QWC meetings. To provide more continuity of leadership on the QWC, the consultants recommended that the QWC rotate the chairmanship of its meetings on a monthly rather than a weekly basis as had been the case previously. The consultants also recognized the value of the Division Director playing an active and decisive role both within the QWC and with his staff, and encouraged his more active participation in future meetings. It became evident to the consultants that decision-making issues would have to be resolved before any major improvements could be realized from the program.

CHRONOLOGY OF THE CHANGE PROGRAM (1975)

By early June 1975, three changes had been formally announced to all division employees and were in various stages of being implemented. One such change concerned improving the evaluation of employee performance and career planning in order to make performance appraisal a more open, two-way process between the supervisor and employee. A second change was the institution of a mechanism to develop TPE guidelines and facilitate delegation of technical decisions. The outcome took the form of a division-wide Guidelines Review Board and five branch level Guidelines Review Committees. Third, a program of staggered working hours known as the Adjusted Time Schedule was instituted for those who desired a more flexible work schedule. Meanwhile the QWC had several proposed changes in progress, including a merit award for outstanding performance and the restructuring of the Field Survey unit in the Civil Engineering Branch. There were continuing efforts during this time in the areas of employee utilization and developing measures of improvements in productivity stemming from the Quality of Work Program.

By far the most vital and complex change area to be undertaken was the examination of the workflow and organizational structure of the division. Under the banner of reorganization, several activities had begun early in the summer of 1975. A subcommittee of the QWC was appointed to study the problem. The Systems Planning division, with the assistance of the consultants and the QWC, began its evolution toward a project form of organization. The task force on environmental problems recommended the development of a new branch within the division, composed of the location sections of the Electrical and Civil branches and the existing environmental group in the Director's office. This proposed branch would deal specifically with environmental issues arising out of new federal, state and local legislation. The ensuing debate on this proposal within the QWC and with the Branch Chiefs brought the QWC to the realization that it would eventually have to deal with the larger issue of division organization.

During this transition stage between the change formulation and implementation phases, the QWC further clarified its role in the decision-making process. The consultants noted in one of their status reports (June 6, 1975) that the "relationship between the QWC and the Branch Chiefs with regard to the development of recommended changes shifted from a model analogous to ping-pong to one like wrestling." Branch Chiefs were now being included at an earlier point in the change formulation process. This enabled the Branch Chiefs to have more input into proposals rather than be the passive recipients of a finished package of recommendations. They attended QWC meetings more frequently and consulted more with the task forces. Also the Division Director's attendance at QWC meetings became more regular.

Implementation progressed throughout the summer of 1975 with continued implementation of changes instituted prior to June, the further development of earlier conceived change plans, and the approach toward new problem areas. Training seminars for those responsible for evaluating performance were instituted as part of the new approach to service reviews. The outcome of the service review task force went into operation on July 1. The new service review approach involved the use of a four page "Employee Profile" form filled out separately by supervisor and employee. This profile covered the employee's work performance for the appraisal period as well as future plans. A final joint profile was then developed based on a two-hour discussion by the supervisor and the employee. This informal process provided a basis for the completion of the employee's official service review (Form 3031) which became part of the employee's permanent record.

The staggered working hours went into effect on June 9. Within a few months, the number of employees working under the new arrangement stabilized at about 60 or 18% of the division. The Guidelines Review Board was established on June 15, followed by the Branch Guideline Review Committees a month later. Its first major undertaking was to develop guidelines stipulating who was to be responsible for developing and conducting service reviews and nominating merit award candidates.

Several new projects were instituted as of August 1975. The task force on rewards and recognition devised a plan for the merit award for outstanding performance. The award would be a single lump sum payment administered by the process of management nomination and peer review. The task force working on eliminating overlap of work with the Power Systems Operations Division (PSO) developed several changes in drafting notation, standardizing the process, and enabling TPE drawings to be directly used by PSO. This particular change project was regarded by the consultants and the task force as an outstanding example of interdivision collaboration. Debate continued concerning creation of the new branch recommended by the task force on environmental problems. The QWC had accepted the underlying concept of the task force, but realizing the objections of some of the Branch Chiefs, proceeded with a degree of caution.

There were also several changes nearing the implementation stage by August 1975. The field survey task force had reached an agreement with the Civil Engineering Branch Chief on July 17 regarding a modified four-day work week, equipment improvements, and plans to examine the survey jobs with the intention of applying a new job evaluation plan. There was, however, continued debate on the per diem issue (i.e., travel allowances). Management in the Civil Branch believed that an allowance of $12 a day for accommodations and $10 for meals, and so forth was an equitable rate. The task force members desired a change in the TVA code designation for the field survey employees from a code IV (applied to persons who travel continuously) to a code I (for intermittent travel). Such a change would result in a higher per diem allowance of up to $16 per day for accommodations and $14 per day for "food and incidentals." Plans were in progress for a revised proposal concerning the per diem issue.

The task force on measurement conducted a study requesting from each branch their estimate of how much rework was being done. They consistently obtained from each branch estimates of 3 to 5 percent from Branch Chiefs and 20 to 25 percent from employees. The report of this task force to the QWC on July 25 was marked by considerable frustration. They had become dissatisfied with their approaches to quantitative productivity measurement. This was primarily attributable to work fluctuations and a lack of comparability among jobs. Better progress was made with establishing behavioral indicators such as absenteeism and turnover.

On the same day, the task force on rewards and recognition reported to the QWC a recommendation concerning the hiring of a full-time staff member in TPE to administer an employee suggestion plan and to produce a newspaper for the division. The response by the QWC was described as "lukewarm," yet they requested that the task force prepare a proposed job description for the staff position.

For the purpose of enhancing intradivision communications, the QWC conducted a 90 minute division-wide meeting on July 25, dealing specifically with the Quality of Work Program and its progress thus far. The meeting was attended by approximately two-thirds of TPE. The QWC members responded to a series of written questions solicited in advance as well as spontaneous questions raised from the floor. Major issues addressed included job and classification inequities and the fact that substantial improvement from the program had not yet been felt within the division. The consultants presented a short commentary stressing the innovation and complexity involved in carrying out the program. The general reaction to the meeting by employees was described as favorable.

The Employee Utilization Advisory Group appointed by the QWC in March 1975 submitted a set of issues to the QWC. After circulating

the report to the task forces in operation, the QWC identified new
areas for future work including career development, vacancy announce-
ments, internal communications, and job classification. With the work
of the Advisory Group as a resource, the QWC developed a charge for
a new five member Task Force on Professional and Career Development that was approved on September 4. Also, in response to the need
for developing work in the area of equal employment opportunity and
affirmative action, the QWC, acting on prevailing negative perceptions
of affirmative action in TPE, recommended that a charge be prepared
by a new task force to deal specifically with these issues.

THE OBSERVER/FACILITATOR

It is important here to note that after the September 4, 1975
QWC meeting the consultants no longer attended the weekly QWC
meetings on a regular basis. It was recognized and agreed to by the
consultants and the QWC that the committee could function effectively
on its own from that point on. The consultants began to concentrate
their efforts more directly on the issues of organization and workflow
and related concerns.

As the consultants' direct involvement waned, the Division Personnel Officer, who had been among the originators of the project and
present at most QWC meetings, began to emerge as an observer/
facilitator for the QWC. Although he had no formal training in process
consultation skills, the DPO, relying on his own experience, interpersonal skills, and readings, made insightful comments to the QWC.
He also served as a contact person for the outside parties involved in
the project such as the consultants, ISR, and NQWC as well as being
a resource person to several task forces. This process role conflicted
with the DPO's formal role of personnel administrator which required
him to make decisions about hiring, firing, promotions, and resource
allocation. Because of this inherent conflict of roles, some people
on the QWC and in the division had difficulty accepting the DPO as
observer/facilitator, yet he continued to provide this service regularly.

SUMMARY

By the end of the summer of 1975, nine task forces were at work
on various aspects of organizational improvement. While some of the
changes were rather simple in their conception, i.e., eliminating
duplication of effort with another division, others were more profound
in their implications. The merit award for outstanding performance,

the adjusted time schedule, the revisions in the performance review procedure, and the addressing of the field survey organization problems were all considered major changes. The QWC was definitely a formidable unit in the division, enough so that questions had to be addressed concerning the use of its power, especially in relation to the Branch Chiefs and the Division Director. Clearly, these problems were not fully resolved as at least two Branch Chiefs were resisting the change program. The proposed changes in the structure of the division, especially around the environmental function, would bring further challenges to this delicate power balance. Underlying the development of these changes was the fact that a new process that encouraged participation by employees in the division was well in place and functioning quite smoothly. The division had clearly moved. The next chapter documents the second contract period, focusing on the issue of organizational structure.

5 EXAMINING ORGANIZATIONAL STRUCTURE AND WORKFLOW

This chapter documents the events of the second formal period of the TVA experiment beginning approximately September 1975 and continuing through June 1977. This period was a natural outgrowth of the myriad activities introduced in Chapter 4, yet represented a distinct shift in the course of the experiment. The major event of this period was a second workshop conducted by the consultants focusing on the complex areas of organization structure and workflow. The workshop will be described in detail along with the events leading up to it and the series of changes that transpired in its wake. The continued work of the task forces during this period will also be described.

BACKGROUND AND PRELUDE TO PERIOD II

During late May and early June 1975, the QWC, acting on a suggestion from the consultants, began discussing the establishment and makeup of a task force to examine broadly the entire TPE organization and workflow. It was the QWC's feeling at this time that the consultants' assistance could be engaged through a normal extension of the existing contract with NQWC with the QWC as the client. The QWC also desired a more pronounced role for the consultants, encouraging them to participate directly on the task force as an equal third party and assume an advocacy position. The consultants believed that the study of organizational structure represented the key to success of the entire project since proper organizational changes would ensure the workability of many of the changes already under way. They also saw the examination of organization and workflow as an opportunity to further engender the support of the Branch Chiefs by including them on the proposed task force.

On July 31, 1975, the QWC decided that membership on the task force would be composed of: the Division Director as Chairman, the four Branch Chiefs plus the forthcoming head of the new staff on environmental issues, the Division Personnel Officer, and six employee representatives.

An Attempt to Change the Client

As the QWC was considering the appointment of the new task force on organization and workflow and anticipating the consultants' contract extension, the consultants were becoming concerned by what they perceived to be a general opposition by some of the Branch Chiefs to the entire program. It appeared that an adversary relationship was developing between these Branch Chiefs and the QWC. Moreover, the consultants wanted to be perceived by the Branch Chiefs as an independent third party rather than an exclusive agent of the QWC. They concluded that:

> . . . as the Director in the final analysis was in the
> position of having to decide in cases of differences
> between positions taken by the QWC on the one hand
> and those taken by the Branch Chiefs on the other,
> we believed we could have the greatest leverage and
> provide the most effective assistance to the QWC if
> the Director became our official client for this par-
> ticular project. [1]

In informal discussions with several QWC members, the consultants received the impression that the change in the client would matter little since they believed that chances for success of the program would be enhanced. The consultants also assumed that TVA would be funding this portion of the project entirely, further supporting their logic for the shift in the client relationship. Because the events transpired in mid-summer 1975, vacation schedules (including that of Ted Mills) and other delays precluded them from testing their assumptions. This did not occur until they presented their formal proposal for the second contract to the QWC for its comments. While the QWC reacted favorably to the work plan presented in the proposal, they noted that the proposal was addressed to the Director and not the QWC. The QWC reacted vehemently and accused the consultants of

---

[1]Letter from the consultants to Ted Mills, September 12, 1975.

trying to make an "end run" around the committee, thereby demonstrating little confidence in its accomplishments up to that time. Ted Mills, upon returning from vacation and hearing of the proposed change, echoed the negative reaction of the QWC.

A meeting was held in New York on August 11 involving the consulting team and others including Mills and Dr. Stanley Seashore, Program Director at ISR. As a result of the meeting it was agreed that the consultants would work with the new Task Force on Organization and Workflow as an extension of the existing contract with NQWC and that NQWC could provide funding from sources in addition to TVA with no change in the client relationship. It was also suggested that a briefing session be held with all key parties of the entire QWL project (i.e., Personnel Division of TVA, union leaders, QWC, NQWC) in order to gain more understanding of the consultants' concerns about the project and to provide useful information for the resubmission of their proposal. At first, the QWC questioned the need for such a session and requested to meet with the consultants.

Meeting with the QWC on August 15, the consultants characterized their rationale for organizational change in TPE as a refinement system employing a cooperative method. This approach was distinguished from the more authoritarian risk/decision management system and the adversary nature of the union collective bargaining system which they saw as the two traditional prevailing systems within TPE. It was pointed out to the QWC that the issues involved in the proposed plan were likely to be perceived as more threatening to existing systems and less experimental than the changes made up to that time. This threat potential, according to the consultants, could have serious effects on the future of the entire Quality of Work Program.

Three days later in Knoxville, at a briefing session, the consultants presented this rationale to the major parties to the project and reached agreement as to how their proposal could be modified. An outcome of this meeting was the suggestion that the cooperative conference be the eventual vehicle for long-term diffusion of the Quality of Work Program.

Plans for Ramada II

Approval for the extension of the consulting contract from NQWC came in early September 1975, and the consultants began their background preparation for dealing with the organization and workflow issues. This initial work was accomplished primarily by a series of "walk-throughs" of each branch and section of TPE. Each of these walk-throughs consisted of a consultant touring a branch on two separate occasions. The first tour was led by the Branch Chief and section supervisors and the other by the branch representative to the QWC. Later, a two-day walk through of the entire division was provided (at the consultants' request) for a fifth consultant, a senior staff member from the consulting firm with an engineering background and experience with various electric utilities. His comments along with the other consultants' impressions were fused to form the following list of observations resulting from the program of walk throughs:

TPE organization and workflow is characteristic of electric utilities
    in general.

The quality of TPE's "product" is regarded both, within TVA and
    within the electric utilities industry as being generally excellent,
    especially from a technical standpoint.

There was a general lack of any perceived need for significant change
    in the organizational structure and workflow by most employees
    and especially by management.

Those employees who did voice a desire for change were typically
    unable to present any rationale other than, "We're operating
    today the same way we operated 25 years ago . . . it's time
    we changed."

Many managers expressed concern that changes made to "improve"
    organizational structure and workflow would have an adverse
    effect on the high quality of the work being done in TPE; thus
    more might be lost than gained.

Little credence had been given to statements made by the Director
    over the past 18 months about the need to improve organization
    and workflow so that anticipated increases in workload could be
    handled without corresponding increases in staff. [2]

The observations would serve as a vital input into the projected workshop which would launch the task force on organization and workflow (TFOW). In designing the workshop, the consultants realized that they needed additional input concerning future trends in internal and external factors that could have an impact on TPE and necessitate changing the organization and workflow. The role of the Director became crucial here as he was in the best position to identify the required trends and make future needs credible to members of the TFOW. Since it required considerable time for the Director to meet with Branch Chiefs and the QWC in advance, the workshop (originally scheduled for late October) was postponed until November 20–22, 1975.

---

[2]Taken from a letter from the consultants to Ted Mills, Director, NQWC, dated January 16, 1976, (p. 3).

The consultants met with the Director late in October to discuss potentially significant trends and to develop a conceptual design for the workshop. In the following week the TFOW reviewed relevant data from the ISR Time 1 survey and the results of some preworkshop exercises completed by members of the TFOW. The results indicated to the consultants that there was a need for a felt "sense of urgency" by members of the task force in order to help focus their review of the existing organization and workflow in the Division. Again, the Director was placed in a crucial role. The consultants felt that strong leadership on the part of the Director could counter prevailing feelings of complacency about organization and workflow and garner critical support from the Branch Chiefs.

The Second Workshop

The Director expressed the need for reviewing the area of organization and workflow in his opening remarks at the workshop. Several needs were identified, including a better balance between technical and human considerations on the part of TPE managers, a projected increase in workload, the need to reduce total systems cost, and the need to approach organizational problems identified by the consultants in their initial reconnaissance. During the workshop the TFOW, which was divided into employee and management subgroups, developed 52 separate needs. The consultants encouraged the TFOW to broaden its perspective and consider the term "organization" as a multidimensional concept. The group subsequently generated a priority list of 12 "starting points" and some beginning action steps. Examples of some starting points included salary schedule inequities, meeting the challenge of new technology, and the role of the QWC in the coming six months.

The consultants raised several issues to the TFOW in the final stages of the workshop. One point concerned incorporating the TFOW into the QWC since all but three QWC members were on the task force already. A second suggestion was the establishment of a substructure of the QWC to integrate the QWC mechanism into the daily operation and decision making of the division. These subunits would consist of 2 to 3 person subcommittees from each section (including the section supervisor). The subunits would operate as a continuous information channel between the QWC and employees by which the QWC could keep abreast of employee and organizational needs. The TFOW reacted to this idea with interest and was to consider these suggestions by the consultants in future meetings. (It should be noted that the subunit idea was never put into practice by the QWC during the period of the experiment.)

The consultants noted that the TFOW had experienced considerable difficulty in arriving at concrete action steps in the workshop.
They attributed this to several causes: (1) the inherent difficulty in
working down from "comfortable levels of abstraction," (2) the continued resistance of some of the Branch Chiefs, and (3) the absence
of a strong leadership role on the part of the Director. The consultants encouraged the Director to take a stronger stand and push the
group toward more rapid closure.

Nevertheless, the consultants felt that the TFOW had achieved
a number of significant accomplishments through the workshop:

They developed a view of organization and workflow considerably
    broader than their initial concept . . . that of organizational
    structure. Thus, they developed a substantially broader scope
    for their work agenda than originally anticipated.
The question of structural change was deferred until work had been
    done by the TFOW in other dimensions of organization and work-
    flow; although structural change was not ruled out as something
    that eventually should be changed, the TFOW came to view
    structural change in a broader, more balanced perspective.
The Branch Chiefs, some of whom were quite resistant to changes of
    significance, and who were perceived by the employee members
    of the TFOW as representing a major barrier to any change,
    began to develop an understanding of the need for some changes
    and a commitment to work further to develop recommendations
    for change. By the end of the workshop, the employee members
    of the TFOW (and the supportive management members as well)
    were beginning to feel more optimistic about the prospects of
    gaining the support of the Branch Chiefs for the quality of work
    program, and for positive improvements in organization and
    workflow in TPE.
A concrete program for further work of the TFOW was developed de-
    fining additional starting points relevant to needs, identifying
    the barriers associated with each starting point, and developing
    further the strategies and next action steps for capitalizing on
    the opportunities represented by these starting points.
Developing some fresh thoughts about the relationship of the TFOW
    to the QWC, and the future of the QWC and the quality of work
    program more generally in TPE in the longer term.[3]

---

[3]Consultants' status report to Ted Mills, Director of
NQWC, January 16, 1976 (pp. 9-10).

Reactions to the Workshop

Ramada II represented a turning point for the TVA Quality of Work Program. It was the general feeling of the QWC and others that this workshop was not as successful as the first one. Because of inclement weather, the consultants arrived late and thus the workshop had gotten off to an awkward start. The organization structure issues were much more complex and difficult to approach than the more concrete issues raised at Ramada I. It was, therefore, more difficult for participants to come away with a feeling of accomplishment. A former management member of the QWC commented:

> I wasn't there. I don't know except for the fact that from the outside looking in, they didn't do anything over what we did at Ramada I. In Ramada I we put down all of our goals and what we were going to do, and how we were going to do it, and what steps and it worked real good. At Ramada II, it looked like they were rehashing the same old thing that we did in Ramada I, at least from what I could see from the flip-charts and so forth from looking at it in the conference room. (Flip charts from both workshops were put on display for employees.)

An employee participant in the workshop recalled:

> For one thing, it reinforced the fact that if you don't want to discuss something, you don't have to. You can stalemate all you want to and we're still going to just sit here and discuss it but we ain't never going to . . . you don't have to resolve anything of importance.

Finally, a Branch Chief had this to say about Ramada II:

> I don't know why Ramada II was called in the first place. In the beginning it was agreed that there would be no reorganizational changes, major ones and then all of a sudden we had a workshop to reorganize the division. Now, you can't do that with a bunch of people who know nothing about the functions of the entire division. And [the consultants] to come up to speed, came in and interviewed throughout the division and wrote a report that the organization of the division was stable and they recommended no major organizational changes. This report came out, or came to light about a week before Ramada II and was given to the Division Director and here we are with a big workshop,

paid them money and all those plans were made and people keyed to go out for things that everybody's going to reorganize and get themselves a raise. And when they got there they found that there wasn't . . . I don't think they were ever told the background of why reorganization was never discussed as such. To add insult to injury they flew through a snow storm, they got here late, one woman, one of the members was pregnant, she was sick and they were three hours late and the observer wanted to go to an Ohio State football game so it kind of didn't get off to too good a start. But there was no need for it, the need was . . . they had already decided themselves that there was no real need for Ramada II.

Perhaps the most significant outcome of the workshop and that which would have further impact was that all four Branch Chiefs became members of the QWC as the TFOW and QWC were merged into one group. It was clear that the workshop did not have the impact on the organization of the division that the consultants had intended. Because of the earlier difficulties in determining who the client would be, the consultants lost some credibility in the eyes of the QWC and others in the division. The consultants concluded in their final progress report to NQWC that the work begun at the second workshop would have to bear "substantive fruits, highly visible to all TPE employees."[4]

A REVIEW OF TASK FORCE ACTIVITY (1976-1977)

During 1976-77 there were as many as thirteen task forces operating within TPE on various problems involving the direct efforts of over 100 employees. The following is a brief sketch of the work of task forces during this time.

Service Review

It had become evident that the yearly performance evaluation of TPE employees had become a standardized process. The task force had established a procedure known as the employee profile which

---

[4]Letter from the consultants to Ted Mills, NQWC, dated January 16, 1976, (p. 11.).

covered an employee's work performance as well as future goals. The employee and supervisor were to fill out a separate form which was followed by a mandatory discussion period. During this time the employee and supervisor reached an agreement regarding the employee's performance and a third profile was filled out jointly. This new profile was to serve as an input to the employee's official performance record. During 1976 the profile became an integral part of the service review process and engendered quite a favorable response throughout the division. The task force had also recommended an appraisal of the performance of managers. This program was implemented early in 1976.

Division Guidelines

The task force was charged with developing a process to ensure that technical information was available to employees requesting it. The lack of guidelines had pushed most technical decisions up to the middle and upper management levels. In response to this need, committees were established in each branch to review employee requests for procedure clarifications. The committees also began the development of engineering guidelines. A division control committee known as the Guidelines Review Board was also established to coordinate the workings of the branch committees.

Rewards and Recognition

The work of this task force focused on three major areas:

1. The Adjusted Work Schedule—the flexible work schedule was implemented in which employees may have one-hour flexibility in starting or ending the work day. During 1976-77 over 150 employees were operating on this schedule.
2. Merit Award—A cash award for outstanding performance during the two years prior to review period was developed. The process included nomination of candidates by supervisors, confirmation by a secret peer vote, and final selection of recipients by a joint committee. After a one-year trial, this plan was discontinued because of unfavorable employee responses. The task force continued working on a new method of rewarding outstanding performance.
3. Program Coordinator—A staff member was hired in May 1977 to fulfill the position of Editor/Coordinator. The first division newspaper, Powerline, was published in December 1977. Other duties of the editor/coordinator included working with the suggestion committee and organizing employee recreation activities.

Environmental Problems

The major outcome of this task force was the establishment of
the new Transmission Systems Siting and Clearance Staff (TSS&C).
Early in 1975, the task force on Environmental Problems recommended
the development of a new branch within the division, composed of the
location sections of the Electrical and Civil Engineering branches and
the existing environmental group in the Director's office, to deal specifically with environmental issues arising out of new federal, state
and local legislation (e.g., the National Environmental Policy Act of
1969). It was recognized that the existence of these separate groups
had resulted in coordination problems and the lack of a unified policy
with regard to environmental clearance prior to a project.

The bringing together of the three closely related units provided
a logical grouping of activities under common supervision. The rationale was to improve information flow so that the Systems Planning
Branch could receive preliminary information more efficiently. The
staff was also seen as a means to reduce duplication of effort, improve
scheduling, increase communication among branches, and provide individuals working on the staff the opportunity to work on an entire project rather than only one segment.

After considerable debate within the QWC and the division, the
new staff officially began operations in January 1976. Though identified
as a "staff," the new group was the functional equivalent of a branch
within TPE.

Field Survey

Within the Civil Engineering Branch was a group of about 50
employees who performed transmission line surveys. Their work
involved constant travel requiring crew members to be away from
their homes for as many as five nights a week. In order to alleviate
some of the special problems of these survey crews, the task force
developed several changes that were put into operation in October
1975. The major change was the introduction of a four day ten-hour
per day work week that would enable the workers to spend more time
at home. Equipment and procedure improvements were made and there
was a change in the per diem pay rate for travel allowances. These
changes continued to take shape throughout 1976–77.

Employee Utilization

From the work of the original advisory group appointed to in-
vestigate these problems, two task forces emerged. The first group

approached problems concerning professional and career development. This task force worked throughout 1976-77 gathering information in the division. A major focus of their work was the idea of equal pay for equal work, particularly between SE (associate and technical) and SD (professional) schedule employees. They also approached items relating to professional memberships, educational opportunities, and the unique developmental problems of minority employees. A comprehensive report including recommendations for improvement was submitted to the QWC in August 1977. Comments were ascertained from throughout the division regarding the implementation of the recommendations.

The second task force investigated problems concerning equal employment opportunity and affirmative action. An outcome of this group was a series of workshops for supervisory employees in August and September 1976. Two external consultants who specialized in this area were employed to conduct the workshops. The consultants submitted a report to the Division Director outlining the affirmative action needs of the division. As a result of the task force activity and the consultants' recommendations, an Action Issues Committee was formed in the division to work with the Director on affirmative action concerns and division policy in relation to TVA equal employment opportunity requirements.

Single Line and PSO Diagram

The creation of the single line diagram by this interdivisional task force eliminated duplication and resulted in savings of time. This was accepted as a working program in September 1976 and was the first program completed by the QWC.

Organization Review

In addition to the second workshop (Ramada II) described earlier, several additional organizational changes were in progress during 1976-77. Changes were completed in the structure of the Systems Planning Branch resulting in more of a project or "matrix" type design. Structural changes were also proposed for division staff personnel (i.e., Division Services). The task force also developed a "future agenda" early in 1976 pinpointing new problem areas for the QWC to undertake in the coming months.

Switchyard Design

The work of this technical task force was finished and turned over to the Division Director for continuation.

Productivity Measurement

The difficulty of a quantifiable productivity measure caused problems for this task force. Because of the complex nature of the problem, this group coordinated with a newly formed task force on cost accountability.

Development of New Task Forces

During 1976, several new problem areas were identified by the QWC in addition to the ongoing programs outlined above. A need was recognized to manage and control division costs and develop a better system of workload predictions. As a result, charges were prepared by the QWC for two new task forces. The cost accountability task force, formed in August 1976, began investigating methods of control and measurement to improve the timing and control of division costs. The "crystal ball" task force began working in July 1976 on improving critical path project scheduling by supplementing five year manpower projections. Work continued in both of these complex areas throughout the remainder of the experiment.

A third new task force, formed early in 1976, began investigating the eventual process of integrating the Quality of Work Committee with the cooperative conference and other "power centers" in TPE. The new group, known as the consolidation of power centers task force, submitted an initial report to the QWC late in 1976, but their work was to be later subsumed under a new plan for institutionalizing the QWC process in the division. (See Chapter 6.)

AFTERMATH OF RAMADA II:
ADAPTING TO UNPLANNED CHANGES

While 1975 and 1976 were years of planned change for TPE, the year 1976 was particularly marked by a series of division changes that were not planned by the QWC and the consultants. Although these critical events were considered as external forces of the Quality of Work Program, they must be included within the myriad events occurring during the experimental period.

It was necessary for the QWC to adapt to a dual turn of events early in 1976. The consultants officially ended their activities in TPE in January. Although their direct contact with the committee had waned during the planning and execution of Ramada II, the QWC was to operate without the aid of these consultants for the remainder of the experiment. The committee did not have a set agenda for 1976. Most of their work involved monitoring the progress of task forces and changes implemented previously and planning the administration of the second wave of measurements by ISR scheduled for June.

The QWC had undergone several membership changes. After the second workshop, three Branch Chiefs became QWC members. At that point all of the Branch Chiefs were members of the committee including the head of the new Siting and Clearance Staff. Two first line supervisors were taken off of the committee. Earlier, an employee representative had resigned from the QWC for personal reasons and another employee was elected as his replacement. While the new members knew of the QWC activities, they had to learn the operations of the committee as members. With the addition of the Branch Chiefs the original employee members now were to deal with a higher level of management in their meetings. One QWC member made the following comment about the addition of the Branch Chiefs to the Committee:

It had a big effect. That was, just like I said before, to them, because they hadn't really been in touch with the program. I can't help but feel they were sort of stepping in my territory, and so it was just like going to the staff meeting with the peons present.

Similarly, an outside observer noted:

Charles Dickens in his Tale of Two Cities begins by saying, 'It was the best of times and it was the worst of times.' I suppose it attempted to deal directly and head on with the question of we've got to have management of the organization in the program committed to it, working in that environment. And that's what that particular change accomplished. However, the issue had been skirted early on, for perhaps several reasons. It set in place a Quality of Work committee which had to seriously adjust its modus operandi with this new factor being introduced. And it was helpful and it was harmful; it had effects both ways in the operation of the committee. It was perhaps a more powerful committee with them on board, potentially, it was potentially a more powerful committee. A practical fact: A great deal of energy was spent accommodating to this new influence, which I think did affect the effectiveness of the committee.

A few months later another important change occurred. In February 1976, it was announced that the Division Director was being promoted to the Office of Power and that his Assistant Director would be assuming the Director post. The Director had been highly instrumental in establishing the Quality of Work Program in TPE and continued to have a formidable influence throughout the duration of the project as a member of the QWC. His successor was knowledgeable about the program but had not been involved with it to a great extent. He would now fill the Director's role on the committee in addition to the role of top management in the division. Consequently, it took several months for him to become familiar and comfortable with the new role.

There were striking contrasts in the styles of the two Directors. Several QWC members indicated that the former Director had a better grasp of the issues and was more strongly committed to the QWL concept than his successor. One employee said that the old Director "had the fire behind him and you can't transfer fire." The new Director described his accession to the top management position and introduction to the QWC as "being thrown into a boiling cauldron. I had a bear by the tail and didn't quite know what to do with it."

By March 1976, the QWC began to turn its attention to self evaluation and the forthcoming ISR survey. A TVA internal development consultant working on the Employee Development Staff in the Division of Personnel, was introduced to the QWC as a resource person with expertise in the area of evaluation. The internal consultant was trained in experimental research methodology and had been previously employed in a private consulting firm. He was thus able to provide assistance to the QWC in data interpretation and feedback techniques. He frequently attended QWC meetings, often offering comments on various issues. He interacted directly with the ISR assessment team and served as a liaison between the QWC and ISR concerning the assessment. Eventually, the internal consultant increased his involvement in TPE, serving as a consultant to several task forces (e.g., Affirmative Action, Field Survey). His primary involvement was in the preparation of data feedback sessions for division employees.

In the summer of 1976, the employees of TPE learned of some additional personnel changes. The Division Personnel Officer was promoted to a new position in the Office of Power and the TVAEA representative to the QWC became the new Personnel Officer. Both of these men, along with the Division Director, had a major impact on the development of the program in TPE. The Division Personnel Officer had the unique role of observer/facilitator to the QWC, regularly attending their meetings and providing an outside perspective on many issues. The new DPO assumed a totally new role. He had previously provided a strong employee voice on the QWC especially since he was past Valley-wide President of TVAEA. His new role shifted him from union employee to management and from QWC member to outside observer/facilitator. The position of union representative to the QWC was filled by a TVAEA election in July 1976, resulting in another new face and the addition of a woman (the fourth) on the committee.

Again, the QWC had to adjust to a personnel shift that affected its process. The outgoing DPO characterized his departure as follows:

> Albeit my own skills being very limited in acting as the
> observer/facilitator to the Quality of Work Committee,
> it nevertheless was a presence which had to be dealt
> with—the fact that I was not a member of the Quality of
> Work Committee, had never been a member of the Quality
> of Work Committee, at least gave me some degree of
> being accepted for objectivity, not so much interested
> in the issues as in process. And although that was not a
> role I was able to successfully always fill, there was that
> presence, the role of someone who was concerned about
> the way that the group was functioning, giving input in that
> area. The greater loss was the removal of the role of ob-
> server/facilitator from the committee, not my personal
> departure.

The new DPO admitted that he had difficulty putting himself in the role of facilitator, stating: "I was too actively involved in the issues to be a facilitator." A Branch Chief summarized the differences between the two personnel officers:

> I sincerely believe [Old DPO] was a very good influence.
> [New DPO] was a hard worker and they were two differ-
> ent people. I think [Old DPO] was more perceptive of
> employees, probably had a more honest feedback between
> him and certain employees which created some sound input
> into what was happening which I don't think [New DPO] had.
> I think [Old DPO] was a more skilled man in personnel
> matters or philosophies in general.

The timing and magnitude of these unplanned interventions caused a slowdown of QWC activity while members adapted to each of the new events. The period January–June 1976 was a period of learning for each person assuming a new role as well as those people interacting with them. Thus the period may be referred to as "holding pattern" for the QWC. The QWC became fatigued and somewhat baffled by all of the changes. Additionally, some of the original QWC members were feeling burned out after eighteen months. One member commented: "I don't think the real spirit behind [the Quality of Work Program] ever got back into play. It was just gone, gone, gone." A former QWC member echoed the sentiment that the nature of the program changed after Ramada II:

> The first 18 months, like I said earlier, it was exciting.
> The first part of it to me, personally, was sort of a scary
> experience in that I hadn't done that type of thing before.
> It took me quite a while to get my feet in the water even.
> Not just me but several of us. Because here we were
> dealing with top management, us like my case, an E (SE
> schedule). It was still exciting and a very, very good
> experience as far as I was concerned personally. The
> excitement went on for quite some time. It went on
> through the workshop and I don't know whether it was
> around the eighteenth month or what month it was but
> then it became sort of a hum-drum type, plodding type
> thing. As I said before, we had a blank check from the
> board of directors and then just a reluctance to cash it.

INTERNAL EVALUATION OF PROGRAMS

After the departure of the consultants in January 1976, the QWC devoted much of its attention to the issue of evaluation. It was recognized that the second administration of measures by ISR (Time 2) scheduled for June was approaching and that the QWC would then be able to compare division responses at two points in time. Since the QWC and the task forces had been working for eighteen months and had established several new programs, they were becoming anxious to learn of their progress as seen by division employees.

The QWC was to have considerable input into the T2 questionnaire. In order to enhance their role in the evaluation, the QWC formed an evaluation planning subcommittee to interact directly with ISR on matters pertaining to the questionnaire. The subcommittee was comprised of one employee representative from the QWC; one management representative from QWC; the Division Personnel Officer; and the TVA internal consultant from Employee Development Staff who was introduced to the QWC in March 1976 to aid in the internal evaluation of the Quality of Work Program and serve as a general consultant to the QWC and task forces.

The Evaluation Subcommittee spent a considerable amount of time going over existing questionnaire items and suggesting new items for T2. The addition of new items dealing with site specific issues (e.g., adjusted time, merit award) lengthened the T2 questionnaire to the extent that it was split into two segments to be administered one day apart. The external consultants had the opportunity to comment on the questionnaire via a conference call with the QWC in May 1976. The T2 measurement took place on schedule on June 2 and 4 in TPE in Chattanooga and on June 3 at the comparison on site in Knoxville.

In the months following T2, several task forces, with the assistance of the internal consultant began to address the problem of how to best use the data provided to the division by ISR. The QWC wanted to ensure proper feedback to division employees and plans were laid in Fall 1976 for special feedback sessions for division employees on a number of change areas. Several task forces, working with the evaluation planning subcommittee and following a set of feedback guidelines proposed by the internal consultant, developed their own package of data to be presented to employees. Some task forces (e.g., merit award) conducted small surveys of their own in order to tap issues not specifically covered in the ISR assessment.

The Feedback Process

The feedback plan developed by the internal consultant was presented to the QWC and approved in December 1976. A schedule for feedback sessions was developed by the Evaluation Planning Subcommittee. The major sessions would concern (1) the merit award program, (2) the employee profile, (3) the adjusted time schedule, and (4) general feedback on the QWC.

The plan for the first three areas called for the following progression of activities:

1. Task force prepares presentation
2. Presentation to QWC—comments
3. Presentation to employees
4. Employee input to task force
5. Task force develops draft plan with inputs and existing data
6. Draft plan reviewed by QWC
7. Draft plan checked by task force
8. Final plan presented to QWC for action
9. Implementation

A modified plan was suggested for the general QWC feedback.

The data were presented in the sessions by a team consisting of two QWC members (1 management and 1 employee) and two mem-

bers of the particular task force. The presentation took the form of
frequency distributions and graphs of responses to selected survey
items presented to groups of 20 to 30 employees from a given Branch.
Groups of employees were scheduled in shifts to view the presentation.
The process normally took several days in order to reach everyone in
the Division. At the end of each presentation, a period of time was
allotted for questions and other employee responses to the presentation. Also, feedback boxes were placed in accessible locations so that
employees could provide their written comments to the task force.
Employee reactions were encouraged in the opening remarks by the
QWC representative at the sessions.

Outcomes

The task forces received valuable information from employees
through the feedback sessions. Perhaps the most dramatic result of
the sessions was the discontinuation of the merit award plan. The task
force received a negative response from employees regarding the plan.
A poll conducted by the task force indicated that a majority of employees wanted to see the plan discontinued. The comments received suggested that the process of choosing recipients of the award was causing
conflicts among employees. The task force presented a review of the
comments to the QWC. After discussing this information, the QWC
passed a motion to discontinue the plan on February 10, 1977. However, the QWC also passed a motion to continue working toward an
alternative reward plan. It was concluded that the original plan had
not done what it was intended to do, that is, increase the morale of
employees. The task force made some recommendations for a new
plan including the right of employees to nominate candidates for an
award.

The employee responses to the employee profile and adjusted
time schedule were quite favorable. Both programs remained in operation in the division. The feedback to the employees on the QWC
was postponed pending the hiring of a new consultant and the future
plans for merging the QWC and the Cooperative Conference.

SUMMARY

The second period of the TVA experiment was marked by complexity and confusion. It was clear that the idealism and energy that
characterized the first year was by mid-1977 turning into disenchant-
ment and fatigue on the part of the QWC. The second workshop (Ramada II) was viewed by most as a failure as there was little attempt

thereafter to examine the macrostructural issues of TPE. The unplanned changes of personnel, especially the loss of the Director and personnel officer, were difficult for the QWC to absorb, resulting in a slowdown of their process. The QWC had a different look and feel as all of the Branch Chiefs were now members along with the new Director and several other member replacements.

The thirteen task forces continued on their various courses and some changes, most notably the employee profile and the adjusted time schedule, were realized and accepted by the division. The merit award program was discontinued and some new and longer term task forces emerged. The QWC, perhaps sensing that the formal end of the experiment was approaching, began to take stock of their accomplishments and to search for ways to fuse their methods into the division. The events leading to the eventual institutionalization of the program are documented in the following chapter.

6 TRANSITION AND PERMANENCE

This chapter describes the final period of the TVA experiment, documenting events from March 1977 through approximately March 1978. The major issue of this period was the fusion of the experimental program into the cooperative conference structure of TVA, thereby making permanent the collaborative process of problem solving that was so essential to the Quality of Work Program. This transition from an experimental program to one of permanence caused considerable soul-searching among QWC members who felt the waning of their three-year enterprise. The events described include the decision to bring in a new consultant to aid the transition and the establishment and eventual functioning of the new cooperative conference structure.

BACKGROUND

The Quality of Work Program had given rise to several new "power centers" within the division. The most pervasive new force was the experimental Quality of Work Committee. Other power centers included the task force on organization and workflow, the Guidelines Review Board, and each of the task forces working within the Quality of Work Program. Interwoven among these new power centers were the preexisting cooperative conference (CC), TPE unions and management, the Central Joint Cooperative Conference, and the unions and management of TVA. Early in 1976 it was recognized by the QWC and others in TPE that the QWC would be terminated as an experimental group at the end of 1977 and that some means of carrying forth their methods would be beneficial to the division. In light of this need, the QWC appointed the consolidation of power centers task force in

February 1976. The main duty of this task force was to find a method to combine the QWC and the cooperative conference into one body in order to provide a continuation of the quality of work concept. The task force consisted of eight people; four management representatives including the Division Director, Personnel Officer, two Branch Chiefs, and four employee representatives including representatives from both unions.

The task force met throughout 1976 to prepare a final report and recommendations to the QWC. A set of guidelines was developed and distributed to the QWC in December 1976 for a new program called the Participative Union Management Program (PUMP). The major feature of PUMP would be a joint committee similar in membership and functions to the QWC. According to the guidelines:

> The purpose of the committee is to provide recommenda-
> tions to the Division Director regarding implementation
> of programs and policies to improve the effectiveness of
> the TPE Division in carrying out its mission and goals.

The guidelines specified the organization and operating method of the committee. The group was to provide a "balanced representation for all groups" in the division. Many of the aspects of the QWC would continue such as the use of subcommittees and task forces and decision making by concensus. The Branch Chiefs and the Director were rec-ommended to continue as management members. Employee represen-tatives would be elected on a branch basis. The task force also rec-ommended training in problem-solving skills as an integral component of the new program.

The consolidation was seen as a means by which to continue the methods of the QWC in a form that was to be permanent and legitimate according to the <u>Articles of Agreement between the Tennessee Valley Authority and the Salary Policy Employee Panel</u>. The QWC provided their comments and suggestions for refinements to the consolidation task force. The report of the task force (i.e., PUMP) was a first step toward the eventual combination of the QWC and cooperative confer-ence. No immediate action was taken concerning these guidelines because of some new developments occurring in early 1977.

In February 1977, the internal development consultant from the Division of Personnel submitted a memo to the Division Director of TPE concerning additional consulting needs for the Quality of Work Program. The internal consultant had been aiding several of the task forces in data feedback to the division and was of the opinion that TPE was in need of additional external consulting. One of the major points of the memo was that a consultant could aid in the transition of the QWC to a new and permanent form. The internal consultant stated that the present QWC needed problem solving discussion skills to operate more effectively. Also, according to the memo, the relationships (i.e., communication) between the QWC and the task forces and the division as a whole were in need of improvement. The new consultant would be charged with fulfilling these needs through team development and training. The memo was distributed to the QWC and discussed at a meeting on February 24. Dr. Edward Lawler, a Program Director of ISR, attended this QWC meeting as an observer.

The memo was seen by both the Director and the internal consultant as a means to generate momentum toward the eventual consolidation of power centers. In conjunction with the ideas expressed in the memo, the Director attended a series of organizational development seminars at the University of Michigan to become more familiar with OD terminology and concepts. After the seminars he stated that he had felt "like a fish out of water" since he was the only top manager in attendance. However, he had gained considerable knowledge and prepared to address the QWC and report his experiences as a prelude to their discussion of the memo.

The address to the QWC was given by the Director on March 24. After reviewing the various seminars and exercises he experienced at Michigan, he put forth his own views concerning the future of the QWC. The major themes were: goals of the QWC, communication, career development, and future involvement of first-line supervisors. He emphasized the need to get moving on the issues specified in the memo.

A special task force consisting of the Director, the internal consultant, and an employee representative to the QWC was formed to work specifically with the ideas expressed in the memo. On March 31, the task force presented three alternatives to the QWC for procuring additional consulting: (1) internal consulting only; (2) combination of internal and external consulting—retain the former personnel officer as an observer/facilitator and hire an external consultant; (3) external consulting only. Each of these alternatives assumed that a transition of the QWC to a new and permanent unit would occur. The task force recommended the second alternative to the QWC, retaining the role of the former observer/facilitator.

The committee discussed the issues over the course of two meetings. They decided to have a joint meeting with the cooperative conference in order to reach agreement on whether the two groups should merge and hire a consultant to facilitate the transition. In the course of these meetings, the QWC became confused and avoided taking a stand on the task force recommendation to hire a consultant. The QWC was reluctant to impose their ideas on the existing cooperative conference. There was also considerable uncertainty about whether a new group would be created or if the existing cooperative conference would simply adopt the methods of the QWC. Some QWC members, particularly two Branch Chiefs, were resisting the idea of starting over and "reinventing the wheel" by bringing in another consultant. The Director, who was part of the task force making the recommendation, did not push the QWC to adopt the task force recommendations.

The internal consultant, also a task force member, broke the confusion by focusing the QWC only on the issue of hiring a consultant. If the QWC endorsed this proposal to the cooperative conference, the combining of the two groups would become a fait accompli. The QWC, after this intervention by the internal consultant, finally endorsed the task force recommendation to hire a consultant after much discussion. (Chapter 9 provides an analysis of these events.) The QWC never dealt with the issue of whether or not to combine the two groups. As one observer noted, "They went straight to product and bypassed the process." They presented this recommendation to the cooperative conference at the joint meeting on April 12 and an agreement was reached to hire an external consultant. Once this agreement was reached, a working plan was developed that stipulated the issues the new consultant would approach and how he would interact with the various parties in the transition. The plan is detailed in Figure 6.1.

Selecting a New Consultant

A nominating group consisting of the Director, one other manager, one QWC member, and one Cooperative Conference member began the process of identifying candidates for the consultant position. The internal consultant and former DPO were appointed as resource persons to this nominating group. Final selection of the consultant was the responsibility of the entire QWC and CC who together would be the initial client. Several candidates were interviewed in the following months extending into the summer of 1977. In July, a new consultant was selected. The need for an outside consultant was not perceived by everyone on the QWC and CC. One QWC member commented that, "sooner or later we have to get off the bottle," i.e., let the QWC handle the transition themselves. Yet others saw the role of the consultant as gaining commitment to the QWL concept, keeping the ideas central to the division, and providing skills training that the QWC never received from the previous consultant team. There was also the leftover issue of involving first line supervisors. The new consultant was perceived as highly perceptive of the division's status at that time—a "sharp cookie" as one QWC member described him.

The new consultant immediately began the task of becoming familiar with TPE, the Quality of Work Program and his new client, the combined memberships of the existing QWC-CC. He formed several

FIGURE 6.1. Transition Plan

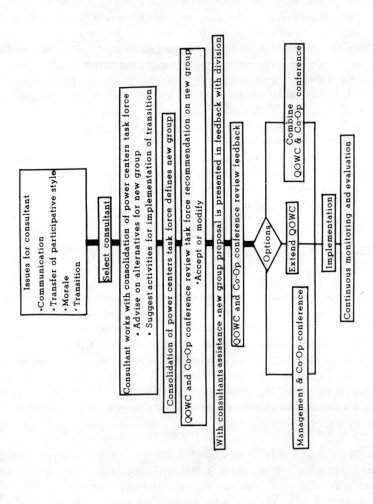

Issues for consultant
•Communication
•Transfer of participative style
•Morale
•Transition

Select consultant

Consultant works with consolidation of power centers task force
• Advise on alternatives for new group
• Suggest activities for implementation of transition

Consolidation of power centers task force defines new group

QOWC and Co-Op conference review task force recommendation on new group
•Accept or modify

With consultants assistance •new group proposal is presented in feedback with division

QOWC and Co-Op conference review feedback

Options

Extend QOWC

Management & Co-Op conference

Combine QOWC & Co-Op conference

Implementation

Continuous monitoring and evaluation

early impressions about the Quality of Work Program. The most salient of these observations included:

1. A considerable degree of support for the Quality of Work concept throughout TPE. There were also positive feelings about the QWC and the task force method of approaching problems;
2. The most positive programs thus far had been the employee profile, adjusted work schedule, the Field Survey 4-day week and the work on affirmative action;
3. A major weakness of the Quality of Work Program was the lack of a well-articulated philosophy and set of objectives;
4. The QWC had not effectively transferred its style and philosophy to other areas of the division; and
5. After almost three years into the program, the QWC members had become fatigued and were in need of rejuvenation.

The consultant recommended a refocusing on philosophy and purposes from a "sociotechnical" perspective. He claimed that each program of social significance must fit with the technical constraints of the organization in order to be more effective. He also recommended establishing a branch structure which would interact with the division structure. This new structure would be in the form of smaller branch cooperative conferences and was similar to the earlier consultants' suggestion. The transition plan was as follows:

1. The new consultant would work first with the combined QWC and CC to develop the philosophy for organization renewal in a workshop planned for August 1977.
2. A new division cooperative conference, to be elected in late 1977, would act as a steering committee for the overall change strategy.
3. Smaller branch cooperative conferences would be elected to implement change activities at a lower organizational level (i.e., branches).
4. Several ongoing task forces of the QWC would continue their work.

DEVELOPING THE PHILOSOPHY STATEMENT

The workshop was conducted on August 10-12, 1977 at the Sheraton Hotel in downtown Chattanooga. The new consultant and his associate were the workshop leaders. The entire QWC and CC were participants along with the DPO once again as observer/facilitator (a total of 33 people). The major purpose of the workshop was to develop material for a written statement of philosophy for TPE. This philosophy statement would provide the foundation for the eventual change activities and the transition to the new cooperative conference. The purpose and theoretical background of the workshop were given by the consultants in brief lectures to the entire group. For the rest of the workshop, the participants were assembled into several task groups. The consultants worked nondirectively, aiding each group in their discussion, and spent a considerable amount of time observing.

In the first day and a half of the workshop, six groups generated ideas and value statements concerning each of the following areas: (1) Successes of the QWC and CC; (2) failures of the QWC and CC; (3) existence of the QWC in TPE; (4) changes in values of QWC members; (5) value changes in the environment-culture and trends; and (6) major organizational difficulties and problems. Ideas were listed, rank-ordered and presented to the reconvened total group.

After the discussion of these items, three larger groups were formed to discuss: 1) the relationship between individuals and their work; 2) the relationship between organization members and the organization as a whole; and 3) the relationship between the organization and its environment. The group discussions extended into the third day. During this final day, all of the information generated by the groups was synthesized. The information from each of the three discussion groups was put before the entire group on flipcharts. The theme for this day was, "One small step for the workshop, one giant leap for the division." The consultant defined the workshop participants as an "initiating body" for the first draft of the philosophy statement. This statement would be presented to division employees for ratification. An editorial committee was appointed whose duty was to assemble the information from the workshop into the written philosophy statement.

Near the end of the workshop, the consultant articulated the objectives for the renewal process as follows:

1. To continue and further develop the concepts and organizational renewal process of the Quality of Work Program;
2. To diffuse these concepts and processes into existing organizational units;
3. To put into place an ongoing organizational renewal process that will optimize both the social and technical systems of the division; and
4. To facilitate the division's survival, growth, and productivity in a rapidly changing environment.

The last afternoon was devoted to future planning and the presentation of the consultant's sociotechnical perspective. The Director ended the workshop, stating "I think we have come up with some statements which will mean a great deal to us."

Many workshop participants expressed feelings of accomplishment as they reviewed the large volume of information generated during the three days. The flipcharts were posted on the walls of the conference room so that all workshop participants could review their work.

Reactions to the consultant were mixed. Some participants saw him as overly theoretical in his approach and felt that he directed his approach more toward management than the employees. In some ways the new consultant was perceived as more effective than the previous team, particularly by Branch Chiefs. One Branch Chief commented that the former consultants pushed a certain course of action whereas this new person gave more choices. Most employees saw him as getting the program back on track.

THE PHILOSOPHY STATEMENT

The first draft of the Philosophy Statement was introduced to the division in late September 1977. The eight-page document was broken down into four major parts corresponding to issues discussed during the August workshop:

1. The Nature of People—individual needs in relation to their work;
2. Nature of Jobs/Work—opportunities and responsibilities, rewards;
3. People and the Organization—the establishment of a climate of honesty, trust, and openness; and
4. Organization, Society and Other Systems—resource utilization, stewardship, leadership, individual commitment.

It was stated in the introduction that the statement would be used for "planning, decision making, and evaluating the functions and practices of the division that relate to how people are treated in their work environment and how the division itself relates to other human societies." Further, the philosophy would be considered as a future oriented working document for TPE. Employees were given an opportunity to comment on the document through feedback sessions and some editorial changes were made. The philosophy statement was approved by both the QWC and CC in December 1977.

In general, the philosophy statement was seen as the product of a useful exercise but was going to be difficult to implement. One QWC member commented:

It's too wordy. It's too many words. It's reaching for the sky. It's just something that we can reach for but may never do it. I really don't feel like the new coop confer-

> ence will really use it as a guideline. I'll just have to
> wait and see. To me, the way it's written up, even
> though I helped on it, it's going to be hard to follow.

There were questions about whether the philosophy statement was truly a reflection of the division. Another QWC member expressed doubts:

> You can't use something that people haven't bought in
> on. Every time you pull out something that any part of
> the population of the division has not bought in on, you're
> going to have the whole can of worms open up all over
> again. It's no good to just get it into writing and try to
> work with it. You've got to sell what you've got in writ-
> ing.

A similar comment was made by an observer:

> Well, I guess I'm not convinced that it is at this point in
> time a statement of the philosophy of the division of TPE.
> I guess I think it is a document which contains a number
> of compromises which are not accepted by anybody in
> particular. I guess I don't believe that that statement is
> accepted by the division as a statement of their philosophy
> at this point.

Others felt the document was useful when viewed in proper perspective. A Branch Chief explained it this way:

> I think it's useful. There seems to be a question that
> keeps coming up at almost every meeting as to just
> exactly how are we going to use this document. As far
> as I'm concerned, I feel like we've already been told
> how we should use it and I think it's just something
> that's back here as a reference for us and we can keep
> referring to back and forth as we take different actions.
> I don't think it's something that was ever intended for us
> to come out as a strict instruction as to what we're to do
> in every case. I think it's just a document back here to
> which we can go to refer if anybody thinks that we are
> deviating from any policies that we might have agreed
> upon. I think it's a useful document. I don't look at it as
> being the Bible.

Another Branch Chief had a different view:

I'm not so sure that it's really all that valuable. I guess, kind of looking at it from a personal viewpoint, I've got my own philosophies and I kind of know what they are. I might change them from day to day a little bit but I never felt that it was something that I needed to get off to myself some day and write down 1, 2, 3 for it and I kind of feel the same way about the division. I'm not sure that it was all that important.

Along with the Philosophy Statement, a set of guidelines was developed for the new cooperative conference to go into effect in January 1978. The guidelines specified the dual structure of the division-wide joint committee (i.e., cooperative conference) and the branch cooperative conferences. The purpose of the new cooperative conference, according to the guidelines, would be "to continually review the programs and policies of the Division, to seek opportunities for improving the effectiveness of the TPE Division in carrying out its mission and goals, and to make appropriate recommendations to the Division Director and Branch Chiefs." Thus, the new cooperative conference was to assume an advisory role in the division.

The new division CC would be composed of 22 members (11 appointed management members and 11 employees elected by their respective unions). Each member was to serve for a two-year term. A new feature of the conference was the recommendation/charge committee. This group would serve as a communications link, transmitting recommendations to the Director and charges to task forces and other action groups. It was decided that the CC would meet on the first Thursday of every month. The monthly meetings were a striking contrast to the weekly QWC meetings. It should also be noted that the new cooperative conference did not create a role for an observer/facilitator.

On December 15, 1977, the QWC had its final meeting, marking the end of the experiment, and the newly established cooperative conference began operating in January 1978. A one-day workshop was held by the new consultant on January 5, 1978 in order to provide some direction for the new group. The major issues of the workshop involved representation, purposes of the conference, priority issues, and interpersonal relationships among conference members. Some of the priority issues identified included career development, working conditions, morale, and establishing the credibility of the new CC. A considerable portion of time in the workshop was devoted to reviewing the Philosophy Statement and guidelines.

In the first few months of 1978, six Branch level cooperative conferences were formed from each of the five Branches (including Siting and Clearance) and the Division Services section in the Director's

office. Each Branch CC began formulating its own task forces. One
of the early issues concerned how best to use the ISR survey data.
The third wave of measurements was administered in early January
1978. By March 1978, the transition phase was essentially complete
and a new and permanent structure was formed to carry on the Quality
of Work process in TPE.

SUMMARY

The transition from experimental program to permanent organization was remarkably smooth despite the initial confusion over which
course of action to take. The new cooperative conference was seen as
a vehicle to carry over the benefits of the QWC and to correct its de-
ficiencies. By entrusting the task of organization renewal to the cooperative conference, a major goal of the Quality of Work Program
was realized by TVA. The experiment, which had lasted for three
years and cost approximately half a million dollars,[1] was now complete.

---

[1]A total of 27,622 man-hours were charged directly to the
quality of work program through July 1977 at a cost of approximately
$450,000. Additional labor charges plus the costs of the new consult-
ants brought the total to approximately $525,000.

PART THREE
OUTCOMES

The results of the TVA experiment are presented in the following chapters. Chapter 7 provides an overview of the experimental design, the measurement program, the research hypotheses, and variables included in the study. Special problems of field research are also discussed. The actual results are presented in Chapter 8. Quantitative data indicate which variables changed over time, whereas the qualitative interview data highlight employee and management reactions to the project. The ninth chapter delves more deeply into the underlying issues of the experiment focusing on power relationships and exploring why events occurred as they did. The outcomes are summarized and discussed in Chapter 10 from the standpoint of the nature of participation and the future of QWL programs.

7 DESIGN OF THE ASSESSMENT

OVERVIEW AND OBJECTIVES OF THE STUDY

The TVA project, like other quality of work life programs, was a naturally occurring field experiment that lasted for a period of just over three years. The Institute for Social Research (ISR) served as an independent third party assessor during the lifetime of the project, applying a relatively standardized program of measurement at specified intervals. The measures ranged from intensive questionnaire surveys of attitudes and beliefs to interviews and direct observation of events. Less successful were the attempts made to measure productivity and other employee behaviors. Because of the magnitude of the project, assessment was by necessity a multifaceted undertaking limited by the natural constraints imposed by field research.

The experiment involved several interested parties: TVA management and employees in the experimental and comparison divisions (TPE & DED), the outside consultants, the National Quality of Work Center, and the ISR assessment group. Each of these directly involved parties viewed the project from its own frame of reference and explicit or implicit objectives.

Determining the impact of such an endeavor as a QWL change project is very much left to the eye of the beholder, in this case, the major stakeholders who will make their own interpretations of the events. It is therefore difficult, if not impossible, to reveal the ultimate "success" or "failure" of the project as truth. To attempt to do so runs the risk of implying a single model for interpretation, thereby risking the loss of potentially vital information about the dynamics of the change process from which one may learn something about how organizations create change.

Given the multifarious nature of this project, the present study will attempt a focused assessment of the TVA experiment along the following global objectives:

1. To determine the effects of the interventions developed by the Quality of Work Committee (QWC) and its consultants on the individuals in the experimental division (TPE) in comparison to their counterparts at the comparison site (DED).
2. To assess the impact of the participatory change process that was at the core of the QWL intervention on individuals at the experimental site (TPE).
3. To provide qualitative data about the process of change, identifying key phenomena within the change structures developed as a part of the experiment that may be of interest to other researchers and practitioners.

The first two objectives will be accomplished in Chapter 8 wherein quantitative results will be reported and discussed. The qualitative data takes on at least two forms. General reactions from participants in the experiment obtained from structured and semi-structured interviews will be presented as a complement to the quantitative results in Chapter 8. A more phenomenological approach, employing data from interviews and direct observation and focusing on process issues will be presented in Chapter 9. The remaining sections of this chapter will discuss the major issues involved in conducting field research and the measurement program and methods applied to the TVA project.

ISSUES AND DILEMMAS IN FIELD RESEARCH

The perils of conducting field research have been well documented in the literature on experimental design (Campbell and Stanley 1966; Cook and Campbell 1976). Mainly, the researcher is concerned with reducing threats to internal validity, i.e., how confident one is that obtained results are attributable to the program and not extraneous factors, and external validity or the likelihood that similar results could be obtained in a comparable setting. Such threats to validity, quite controllable in a laboratory by random assignment of subjects to experimental conditions and the use of control groups, are more difficult to overcome in field settings.

The realities of organizational life and ethical restraints preclude researchers from randomly assigning participants in a study to an experimental program. Because change is such a natural part of the adaptation process of an organization, it is difficult to sort out planned change from that which occurs in response to normal demands. Control sites are almost impossible to locate and maintain given the fluidity of organizations. Even including an approximate "comparison" unit such as that employed in TVA runs the risk of unnecessary intrusion into the lives of organization members and contamination of results by their knowledge of the experiment (Lawler, Nadler, and Mirvis 1983).

These dilemmas have prompted Lawler (1980) to develop the term "adaptive" experiments to fit the type of research required for the assessment of QWL programs. Adaptive experiments are quasi-experimental and fit Campbell and Stanley's (1966) depiction of the nonequivalent control group design which features before and after measures, nonrandom assignment to the experiment, and a comparison group. The experiment is adaptive in the sense that the form of the assessment may change as the experimental program evolves. The key to an effective adaptive experiment, according to Lawler (1980), is in designing a broad and flexible measurement program that is longitudinal and independently carried out. Through such a program, unintended consequences may be ascertained by the measurement program. Adaptive experiments are clearly superior to those that are less experimental because of their generalizability and their capacity to control for the effects of such threats to validity as history, maturation, and the loss of experimental subjects over time (i.e., mortality). Nonetheless, other constraints remain. The organizations under study are still unique entities subject to the demands of their environments and the special status afforded by an experiment. The danger of artificial changes and "Hawthorne effects" must be considered in any analysis. Yet, because adaptive experiments are longitudinal, appropriate statistical controls can be applied to minimize the potentially contaminating effects.

Independent assessment, though a highly desirable attribute of adaptive field research, raises new questions about the relationships among the various parties involved in a project. As Seashore and Mirvis (1983) point out, assessors must come to terms with their role as it intersects with other role systems. Because the independent assessment role is so rare in organizations, defining the proper boundaries of the role and appropriate behavior within the role becomes a challenge. Seashore and Mirvis (1983) provide specific guidelines for building and broadening role relations within an experimental site, including ISR's formal statements of its policies and procedures regarding the dissemination of data. Such specificity in role behavior is essential to understanding how the parties will interact during the course of an experiment.

Often the boundaries of the assessment role become blurred as maintaining autonomy and independence is difficult in light of reactions from key parties at the site and other forces arising from events in the experiment. This was no less the case at TVA than at other sites. Often the assessment team was viewed with a modicum of suspicion by employees who wondered what they were hoping to get from their observations. On occasions QWC members prevailed upon the assessors to provide expert guidance during particularly stressful meetings. Letting the situation run its course was frustrating but necessary to maintain independence and not interfere with the committee's affairs. In certain instances, the Study Director stepped out of the pure assessment role and took a more activist stance (see Chapter 9). In most instances, a high degree of mutual trust evolved among the parties at TVA and the assessment role was respected and maintained.

Finally, it must be recognized that measurement, regardless of who performs it, is an intervention in itself. Baseline data are used to determine the nature of other planned interventions and feedback of interim results can alter the course of a project. This was the case with the merit award program at TVA as it was discontinued after an examination of survey data. Given this inevitability, however, care can be taken by the assessors to try to minimize unnecessary intrusions into the life of the program by establishing policies for requesting survey results and monitoring the use of such data.

THE ISR MEASUREMENT PROGRAM

The Institute for Social Research developed a time-sequenced assessment model that was applied at each QWL site. As indicated in Figure 7.1, the administration of measures was sequenced to coincide with the progression of start-up activities, the introduction of external consultants, and the standardized 18-month intervention and postintervention periods. The forms of measurement included cyclical measures, i.e., questionnaire surveys and interviews occurring in three distinct "waves," periodic measures of behavioral, productivity, and financial information, and continuous measures obtained through naturalistic and structured observations (Lawler, Nadler, and Mirvis 1983). The program employed multiple methods over a three-year time period to capture events as they unfolded before, during, and after the intervention.

The centerpiece of the program was the Michigan Organizational Assessment Questionnaire (MOAQ), a broad-based attitude survey that provided information about the respondent's job and work environment as well as his attitudes and perceptions. Since the questionnaire was comprised of separate modules relating to a particular domain (e.g., task characteristics, supervision, general attitudes), it was easily adaptable to a specific site. The MOAQ also provided longitudinal

FIGURE 7.1. Time-Sequenced Assessment Model

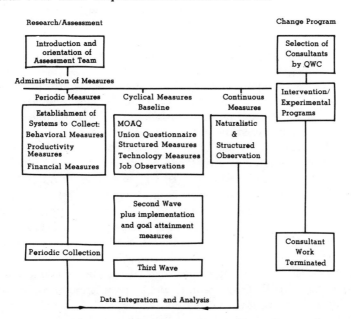

Source: Adapted from Lawler, E. E., Nadler, D. A., and Mirvis, P.H., "Organizational Change and the Conduct of Assessment Research," in Seashore, S. E., Lawler, E. E., Mirvis, P. H., Cammann, C., Assessing Organizational Change, New York, Wiley, 1983. Reprinted by permission.

measures of items that were easily compared across different sites. A complete description of the MOAQ and other types of measurement instruments can be found in Seashore, Lawler, Mirvis, and Cammann (1983).

ASSESSMENT AT TVA

The TVA project yielded one of the most extensive applications of the ISR measurement program and was the only QWL site to produce three waves of attitude measurement. The ISR assessment team was introduced to TPE in August 1974, one month prior to the arrival of the external consultants, and immediately began laying the foundation for the measurement program. The Study Director, a Ph.D. from Ohio State University, was an Assistant Research Scientist at ISR. His assistant, a graduate student at the University of Tennessee, entered the project in early 1976, about midway through the experiment.

The measurement program at TVA was both broad and complex. What follows is a brief description of the various methods applied to TVA during the experimental period.

(1) Questionnaires. The MOAQ was administered at both sites to measure individual attitudes and perceptions as well as obtain descriptive demographic data. The "before" or T1 measure was administered in TPE in September 1974. A second segment of the instrument dealing specifically with the domains of labor-management relations and technology was administered in December 1974 and the third portion, a special pay questionnaire, was administered in June 1975. The staggered application of the T1 questionnaires was attributable to the fact that items were being developed specifically for this site. The T1 measures at the comparison site (DED) were given in April 1975. Time 2 measures were administered at both sites in June 1976. Because of the length of the questionnaire for the experimental site, the administration was split into two days at TPE. Time 3 or "after" measures were administered at TPE and DED in January 1978. The questionnaires were coded in such a way that individuals remained anonymous, identifiable only by an 8-digit number. The number enabled ISR to segment data by branch. Only union leaders and members completed the items dealing specifically with union issues. All TVA employees completed the questionnaires at their work stations during work hours. A summary of response rates for each of the surveys is shown in Table 7.1 As can be seen from the table, response rates were very high across all three waves of measurement.

(2) Interviews. Several types of interviews were implemented at TVA. Structured interviews concerning organizational structure and patterns of influence and interdependence were carried out by a separate ISR study team at both sites in Fall 1974 (T1) and in Fall 1976 (T2). Rework interviews were conducted approximately every six months beginning January 1976 and extending through January 1978, to a selected random sample in TPE. Semistructured interviews were administered to a stratified random sample in TPE during December 1976 (T1) April-May 1977 (T2) and September-October 1977 (T3). The purpose of these interviews was to determine if and how change was being disseminated throughout the experimental division and to obtain general reactions to the project. Final wrap-up interviews which were open-ended in format were conducted early in 1978 with key figures in the change program. Additionally, informal interviews took place with the consultants, the TVA internal development consultant, and others involved in the project.

(3) Behavioral and Financial Data. Systems were established early in the project to attempt to collect data on absenteeism and turnover and various financial indicators on a monthly basis. Efforts to establish productivity measures were unsuccessful given the nature

TABLE 7.1. Survey Administration Summary*

		Number Responding	Response Rate
TPE CHATTANOOGA-TIME 1			
September 1974	Part I (Division N = 403) MOAQ	345	86%
December 1974	Part II (Division N = 412) Union/Technology Portion	294	72%
June 1975	Part III (Division N = 387) Pay Portion	304	79%
Parts I & II Combined		365	91%**
Parts I, II, & III Combined		400	98%**
DED KNOXVILLE-TIME 1			
April 1975	All Portions (Division N = 353)	326	92%
TPE CHATTANOOGA-TIME 2			
June 4, 1976	Part I (Division N = 382) MOAQ	330	89%
June 6, 1976	Part II (Division N = 382) Union/Technology/Pay	328	88%
Parts I & II Combined		357	95%
DED KNOXVILLE-TIME 2			
June 1976	All Portions (Division N = 361)	336	93%
TPE CHATTANOOGA-TIME 3			
January 1978	All Portions (Division N = 365)	326	89%
DED KNOXVILLE-TIME 3			
January 1978	All Portions (Division N = 358)	333	93%

*Outside Union Leaders dropped from response rates.
**Maximum N of Division used for response rate when administration was carried out on separate days.

of the work performed by TPE, although one task force was working on long-term performance measures. Absenteeism and turnover records were kept, but the form of data was not of sufficient quality for use in statistical analysis.

(4) <u>Observation</u>. Direct observation occurred on a reasonably continuous basis in the experimental division (TPE). Most observation was focused on the weekly QWC meetings; however, special meetings, feedback sessions, workshops, and other events were also observed. Both study directors were on site on an average of once every two weeks, although at times their presence was more frequent. They kept extensive field notes of their observations over time. The assessment team also communicated by phone with key parties at the site and received pertinent minutes and memos concerning the QWL program.

The plethora of measurements administered at TVA resulted in an astounding amount of information. It is impossible to assemble all of the data in any meaningful form as it would take several complementary studies to tell the whole story at TVA. The structured interview data, for example, have already appeared in several studies (Feather 1978; Moch, Cammann, and Cooke 1983; Moch, Feather, and Fitzgibbons 1983). The present study seeks to provide a meaningful assessment of the TVA interventions that is grounded in organizational change theory while selectively incorporating the various measures that are available. That task is addressed in the next section.

FRAMEWORK FOR ASSESSMENT

Goals of the Program

An explicit statement of goals for the TVA Quality of Work Program was never articulated by either the QWC or the consultants. As a result, the various parties to the experiment operated according to their own view of what the ultimate outcomes were to be. The tone of the program was clearly set by the general principles of the National Quality of Work Center which specified union-management collaboration in problem solving. In its original public relations document of 1975, NQWC established the following underlying hypothesis for each experimental project:

. . . that when employees in any kind of organization, public or private, are provided expertly-structured opportunity to contribute to designing and implementing activities for organizational change, the organization will become measurably more effective, and the quality of working life for all employees will improve (p. 3).

The dual aims of improved organizational effectiveness and the quality of the individual's working experience were considered the ultimate criteria for all programs. Translating these broad objectives into a set of meaningful goals in specific settings, however, is more challenging.

Because the goals at TVA were more implicit than expressly stated, they were inferred from observation and conversations with key figures in the experiment. An examination of individual statements about their initial hopes for the project and their perceptions about its goals resulted in several recurrent themes:

(1) Participation in Decision Making. It was clear that most parties wanted to develop the means by which lower level employees could have influence over decisions affecting their work. One employee stated that a general goal was "to improve the work environment through employee participation in decision making." A similar comment was made by another employee:

> Well, I think more than anything else [the goal] is to try
> to get employees more involved in the decision-making
> processes within the division. Participating management,
> I guess, is a good word for it.

The QWC and task forces were seen as the vehicles to provide such influence from employees. The participation theme was also well embedded in TVA's cooperative conference program and the ideals of the Authority's founders (e.g., Lilenthal 1953).

(2) Improvements in the General Relationship Between Management and Employees. Many employees and managers stressed that relationships within TPE had been on the decline in the years prior to the experiment and saw the program as a way to enhance these relationships. One manager explained that he hoped that the program "could somehow make the division a more cohesive group." Others made similar references to improving communications, trust, and creating a more harmonious atmosphere in which to work.

(3) Personal Development of Employees. A constant theme expressed throughout the program was the improvement of "morale." The experiment was seen as a way to enhance the dignity, personal satisfaction, and individual development of employees.

(4) Revitalization of the Cooperative Conference. As it was described in Chapter 3, the cooperative conference was the existing vehicle for union-management collaboration. It was the general feeling in TVA that the conference was becoming a formality that was addressing trivial issues. Several employees expressed hope that the new collaborative process would give new life to the tired cooperative conference. The former president of TVAEA described his early interest in the program as follows:

> I could see the cooperative conference program at TVA
> sort of floundering. It was not the active body that it
> once had been. My hopes were that the Quality of Work
> experiment would put new life into the cooperative con-
> ference program and I guess, basically just rejuvenate
> that program. If you remember, [Ted] Mills was down
> here to sell us the package that he called "new," and it
> wasn't all that new to us. We had been involved with it
> years before and our program seemed to have matured
> to the extent that people had begun to let it die and were
> not really using that body. So, that was our hope at the
> time that we got involved in this. Now, I'm speaking as
> the union president, you'll note, and that's what I was at
> the time, of course.

The TVAEA president during the experiment echoed the sentiment of
improving the cooperative program and added that he had hoped that
the Quality of Work Program would enhance the image of the union in
TPE and develop new union leadership resources.

(5) Equity of Rewards. "Equal pay for equal work" was a common theme expressed throughout the experiment. There were perceived inequities in both pay and status between professional engineers
and associate engineering and technical support employees. In many
cases the two classes of workers performed highly comparable work.
The associate and technical employees did not feel adequately recognized even when they were performing essentially the same kind of
work as the engineers.

(6) Productivity, Efficiency, and Workflow. Although never
expressed as a major goal of the experiment, there was hope throughout the lifetime of the project that methods could be developed to improve the technical performance of TPE. Several task forces examined
how work was done and searched for improvements. One clearly desired outcome was the development of procedures to adequately measure productivity. Improved coordination among Branches and smoother
workflow were also seen as desirable and made evident by the second
workshop. As with many QWL type experiments, productivity was
seen as a "fallout" issue. It was hoped that by developing the collaborative problem-solving venture that the process would result in better performance. There was resistance to viewing the project as a
productivity program and quality of work life issues always assumed
top priority.

Research Questions for TVA

Given the implied goals elaborated above, the next task is to develop a set of research questions to guide the assessment. As Goodman (1979) pointed out in his assessment of the Rushton experiment, a QWL program is characterized by a multiple intervention strategy. It is difficult to identify the definite impact of a single change since each of the changes act in concert. The first logical questions for assessment, then, are: What impact did the Quality of Work Program have upon the experimental division? What was different in TPE as compared to DED as a result of the experiment?

It is clear that underlying all of the interventions in TPE was a structure for change that enabled a significant number of employees to participate in the identification, planning, and implementation of changes in the division. Participation in change has been theorized as a way to reduce employee resistance to change (Coch and French 1948; Lippitt 1969). The establishment of the QWC as a collaborative entity and the subsequent development of the task force method of change formulation was the unifying force of the entire experiment. A second set of research questions addresses this aspect of the experiment: What was the impact of the participatory method of enacting changes in TPE? Were there any differences between employees who directly participated compared with those whose participation was more distant? How effective was the QWC in generating employee influence?

Finally, and perhaps most important, questions must be addressed concerning why change happened as it did. What process issues shaped and colored the experimental events? What recurring themes surfaced as the experiment ran its course? How effective were the consultants? What were the political issues permeating the change program? Could the intervention be diffused to other settings or were the changes indigenous to TPE and TVA? What was the impact of the third party assessment? These questions are complex and are not as easily subjected to hypothesis testing in its usual form as the preceding sets of issues. The variables extracted from the collection of data provide a means to develop models to test the "what" issues derived from questions dealing with the overall effects of change on the division and the particular impact of participation. The "why" issues can be assessed, with the absence of testing for statistical significance, by relying on anecdotal information, observation, and interview results. These results, or rather interpretations, help to explain the outcomes of the statistical analyses.

VARIABLES AND METHODS

Numerous theoretical models can be found for assessing and explaining organizational behavior and effectiveness (Nadler 1980; Van de Ven and Morgan 1980; Kotter 1980) and for examining labor-management cooperative programs (Macy and Nurick 1977; Lawler, Nadler, and Mirvis 1983). The models are highly useful in mapping hypothesized relationships among a broad array of organizational variables and in developing an understanding of their causal sequence. The models are a generative source of research aimed at testing these implied relationships and examining them over time.

To address the particular research issues in this study, Likert's (1961) depiction of independent, intervening, and dependent variables provides an elegantly simple yet highly useful analytical framework. A similar framework was employed by Perkins, Nieva, and Lawler (1983) at another experimental site. The conceptual scheme for the global assessment appears in Figure 7.2. The constellation of major

FIGURE 7.2. Global Assessment Model

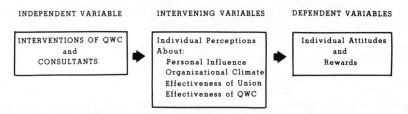

interventions of the Quality of Work Program is the independent variable of the study, producing changes in the dependent variables, i.e., individual outcomes, through its impact on a range of intervening variables, i.e., individual perceptions about the organization. The analysis will explore differences occurring across time in both TPE and DED in individual perceptions about personal influence, organizational climate, union effectiveness and QWC effectiveness.[1] Similar comparisons will be made concerning individual outcomes. The results of this analysis will provide an indication of the impact of the QWC and consultant interventions on individuals in TPE as compared to DED.

---

[1]QWC effectiveness was not relevant to DED employees and was not measured at the comparison site.

A second set of analyses will be performed within the experimental site (TPE) to determine the specific impact of participation in change on relevant variables. The remainder of this chapter is devoted to describing the variables and general hypotheses to be tested in these analyses.

Selection of Variables

The rationale and criteria for the selection of variables in the TVA assessment were based partly on the logic of the above model and prior research, and partly on the nature of the data collected at TVA. As mentioned previously, the quality and availability of the data limited the assessment to the study of individual attitudes. The structural data will appear in subsequent analyses of the TVA data (See Moch, Feather, and Fitzgibbons 1983). Despite their inherent desirability, "hard" measures of employee behavior and productivity simply were not available. The task force working on a measure for productivity met with little success. Therefore, performance data can only be gleaned from impressionistic information and will be discussed accordingly.

The selection of variables for inclusion in the present analysis was based on the following specifications:

1. That the measure was available at both sites for all three measurement points (T1, T2, T3) with the exception of reactions to the QWC.
2. That the variable fit the objectives of the study and the analytical framework and prior research.
3. That the measure was of sufficient reliability and stability to be worthy of statistical analysis.

Independent Variable

The major "intervention" at TVA is defined as the entire set of activities generated by the Quality of Work Committee and consultants under the rubric of the Quality of Work Program. Since it is impossible to isolate the effects of any single new program, the study focuses on the cumulative effect of the broad array of events that occurred as the change program. This includes the workshops, task forces, meetings, and similar program events that were considered part of the experiment and that would not have happened, at least with this degree of intensity, in the absence of the experiment. The primary process underlying these interventions was increasing employee participation and influence.

Intervening Variables

Likert (1961, p. 61) referred to intervening variables as those measures that "reflect the current condition of the internal state of the organization" including such aspects as communication, decision making, and capacity for effective interaction. In this study intervening variables are formed from individual perceptions about how much influence they have, the general state of the work environment and, in this case, the effectiveness of the unions and the Quality of Work Committee as two other components of the organization.

Perceived Personal Influence is defined and measured as the amount of felt or perceived influence an individual may exert within a particular decision domain. Four variables measure the amount of influence in the following domains:

1. resources—decisions about hiring, firing, promotions, pay raises;
2. work activities—decisions about how work is performed, the methods used, and changes in methods;
3. coordination—how work problems are solved, dividing tasks and settling disputes;
4. work hours—decisions about when the work day begins and ends.

These domains encompass varying types of decisions and reflect aspects of the intervention. Perceived influence is akin to the French, Israel, and As (1960) concept of psychological participation or the amount of influence "felt" by the individual.

Perceived Organizational Climate is an indication of an individual's perception of the work environment. The measure is in keeping with the concept of "psychological" climate (James and Jones 1974) or an individual's personal reaction to conditions in the organization. Several variables measure diverse aspects of the work environment according to individual perceptions:

1. Group Cohesiveness—the degree to which an individual feels that he is an integral part of the work group and has a positive feeling toward coworkers.
2. Group Effectiveness—how well the work group makes decisions; overall perception of group performance.
3. Supervisor Encouragement of Participation—the degree to which one's supervisor encourages people to exert influence in decision making.
4. Clarity of Decision Making—the level of awareness an individual has about who makes crucial decisions about coordinating activities and resource allocation.
5. Trust—the degree of trust one has in others in the division.

6. Human Orientation—the extent to which a person feels treated as a human being by the organization (division).
7. Quality of Communications—the general level of communication in the division.
8. Acceptance of Lower Level Influence—the extent to which people at higher levels are responsive to the influence of lower level workers.

A third class of intervening variables deals specifically with the functioning of the union as an organization. One of the implied goals of the program was to increase the effectiveness of the unions in the eyes of members. Currently, there are few instruments that specifically measure union functioning. A notable exception is the union commitment scale developed by Gordon, Philpot, Burt, Thompson, and Spiller (1980). Bullock, Macy, and Mirvis (1983) describe the set of union measures developed for quality of work life sites. Six scales are employed in the present study to determine member perceptions of union effectiveness:

1. Evaluation of Union Efforts to Obtain Task-Related Outcomes—how well the union performs in obtaining fairer job classifications, more participation in decisions, and more meaningful work for members.
2. Evaluation of Union Efforts to Obtain Extrinsic Outcomes—how well the union performs in obtaining better pay, promotions, and fringe benefits.
3. Evaluation of Union Procedures—how well the union handles grievances, selects officers, and selects issues for collective bargaining.
4. Evaluation of Union Processes—the extent to which the union listens to members' views and the way it handles things in general.
5. General Evaluation of Union—member satisfaction with the leadership and general performance of the union.
6. Attitudes Toward Unions in General—the extent to which unions are perceived to be instrumental in protecting employees, improving working conditions, and ensuring fair treatment.

A final set of intervening variables measures individual perceptions about the Quality of Work Committee as the agent of organizational change. These variables, measured only at the experimental site, are as follows:

1. Relationship between QWC and Employees—how well the QWC listened to individual ideas and communicated with the division.
2. Representation—how well the views of all constituent parties were represented by the QWC.

3. Impact of QWC—how effective the QWC was in improving the division.
4. Influence of QWC—the amount of influence the QWC had on decisions that reflected important rather than trivial issues.

Dependent Variables

Since this study is designed to test the impact of the Quality of Work Program on the individual, the dependent variables reflect important individual outcomes defined as personal attitudes and rewards. An implied goal of the program was to make TPE a better place to work and to enhance the personal rewards of the employees. This objective is very much in keeping with prior studies of participation specifying the positive effects of participation on employee attitudes (Morse and Reimer 1956; Powell and Schlacter 1971; Siegel and Ruh 1969; Scheflen, Lawler, and Hackman 1971). It is assumed that participation reduces ambiguity and alleviates the fear that changes will result in negative consequences. Locke and Schweiger (1979) indicate that participation enhances employee attitudes by providing opportunities for the attainment of key values, i.e., intrinsic rewards stemming from increased influence in decisions. In examining the characteristics of successful QWL programs, Nadler and Lawler (1983) point out that individual rewards, particularly internal rewards, must be derived from the process. Individuals involved in a project must be able to find answers to the inevitable question, "What's in it for me?"

The dependent variables have been chosen with these considerations in mind. Several variables deal specifically with individual affective reactions to their jobs and the workplace:

1. Job Satisfaction—general satisfaction on the job and in the work environment.
2. Intrinsic Rewards/Personal Accomplishment—feelings that one has accomplished something worthwhile and has had the opportunity to learn new things.
3. Intrinsic Rewards/Performance and Advancement—satisfaction with one's performance and opportunities for development.

Three variables indicate an individual's motivation level, intentions, and personal assessment of performance:

4. Internal Work Motivation—the extent to which an individual strives to perform well.
5. Intention to Turnover—the likelihood that an individual would actively seek employment elsewhere.

6. Self-rated Performance—personal assessment of quality and quantity of work.

A third type of dependent variable examines individual reactions to pay and other extrinsic rewards.

7. Extrinsic Rewards—satisfaction with pay and fringe benefits.
8. Pay Attitude—feelings of equity in pay.

The final dependent variables are measures of the amount of involvement an individual experiences with his job and organization. Studies by Patchen (1965, 1970) and Siegel and Ruh (1973) demonstrated that participation increases feelings of involvement. The former studies conducted in TVA ten years prior to the Quality of Work Program provide an interesting point of comparison since they examined the cooperative conference as a vehicle for participation. The involvement variables for the present study are:

9. Job Involvement—the extent to which one feels that his job is a significant component of his life.
10. Organizational Involvement—the extent to which an individual is concerned about what happens to the organization (division).

The basic hypothesis to be tested in the global assessment model is that the experiment, i.e., the multiple interventions in TPE, had a positive impact on individuals in the division. According to the research design and the global assessment model, it is anticipated that the interventions produced increases in both the perceptual intervening variables and the individual outcome dependent variables. It is assumed that change in TPE will have occurred between T_1 and T_2 and will have continued or been sustained between T_2 and T_3. By contrast, no change is expected to have occurred in the comparison group in DED.

The Effects of Intensity of Participation

The second major analysis concerns the effects of employee participation in implementing change within TPE. Figure 7.3 depicts the anticipated effects of participation. The independent variable in the second analysis reflects the participatory process by which change was introduced into the experimental division. At the first workshop described in Chapter 4, the QWC developed a formal procedure for problem identification and subsequent change implementation. The QWC appointed a subcommittee of its own members to examine a par-

FIGURE 7.3. Participation Model

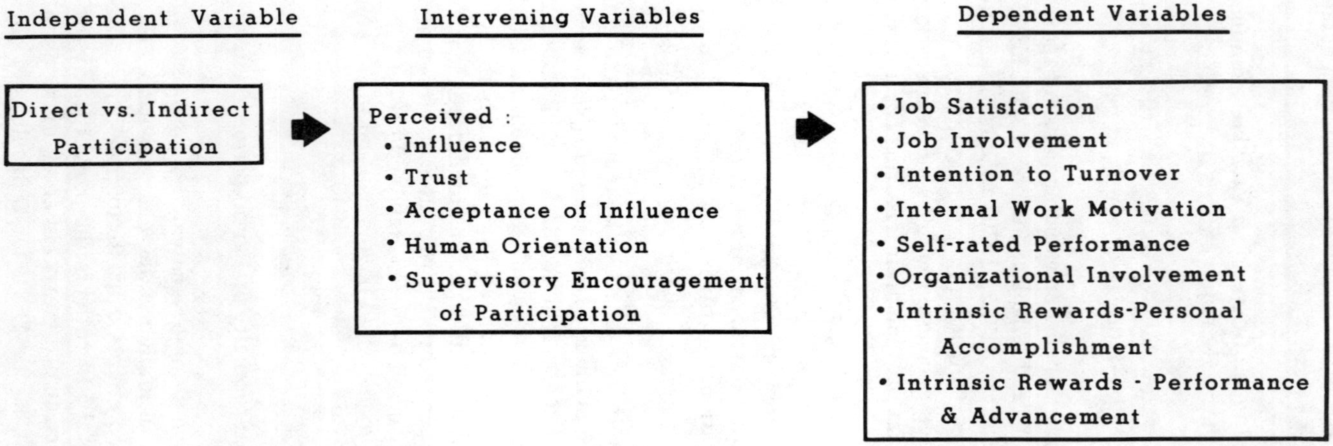

Independent Variable

Intervening Variables

Dependent Variables

Direct vs. Indirect Participation

Perceived :
• Influence
• Trust
• Acceptance of Influence
• Human Orientation
• Supervisory Encouragement of Participation

• Job Satisfaction
• Job Involvement
• Intention to Turnover
• Internal Work Motivation
• Self-rated Performance
• Organizational Involvement
• Intrinsic Rewards-Personal Accomplishment
• Intrinsic Rewards - Performance & Advancement

108

ticular area of concern, e.g., rewards and recognition. The subcommittees in turn appointed a task force of other division employees and provided them with a charge to define the problem and potential strategies. Each task force worked separately and provided recommendations to the QWC which would decide either to implement the program or return it to the task force for refinements. During this process the six to eight member task forces interacted directly with the QWC and received feedback on their work. At one time there were as many as thirteen task forces involving over one-third of the employees of TPE.

This formal change procedure resulted in clear-cut distinctions in the intensity of employee participation in implementing change. The QWC and task force members were clearly contributing to the development of new ideas and procedures. Although the remaining organization members knew of the change program, they acted more as recipients rather than initiators of change.

For the purpose of this study, QWC and task force members are referred to as direct participants while the remaining members of the division are classified as indirect participants. Given this distinction, it will be possible to compare the two groups on their responses to the intervening and dependent variables. Level of participation in this study follows the definition of objective or observed participation put forth by French, Israel, and As (1960). The hypothsized relationships in the participation model are derived from previous models and research which suggests that participation increases feelings of personal influence and trust, and promotes individual rewards (Mann and Neff 1961; French, Israel & As 1960; Marrow, Bowers, and Seashore 1967).

According to the model, it is anticipated that those who participated more directly will experience greater increases in perceived influence, trust, and in feelings that the organization encourages and accepts their influence than will indirect participants. Consequently, it is further hypothesized that direct participants will experience increases in personal rewards and be less inclined to want to leave the organization than those participating indirectly in the change process. It is also expected that the increases will either stabilize or continue during the second measurement interval (with the exception of Intention to Turnover which is expected to decrease).

The global model and the participation model will be tested using appropriate statistical analyses. In addition to the quantitative analysis, relevant data from the semistructured and open-ended interviews as well as observations will be incorporated to lend further insight and meaning to the results obtained.

Measurement of Variables

With few exceptions, this study relies on the variable and scaling conventions of the Michigan Organizational Assessment Questionnaire (MOAQ). A complete description of the development of the instrument is available in Cammann, Fichmann, Jenkins and Klesh (1983). All items were measured on 7 point Likert-type scales and averaged to form the variables employed in the study. Negatively worded items were reverse scored prior to averaging to fit the intended direction of the measure (i.e., organizational involvement). A listing of the items constituting each scale used in this study is presented in Appendix E along with internal consistency (Cronbach alpha) reliability measures for each time period. The alpha coefficient is based on the average correlation among items and the total number of items in a scale (Nunally 1967). An examination of Appendix E reveals that for the most part the scales fall within a very acceptable range of reliability. Correlations computed over time for the TPE measures indicate sufficient stability of measures.

Limitations of the Study

As an adaptive process, this study is subject to the vicissitudes of field research. It is impossible to control for all factors that conceivably could have altered the results. The inclusion of the comparison sample and the application of statistical controls help to alleviate this error component somewhat. Yet, the analysis is by nature more suggestive of effects than conclusive.

Beyond the usual inexactitude of a field study, there are further constraints that come to bear specifically at TVA. Since measurement instruments were being developed as the experiment got underway, the schedule of measurement, as depicted in Figure 7.4, was staggered. The union and technology portions of the survey were administered

FIGURE 7.4. Measurement Schedule

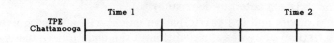
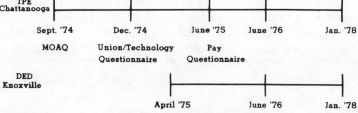

three months apart during a period in which preliminary interventions were already in progress. Therefore, the T_1 measure in TPE was not a pure baseline measure. Furthermore, T_1 measurement at the comparison site (DED) could not be scheduled until April 1975, a full six months after the T_1 measures at TPE. Although it could be argued that the task forces in TPE were barely operating by this time, the gap in T_1 measurement between the two sites must be considered and weighed in the analysis.

Because of the more focused approach taken in this study, there are undoubtedly effects of the interventions that will go undetected by the analyses. The rationale for the models employed and variables chosen for study here has been discussed previously. The discovery of additional effects, particularly in the areas of organizational structure and technology, is left for future research.

SUMMARY

This chapter has presented the overall design of the assessment of the TVA Quality of Work Program. The difficulties of assessing a naturally occurring field experiment were discussed along with the adaptive measurement strategy of ISR which was applied to TVA and other experimental sites. A global assessment model was developed based on the implied goals of the experiment and the nature of the interventions at TVA. The intervening and dependent variables were selected based on criteria that balanced the availability and quality of measures with theoretical relevance. A second model was presented concerning the specific effects of different levels of participation in organizational change. Hypotheses were derived and explored from the standpoint of both models. Finally, the limitations of the study were discussed in relation to both the inexact nature of field research and the particular constraints imposed by the measurement process at TVA. The results of the analysis are presented in the following chapter and follow the logical sequence of the framework presented here.

8 RESULTS: PERCEPTIONS, ATTITUDES, AND REACTIONS

The purpose of this chapter is to provide an assessment of the TVA project. In the preceding chapter, two major models were presented; the global assessment model concerned the overall impact of the QWL program interventions whereas the second model dealt specifically with the effects of participation. Accordingly, this chapter will present a longitudinal comparison of TPE and DED along each of the intervening and dependent variables. A second analysis will be performed in which direct participants in the experimental program will be compared with indirect participants on relevant variables. Finally, qualitative results will be presented and explored to more fully understand employee and management reactions to the experiment.

GLOBAL ASSESSMENT

The first analysis addresses the issue of what impact the interventions had in the experimental division (TPE) in comparison to DED. To approach this task, the analysis is set up according to the nonequivalent control group design (Campbell and Stanley 1966):

TPE experimental site	O_{c1}	X	O_{c2}	(X)	O_{c3}
DED comparison site	O_{k1}		O_{k2}		O_{k3}

where, O_c and O_k are the measurements taken at three points in time at Chattanooga (c) and Knoxville (k), X = intervention, and (X) = intervention continues. It was hypothesized that as a result of the interventions, measures at Chattanooga (TPE) will increase in greater magnitude compared to those at Knoxville (DED).

Sample

The sample for the analysis consists of those employees at both sites who responded to all three survey measurement waves. (N = 245, Chattanooga and 227, Knoxville.) The samples are smaller than the total number of employees at the sites because of turnover during the three-year period and the availability of questionnaires with complete data. As described in Chapter 2, demographic patterns were highly similar for both groups. Most employees in the sample were male, college educated, and members of a union.

Method

The test of the first general hypothesis is accomplished by calculating paired t tests between T_1 and T_2 measures and again for T_2 and T_3 measures at both sites. The t statistic tests for the significance of changes occurring between the two measurement points. Although the t test is the most commonly used statistic for determining changes in survey variables, there are errors that warrant caution in the interpretation of results (Macy and Peterson 1983). Most troublesome are effects attributable to statistical regression. It is possible for an initial score that is below the mean for the entire population to rise and one which is above the mean to naturally decline, thereby confounding observed changes. According to Macy and Peterson (1983), confirmation of a given hypothesis depends in part on the judgment of the assessor. They suggest that the assessor use theory to guide the selection of variables for evaluating change. Despite the fact that care was taken in selecting variables for this analysis (see Chapter 7), errors of measurement cannot be completely controlled. Therefore, the quantitative results will be interpreted with necessary caution and, where possible, corroborated by other forms of data.

RESULTS

Intervening Variables

The comparisons between TPE and DED on personal influence variables appear in Table 8.1. The table presents sample means,

TABLE 8.1. Paired T Tests—Personal Influence

Variable		N^2	Mean (T_1)	Mean (T_2)	S.D.	t	N	Mean (T_2)	Mean (T_3)	S.D.	t
Influence over resources	C[1]	220	1.58	1.73	0.74	3.18**	238	170	177	0.84	1.20
	K	227	1.66	1.62	0.55	-1.16	—	1.62	1.59	0.70	-0.62
Influence over work activities	C	222	2.83	3.42	1.25	7.05***	240	3.40	3.33	1.04	-1.04
	K	227	3.70	3.11	1.24	-7.19***	227	3.11	3.18	1.06	0.97
Influence over coordination activities	C	222	2.50	2.99	1.19	6.16***	240	2.96	2.97	1.01	0.18
	K	227	3.14	2.87	1.01	-4.12***	227	2.87	2.90	0.86	0.62
Influence over work hours	C	217	1.46	2.91	1.96	10.95***	236	2.85	2.99	1.73	1.24
	K	227	2.20	1.30	1.87	-7.25***	227	1.30	1.19	0.97	-1.75

[1]C = Chattanooga TPE
K = Knoxville DED
[2]Because of missing data, sample sizes vary for each analysis

*p ≤ 0.05
**p ≤ 0.01
***p ≤ 0.001

paired standard deviations, and the t statistics for both sites. It is apparent from viewing the results that TPE respondents increased significantly in their perceptions of influence over resources, work activities, coordination activities, and work hours between T_1 and T_2. Commensurately, the DED sample shows a significant decline on all but the influence over resources scale. No significant differences are present between T_2 and T_3. Although some of the results could be attributable to natural regressive effects, there is evidence that suggests a clear pattern of effects on perceived influence.

Table 8.2 displays the results on individual perceptions of organizational climate. Between T_1 and T_2 significant differences are shown in TPE for the following variables: human orientation, quality of communications, acceptance of lower level influence, supervisory encouragement of participation, group cohesiveness, and group effectiveness. Significant decreases are shown in DED on supervisory encouragement of participation and group cohesiveness, while there was no significant T_1 to T_2 increase for clarity of decision making and trust in TPE. These variables increased significantly between T_2 and T_3. Similarly, human orientation and quality of communications continued to climb significantly during the second interval. No other significant changes were found.

Union perceptions are shown in Table 8.3. Here, the results suggest a different pattern. There were no significant increases at all in TPE during either period, while member evaluations of the union in DED increased in satisfaction with efforts to obtain extrinsic outcomes, evaluation of union processes and procedures, as well as general evaluation of the union. The latter measure declined significantly in DED between T_2 and T_3. Quite notable is the significant decline in general attitudes toward unions at both sites during the first eighteen months. Even though Knoxville respondents perceived their union as growing in effectiveness during this period, feelings about labor unions per se decreased. It is also very clear from the data that the interventions in TPE had little, if any, effect on union member perceptions.

Measures of the effectiveness of the Quality of Work Committee were ascertained only at Chattanooga. The results are presented in Table 8.4. According to the data, the relationship between the QWC and division employees declined sharply between T_1 and T_2 along with perceptions about how well the QWC represented employees. The latter measure continued to decline during the second time interval. However, the perceived impact of the QWC on the division rose significantly between T_1 and T_2. There were no significant changes in perceived power of the QWC. The results suggest that although the QWC clearly had an impact on the division, employees responded negatively to the manner in which the committee related to others in the division.

TABLE 8.2. Paired T Tests—Organizational Climate

Variable		N	Mean (T₁)	Mean (T₂)	S.D.	t	N	Mean (T₂)	Mean (T₃)	S.D.	t
Clarity of decision-making	C	224	4.47	4.48	1.33	0.12	239	4.46	4.65	1.45	1.94*
	K	225	4.12	4.22	1.41	1.09	225	4.22	4.26	1.29	0.47
Trust	C	222	3.89	3.95	1.00	0.91	238	3.93	4.06	0.99	2.02*
	K	227	4.01	3.93	0.97	-1.24	227	3.93	3.93	0.89	0.37
Human orientation	C	224	3.92	4.10	1.22	2.16*	239	4.10	4.31	1.02	3.13***
	K	227	3.88	3.91	1.25	0.345	227	3.91	3.88	1.01	-0.39
Quality of communication	C	226	3.48	3.75	1.18	3.56***	240	3.74	3.89	1.18	2.05*
	K	227	3.81	3.95	1.26	1.66	227	3.95	3.95	1.11	0.60
Acceptance of lower level influence	C	224	3.43	3.85	1.12	5.72***	238	3.82	3.89	1.01	1.09
	K	227	3.48	3.44	1.16	-0.52	227	3.44	3.38	1.00	-0.85
Supervisory encouragement of participation	C	224	3.91	4.17	1.49	2.59**	239	4.15	4.07	1.18	-1.04
	K	226	4.51	4.10	1.17	-5.25***	226	4.10	4.08	1.12	0.27
Group cohesiveness	C	222	4.98	5.16	0.89	3.08**	238	5.18	5.21	0.84	0.43
	K	226	5.20	5.05	0.85	-2.61**	226	5.05	5.11	0.84	0.96
Group effectiveness	C	224	5.18	5.42	1.13	3.19**	240	5.41	5.38	0.98	-0.50
	K	225	5.15	5.14	1.14	-0.87	225	5.14	5.12	1.03	-0.23

C = Chattanooga TPE
K = Knoxville DED
*p ≤ .05
**p ≤ .01
***p ≤ .001

TABLE 8.3. Paired T Tests—Union Effectiveness

Variable		N	Mean (T_1)	Mean (T_2)	S.D.	t	N	Mean (T_2)	Mean (T_3)	S.D.	t
Union efforts task outcomes	C	123	3.68	3.75	1.29	.70	137	3.78	3.95	1.09	1.81
	K	133	3.81	3.88	1.06	.71	144	3.92	3.90	1.05	-.20
Union efforts extrinsic outcomes	C	123	4.12	4.11	1.14	-.12	137	4.19	4.21	1.14	.21
	K	133	3.78	4.07	1.21	2.70**	144	4.07	4.17	1.15	1.03
Union processes	C	121	3.77	3.62	1.00	-1.67	134	3.64	3.73	.89	1.12
	K	133	3.57	3.81	.91	3.05**	143	3.80	3.67	.89	-1.96
Union procedures	C	123	4.17	4.10	1.05	-1.06	138	4.10	4.11	1.05	.10
	K	133	3.86	4.13	1.14	2.71**	144	4.13	4.05	1.05	-.88
General evaluation of union	C	122	3.85	3.77	.95	-.98	137	3.79	3.85	1.01	.65
	K	133	3.34	3.82	1.02	5.41***	144	3.85	3.66	.94	-2.46*
General attitude toward unions	C	120	4.61	4.24	.93	-4.36***	132	4.19	4.25	.98	.79
	K	131	4.60	4.30	1.10	-3.10**	145	4.28	4.32	.77	.57

C = Chattanooga TPE
K = Knoxville DED

*p $\leq$ .05
**p $\leq$ .01
***p $\leq$ .001

117

TABLE 8.4. Paired T Tests—QWC Effectiveness[1]

Variable	N	Mean (T_1)	Mean (T_2)	S.D.	$\underline{t}$	N	Mean (T_2)	Mean (T_3)	S.D.	$\underline{t}$
Relationship between QWC and employees	C 140	4.66	3.98	1.67	-4.85***	212	4.09	4.02	1.04	-1.03
Representation of QWC	C 70	5.04	4.50	1.59	-2.87**	158	4.61	4.40	1.17	-2.19*
Impact of QWC	C 87	2.17	3.26	1.77	5.76***	211	3.36	3.26	1.40	-0.98
Power of QWC	C 92	3.57	3.69	1.94	0.60	210	3.69	3.67	1.08	-0.23

[1]Measured at Chattanooga only.
*$p < .05$
**$p < .01$
***$p < .001$

Dependent Variables

It was hypothesized in the global assessment model that the Quality of Work Program would have a positive effect on individual outcomes, particularly their attitudes and personal rewards. The results of this analysis are shown in Table 8.5. As indicated by the t tests in the table, few of the hypothesized results appear. Internal work motivation declined significantly at both sites during the first time interval. Self-rated performance increased significantly at TPE and organizational involvement decreased at DED during T_1 and T_2. TPE employees increased significantly in intrinsic rewards from both personal accomplishment and performance and advancement during the first time period. Pay attitudes increased at DED as significant results are shown for both extrinsic reward satisfaction and general pay attitude. DED respondents decreased in job satisfaction and job involvement between T_2 and T_3. There were no other significant changes during this time. Altogether, the results on the dependent variables provide little support of the hypothesis that TPE respondents would gain significantly in attitudes and rewards. The major impact of the program appears to have been on intrinsic reward satisfaction and self assessment of performance. Individuals in TPE derived more satisfaction from performing the work itself although there was no evidence that they were more satisfied or involved with their jobs or more motivated. However, employees did feel better about their opportunity to learn new things and accomplish something worthwhile, as well as to develop their skills and perform at a higher level. Knoxville respondents were less satisfied and involved with their jobs, but felt better about their pay, despite the fact that there was no planned intervention in DED designed to affect the pay system. Several pay interventions were attempted in TPE, but the results indicated that pay attitudes were not enhanced. This was reflected to an extent by the initial failure of the merit award program and the general perception throughout the experiment that pay irregularities among engineers continued to plague the division.

Discussion

The most striking effects of the Quality of Work Program seem to be on influence and relationships among employees and management within TPE. Employee perceptions of the amount of influence they actually have over resources, work, coordination, and work hours increased considerably during T_1 and T_2 and leveled off during the subsequent eighteen months. This is a logical finding because of the fact that the entire intervention was designed to increase employee

TABLE 8.5. Paired T Tests—Attitudes and Rewards

Variable		N	Mean (T_1)	Mean (T_2)	S.D.	t	N	Mean (T_2)	Mean (T_3)	S.D.	t
Job satisfaction	C	227	5.05	5.17	1.16	1.52	240	5.18	5.24	1.08	0.87
	K	227	5.11	5.21	0.97	1.65	227	5.21	5.06	1.65	-2.15*
Job involvement	C	226	3.62	3.65	0.93	0.50	239	3.65	3.66	0.79	0.25
	K	227	3.64	3.61	0.90	-0.45	227	3.61	3.46	0.83	-2.86**
Intention to turnover	C	229	2.39	2.40	1.13	0.12	241	2.40	2.33	1.19	-0.87
	K	227	2.37	2.49	1.26	1.47	227	2.49	2.57	1.18	1.06
Internal work motivation	C	227	5.90	5.79	0.67	-2.31*	240	5.80	5.84	0.69	0.93
	K	227	5.90	5.75	0.70	-3.42***	227	5.75	5.75	0.76	0.29
Self-rated performance	C	227	5.06	5.22	0.98	2.48**	241	5.20	5.31	0.94	1.68
	K	227	5.25	5.26	0.91	0.150	227	5.26	5.34	0.84	1.53
Organizational involvement	C	228	5.86	5.76	0.99	-1.54	241	5.74	5.79	0.87	0.85
	K	227	5.86	5.69	0.89	-2.93**	227	5.69	5.66	0.90	-0.48
Intrinsic reward satisfaction—personal accomplishment	C	227	4.33	4.66	1.38	3.62***	239	4.62	4.67	1.17	.68
	K	227	4.59	4.62	1.19	.38	227	4.62	4.54	1.20	-1.08
Intrinsic reward satisfaction—performance and advancement	C	227	4.32	4.57	1.01	3.76***	239	4.54	4.58	.85	.79
	K	227	4.43	4.54	.94	1.67	227	4.54	4.42	.91	-1.88
Extrinsic reward satisfaction	C	228	5.17	5.16	.97	-.07	241	5.17	5.22	.99	.86
	K	227	5.10	5.24	1.05	2.01*	227	5.24	5.33	1.00	1.23
Pay attitude	C	229	4.69	4.82	1.08	1.87	242	4.82	4.87	.98	.82
	K	227	4.79	5.02	1.13	3.05**	227	5.02	4.95	1.01	1.05

C = Chattanooga TPE.
K = Knoxville DED.
*p ≤ .05.
**p ≤ .01.
***p ≤ .001.

120

involvement in decision making. Coupled with these results are the additional findings that the employees felt that supervisors encouraged their participation and that individual exertion of influence was accepted by those higher in the division. As a corollary result, employees felt that they worked in a more human environment, i.e., they were treated more as individuals, and that communications and group relationships were enhanced throughout the division over the experimental period. Consequently, employees felt better about performing their work but were not necessarily more satisfied with their jobs.

These findings tend to reflect the nature of the experimental programs. The adjusted work schedule gave employees more discretion over their work hours and thus increased their influence. Several other task forces focused specifically on improving how work was done in the division, e.g., single line diagrams, eliminating overlap with another division, development of division engineering guidelines. However, the jobs of employees did not change. There were no attempts to redesign or enrich jobs. The employee profile as part of the service review process ensured more interaction between supervisors and their subordinates, perhaps increasing feelings of individual treatment. Although pay was a dominant issue in the intervention, the recognized failure of the merit award program indicated that pay equity was to remain a significant problem area. Therefore pay attitudes did not improve.

The perceptions of union members at TPE clearly did not support the hypothesized results. This could have been attributable to a number of possible factors. Because the QWC as a structure for labor-management cooperation was an outgrowth of the long existing cooperative conference, union members may not have perceived union participation in the experiment as anything special or new. The former union president alluded to this perception. The only different aspect was that the QWC could address issues that were more substantial. Union direction really did not change in TPE as a result of the experiment. Attitudes toward unions as useful organizations declined in both settings, perhaps reflecting a societal trend. It must also be recognized that the major union under consideration was a more professional association, engaging in collective bargaining, but generally perceived as more sympathetic to management's goals than the typical labor organization. OPEIU tended toward the latter prototype, but its numbers were small and its influence minimal in the experimental program.

The mixed reactions to the QWC reflected the general ambivalence of the division toward the new entity. The data suggest that the QWC was clearly influential in the daily affairs of the division. Yet, there were concerns about how well the QWC was doing what it was intended to do, that is, represent the interests of employees and keep them informed of its activities. Perceptions of its representation declined over the course of the project. (The effectiveness of the QWC as a working group will be addressed in more detail in the following chapter.)

Overall, the results of the global assessment indicate that TPE employee perceptions of their influence and the general climate of the division increased considerably during the first eighteen months and were maintained during the subsequent time period. Direct increases in personal outcomes did not materialize with the exception of intrinsic rewards stemming from individual performance. Influence perceptions declined sharply in DED, but perceptions of union effectiveness and pay attitudes rose. It is apparent that participation and influence were key variables in the experiment. The second phase of the study focuses more specifically on these effects.

THE IMPACT OF PARTICIPATION

Rationale

The participation model presented in Chapter 7, following the theoretical definition of French, et al. (1960), distinguished between objective and psychological participation. Objective participation was defined as the degree of involvement in the experimental programs that occurred on two levels, direct and indirect. Psychological participation was defined as the amount of perceived or felt influence over resources, work, coordination, and work hours. It was generally hypothesized that more direct participants would experience greater increases over time on perceived influence than indirect participants. It was further hypothesized that the same would hold true for perceptions of trust, human orientation, acceptance of influence, and supervisory encouragement of participation. Likewise, direct participants were expected to increase in relation to their indirectly participating counterparts, on a range of personal outcomes. These predictions were in line with previous models and research suggesting that participation produces psychological benefits for employees, especially when they participate in creating organizational change. The second analysis is designed to test these predictions.

Method

The purpose of this analysis is to compare direct versus indirect participants in TPE over the range of variables specified in the model. The sample is the same as in the previous global assessment model (N = 245). Individuals were designated as direct participants if they were members of either the QWC or one of its task forces as of the T_2 measurement (N = 84 or 34%). Indirect participants (N = 161, 66%) consisted of the rest of the sample.

Since this analysis calls for the direct comparison of employees within the same division, a different form of analysis was chosen. To control for extraneous effects, the analysis of covariance (ACV) was chosen as the statistical method (Lord 1963). By using this technique, initial differences between direct and indirect participants that could have a direct bearing on the results could be held constant. Two covariants were controlled: 1) job level[1] and 2) pretest (T_1) score on the dependent variable of interest. The specific procedure employed was the multiple regression approach to ACV of Cohen and Cohen (1975). The participation variable is entered into the regression equation after statistically controlling the effects of the two covariants.[2] The procedure has the impact of comparing two groups who have been equalized with respect to the covariants. Such a procedure was recommended by Linn and Slinde (1977) and Lord (1963) as a way of measuring change in each of the dependent variables. The procedure was applied to the data over both time intervals.

Results: Direct versus Indirect Participation

The results of the analysis of covariance appear in Table 8.6. Significant differences between direct and indirect participants are shown during T_1-T_2 on influence over work activities, influence over coordination, trust, human orientation, and acceptance of lower level influence. Moreover, direct participants also increased in job satisfaction, organizational involvement, and both intrinsic reward variables in comparison to indirect participants. Other hypothesized differences were not found.

In the T_2-T_3 analysis,[3] only two significant differences appear. Direct participants increased relative to indirect participants on influence over resources and influence over coordination. There were no gains during this period on any of the dependent variables.

---

[1]Job level was coded as four discrete categories: management, engineering, associate and technical support, and administrative-clerical.

[2]The difference is tested by an F ratio which, if significant, indicates differences between the two groups.

[3]In this analysis, T_2 scores were held constant as the pretest score.

TABLE 8.6. Analysis of Covariance: Direct vs.
Indirect Participants[1]

	T_1-T_2		T_2-T_3	
Intervening Variables	N	F	N	F
Influence over resources	220	2.05	238	6.19*
Influence over work activities	222	8.73**	240	0.98
Influence over coordination	222	5.03*	240	6.94**
Trust	222	8.47**	238	0.25
Human orientation	224	7.48**	239	0.39
Acceptance of lower level influence	224	13.82**	238	1.93
Supervisory encourage- ment of participation	224	3.62	239	0.43
Dependent Variables				
Job satisfaction	227	5.37*	240	0.71
Job involvement	226	3.22	239	0.12
Intention to turnover	229	1.09	241	0.17
Internal work motivation	227	0.13	240	1.15
Self-rated performance	227	0.32	241	2.15
Organizational involvement	228	4.28*	241	1.83
Intrinsic rewards—personal accomplishment	227	7.48**	239	0.68
Intrinsic rewards—performance and advancement	227	10.61**	239	0.95

[1]Controlling for job level and pretest score
*$p \leq 0.05$
**$p \leq 0.01$

Discussion

These results support the second hypothesis and are indicative
of the positive impact of employee participation in organizational
change, especially during the first eighteen months of the program.
An additional analysis of the data revealed that the changes in perceptions and attitudes were quite durable over time. Measures did
not drop significantly during the T_2-T_3 interval as might be expected.

Direct participants experienced an increase in their perceptions of influence over resources and coordination activities during the second period.

Of theoretical importance is that these results demonstrate that objective participation is linked to psychological (or perceived) participation. Those employees who were observed participating more directly in problem solving and change implementation felt that they were exerting more influence in work-related decisions. They experienced greater feelings of trust and individual treatment by the system. Direct participants also perceived that beyond exerting more influence, that others in the division were receptive of their influence. As the work of the task forces shifted to issues of affirmative action, pay equity, and workflow, the direct participants experienced an increase in their perceptions of influence over pay and promotion policies and coordination of tasks during the second eighteen months. The findings are also consistent with earlier studies on participation which suggest that participation enhances job satisfaction, involvement, and intrinsic rewards. Apparently, direct participants viewed their task force involvement as a new component of their jobs, perhaps increasing their satisfaction. While they were not more involved in their jobs, they did experience a greater identification with the entire division. They also derived considerable gains in feelings of personal accomplishment and enjoyment from their work. There is no indication that direct participants performed at a greater level than indirect participants.

All in all, the results of the second analysis suggest that participation was a major intervention of the experiment, resulting in rather profound effects. It is clear that for the one-third of the division most directly involved in the project, there were considerable psychological benefits from exerting more influence over important decisions. These employees experienced the project at closer range, had more knowledge about the intricacies of planned change, and felt the impact of the experiment at a more personal level. These results become more meaningful when interpreted within the context of what actually happened in the experiment and why. These issues will be explored in the remainder of this chapter and will be continued in more detail in Chapter 9.

GENERAL REACTIONS

The results presented in the previous sections provide evidence of the impact of the experiment from an empirical point of view. One may peruse the data and reach conclusions about what variables changed during the course of the project as a result of the interventions. This section will focus more on employee and management views about the experiment itself—whether it was accomplishing what they had intended, in essence, whether it was "working."

Method

To gain understanding of reactions to the experiment, qualitative data from the semistructured interviews will be summarized. Respondents to the interviews answered questions concerning specific changes they recognized in the division, the problems of the division, and their overall opinions about the quality of work program. The interviews were administered to a stratified random sample (N = 44) of the TPE division. An effort was made to select a sample that represented the division in branch and salary level distribution. Table 8.7 shows the branch and salary level breakdown of respondents to the semistructured interview.

TABLE 8.7. Semistructured Interviews

Sample Characteristics			
Branch	N	Salary Level	N
Director's Office	5		
Siting and Clearance Staff[1]	2	Management	9
Transmission System Planning	8	Professional	18
Civil Engineering	13	Associate and Technical	11
Electrical Engineering	9	Administrative/Clerical	6
Communications Engineering	7		
Total N = 44			

[1]Newly formed as a result of QWL program.

Respondents were interviewed three times: (T_1) November-December 1976; (T_2) May-June 1977; and (T_3) October 1977, spanning the period of the last full year of the experiment. By this time, task forces had been working for over a year and most, if not all, of the change programs were in the process of being implemented.

Division members were asked: "What do you consider to be the three most important changes which have occurred in TPE since the Quality of Work Program began?" It was very clear that at Time 1, the three most recognized changes were, in order: 1) the adjusted work schedule or flextime (21 first mentions, 5 second mentions, 2 third mentions); 2) the merit award (4 first mentions, 14 second mentions, 7 third mentions); and 3) the employee profile-service review procedure (3 first mentions, 2 second mentions, 4 third mentions). Several other changes received two or more mentions: reorganization of Systems Planning Branch, Division Guidelines, changes in Field Survey Section, including the 4-day week, and greater employee participation. Other responses included better communications, a "climate for people to object," emphasis on training and advancement, establishment of the new Siting and Clearance Staff, and that the division was "more employee-oriented." The pattern was much the same at both T_2 and T_3.

The three major programs continued to be the most visible throughout all levels of the Division. The adjusted work schedule directly affected over one-quarter of the Division's employees who opted for the program. Although the merit award was very visible as a change, it was also recognized as creating perceptions of inequity with favored employees receiving the awards. Because of these problems, the program was discontinued after one year. The employee profile was a permanent part of the performance review process for each employee and was considered successful because it increased communication between supervisors and employees as a result of the required two-hour discussion period.

Employees were also asked what they saw as the major problems in TPE. Responses varied, however, several recurrent themes emerged across the three interview periods. By far the most important problem area was communications at all levels. Employees complained that there was a lack of information flowing between managers and employees, among the branches, and between the QWC and the division. The latter response lends credence to earlier findings about the relationship between the QWC and the employees of the division. Two other related problems were management-employee relations and coordination among units. The equal pay for equal work problem continued to plague the division despite efforts by the QWC to alleviate it. Several problems mentioned fell under the general category of "management." Employees perceived that Branch Chiefs continued to do engineering work and did not manage while others had problems with one particular Branch Chief whom they saw as resistant to change. Other problem areas included the use of employee capacity, morale and satisfaction, and the belief that there were too many committees operating in TPE and no one was making any decisions.

Finally, employees were asked: "All things considered, what is your current opinion about the Quality of Work Program in general?" The open-ended responses were coded into one of three categories: 1) positive comment, 2) uncertain, neither positive nor negative, and 3) negative comment. The pattern of responses for each interview period appears in Table 8.8.

TABLE 8.8. Responses to Quality of Work Program in General

	T$_1$ (Oct.-Nov., 1976) N = 44		T$_2$ (May-June, 1977) N = 42		T$_3$ (Oct.-Nov., 1977) N = 38	
	N	%	N	%	N	%
1. Positive	21	48	20	48	22	58
2. Uncertain	13	30	9	21	6	16
3. Negative	10	22	13	31	10	26

Although the data here are inconclusive, one can receive a rough idea of the general pattern of responses. About half of the respondents were clearly positive in their views about the program. The percentage of positive responses was greater toward the end of the experiment. The number of uncertain responses declined during this time, suggesting that respondents became more definite in their own assessments of the project. Negative responses increased between T$_1$ and T$_2$ and declined between T$_2$ and T$_3$. More can be learned about employee reactions by examining the nature of the actual responses. The following are typical positive responses:

Very high. Very grateful to have the opportunity. Hope that it is not becoming "tired." A helpful and healthful situation. Total benefits are not obvious yet—will appreciate it more in retrospect than now. (T$_1$)

Made tremendous progress considering the type of people you're dealing with. I've seen these things before— this time has made most progress for both management and employees. (T$_1$)

From what I know and the newsletters, I feel it is probably a good thing. (T$_1$)

It's helped employees to understand how management works. We understand each other better—feel freer to talk about different problems. (T$_2$)

Overall, it's fine. QWC has realized some weaknesses through feedback from employees. Has been effective overall. Sometimes little things have to be handled before big things. (T$_2$)

Very worthwhile endeavor—something that was needed— we had stagnated—something we should definitely continue.

Aware of opposition to QWP—people don't fully realize
the extent of benefits in the future. Has been added work
on many top engineers, very satisfied with status quo.
Also those who are never happy no matter what is done.
All in all, QWP a tremendous asset. (T_2)

They are to be commended at least on the type of problems they attempted to solve. Many of the problems do
not have easy solutions. They have tackled a much higher
level problem than the old [cooperative conference] which
dealt with trivial men's room issues. (T_2)

We've done a lot of things. If you have an issue, it has
given us a lot of muscle to resolve it with. A door to a
problem we did not have before. (T_3)

A good program—has delved into some basic problems—
a more congenial, understanding relationship between
management and employees. (T_3)

Has brought employees and management closer together
in their opinions of one another. This is what the C-C
[cooperative conference] was supposed to have done. (T_3)

By contrast, below is a representation of the general tone of the
negative responses:

Started out to be a good thing—now manipulated by management—they do what they please. Merit award a popu-
larity contest. Employees don't get much feedback unless
a promotion is made or someone is nominated for a merit
award. (T_1)

Gross waste of money. I see nothing constructive that has
come from it. (T_1)

Started out "gung ho"—program has slowed down. From
sitting in on some of the meetings, can't believe some
people are in management. Too much emphasis on minor
details—wording. Newsletter is not exactly what I'm looking for as far as gaining information on things I don't know
about. (T_1)

It has moved too slow. They are working on a lot of stuff
that doesn't amount to a hill of beans in the long run [e.g.,
equal opportunity]. Spent a lot of manhours but I don't see
the benefit. It has perhaps helped avoid RIFs by having so
many people involved. The rank and file don't recognize

the benefits yet. They [QWP participants] say that the expenditure is worth it. (T_2)

A great waste of money and time since we haven't seemed to progress with it. Employees have really not benefited. (T_2)

Greatest thing for some (sarcastically). QWP absolutely foolish, unreal. The way it has been conducted—hasn't been fair—not concerned with the people—the little kings want to climb higher. I've said too much. (T_2)

Unless they start dealing with something that amounts to something—quit it. Too generalized. I like to think that I'm being heard on an individual basis. (T_2)

A mystery to me from the outset. Management knew the problems—they didn't need QWP. Didn't tackle any problems with employees until the end when it is too late—then it was rather forced. (T_3)

I don't think it has been as effective as a lot of us thought it would have in the beginning. They have attacked trivial matters which were results of the main problems rather than attacking the main problems themselves. (T_3)

The neutral or uncertain responses contained elements of both sentiments:

Disappointed—had great potential—concept is marvelous if properly applied—have created discussions between QWC employees and non-QWC employees, should continue. Neutral; some good—might waste more time than is necessary. Haven't been here all that long—mainly concerned with doing a good job. I don't feel much needs changing. (T_1)

Uncertain; they haven't produced as much as expected. Too much attention in meetings to minor details (bickering), considering the level of the people involved. They have created a more relaxed atmosphere in the division as far as freedom of employees to give their opinions. (T_2)

They're trying. Can't truthfully say that they have accomplished a lot. A lot of good men involved—I respect them. If we didn't try anything, we couldn't accomplish anything. (T_2)

I don't think it has accomplished what I thought it could
in the beginning. Maybe it dragged out too long. Has
accomplished much in certain areas. Has taken up so
much of management's time—can be turned over to lower
levels. Overall, a good idea. (T_2)

Still uncertain—as long as majority of the people [and
management] want it, I'm for it. (T_3)

Discussion

The results of the semistructured interviews present the logical
outcomes stemming from evaluating the same phenomena from divergent points of view. One aspect that both positive and negative parties
seemed to agree upon was that the program was general in scope and
moved slower and accomplished less than originally expected. Positive
respondents saw this as evidence that the issues under consideration
were broad, complex, long-term and not conducive to quick and easy
solutions. The negative respondents' view was that the program was
a waste of time and money with little to show for it. There is reason
to believe that those who participated more directly changed their assumptions about what the program was all about. They could witness
firsthand how difficult it was to initiate something new and have it continuously refined as it worked through the system. The indirect participants in their role of reactors, responded to direct tangible benefits
and other segmented bits and pieces of information.

The QWC and management were looked upon with suspicion and
perhaps a bit of envy, i.e., "little kings who wanted to climb higher."
Employees felt inadequately informed about what the QWC was doing
and became suspicious of their motives. Coupled with this was a political atmosphere, concerned with inequities, that was exacerbated
by the merit award program. There was a feeling that some people
were benefiting from the program at the expense of others. Clearly,
the Quality of Work Program changed some perceptions in the division,
but many of the same problems, i.e., communication between management and employees, equal pay for equal work, remained along with
the question of whether surfacing these issues was good in and of itself.

MANAGEMENT REACTIONS

Management members of TPE (Director, Branch Chiefs, and
Section Supervisors) were asked open-ended questions as part of the
structural interviews that were conducted during October-December,

1976, N = 41 and March 1978 (N = 18). Their responses are summarized in this section.

Managers were asked: "Has the Quality of Work Committee caused any problems that weren't anticipated in advance?" The overwhelming response was that the activities of QWC took up too much time. Typical responses from managers were:

> The large amount of time spent, and whether we're getting our money's worth.

> It's taken so much time. It got to be that you couldn't get anything done on Thursday (QWC meeting day) because everyone was in a meeting.

> Every time you want to see somebody, they're in a meeting.

> The time that's been spent. Some of my guys are gone 3 to 4 hours a day. I know that's not true, but it seems like it.

> There have been a lot of manhours spent, without a lot of results.

> The amount of time and the wheel spinning.

> All the time spent.

> They gave us extra tasks (employee profile, etc.) without us having any more time. There's a great amount of time spent in bull sessions dealing with Quality of Work.

Other managers expressed dissatisfaction with the merit award and employee resentment about the entire program. One manager recalled that the selection of the QWC created hard feelings. Some managers felt that because of the program's emphasis on participation, employees were taking their jobs away.

The management sample was then asked for additional comments about the QWC and the entire program. Two Branch Chiefs who were QWC members responded:

> We haven't talked to the employees enough about our activities. We don't think we got our money's worth out of [the consultants] but a committee like this needs an outside push. Otherwise, we would spend our time in day-to-day work activities. We never had developed goals. It makes it hard to evaluate what we've done. There ought to be a general goal to evaluate things against. I'm afraid we might degenerate into a trivial session—annual picnic

and elevator service. We've got to evolve into something
else.

I feel that we've had good management over the years.
Therefore, the problems that are left are tough problems. People are disappointed that things can't be done
overnight. I feel our people are better informed about
things, but not many final solutions. I feel that not including Branch Chiefs was a mistake, even though I didn't
think so at the time. We have to recognize this communication [with employees] problem. Part of our people
expected magical answers to problems that <u>have</u> no answers. Merit awards are self-defeating endeavors. The
good people will be motivated anyway. Those who need it
just get pushed down.

Another Branch Chief had a different view about the intensity
of their involvement:

It's very time consuming. It's hard to make time for it.

I don't feel that all the Branch Chiefs or the Director
have to be there every meeting. I felt that having Assistant Branch Chiefs (on QWC) was best. We should
move the responsibilities down.

Section Supervisors commented more on the "nuts and bolts"
of the program:

I have vested interest in the employee profile. I feel the
ideas are valid and should be instituted. The forced face-
to-face confrontation is good, even if there are other
problems.

The flexible time schedule has been a great success.

I like the idea of the merit award, so that people can
be rewarded for work above and beyond.

I doubt if the cost/benefit ratio (for QWC) has been that
good.

It would be better in an organization where there was
poor top-to-bottom communication. That wasn't the case
here.

There is a continuing need to concentrate on developing
a better quality manager at all levels, including the SD4s
[professional engineers].

A good engineer doesn't make a good manager, but the technical work requires someone who knows the technical stuff.

I feel that we should be closer physically to the Substation Layout section for coordination purposes. The QWC hasn't worked on this yet.

It has good possibilities [Has it not lived up to those?]. I don't know. I really can't evaluate it.

The organization can't be changed to satisfy the workers. It has a job to do. I don't know how far you can go in satisfying people.

There is a lot of feeling against the cooperative spirit that is necessary. This is true of the SEs [draftsmen and engineering associates] especially. They feel they are getting the shaft.

Consistent with the earlier employee responses, supervisors who were more distant from the program concentrated on specific benefits:

Overall, it has merit. Because I've not been directly involved, I only see it from a distance. Adjusted work schedule and employee profile has had beneficial effects.

When you get beyond merit award, flextime, and the four-day week [survey section], what do you have that you can put your finger on?

I think we've spent so much time on QWC work that whatever gains we've had have been lost.

It's sort of off in the distance to us. It really hasn't changed us that much.

I'm neutral right now. I thought we'd get into the nitty-gritty.

Every five years, the committee should be organized as a "bell ringer" for management to operate for a year. To tell management what should be looked at.

I predicted that the merit awards wouldn't work because it gets into personalities. They involved religion, part of town, everything in deciding who to give it to.

Managers recognized that communication was a more open process and that perhaps that was the most significant accomplishment of the whole program. One manager commented that the QWC had accomplished more in two years than he had seen during his entire 17 year career in TPE. Another commented that the QWC was making employees understand how elusive some of the problems were. Others, however, saw major problems with how the committee operated:

> Members of the committee never make decisions. They table issues until it goes away. They never vote, they just argue, so they never get anything done. There's too much bickering among Branch Chiefs.

> I think more people should have been on it. I think some employees feel that the QWC is another branch of management and resent it.

> At the beginning, people thought it would cure everything in three months' time. There's been disillusionment.

> It's not a complete loss, but it hasn't achieved as much as was expected.

> There was a smugness on the part of the QWC, and this was disastrous. If they could have been replaced every six months, it would have helped.

Discussion

These management reactions reinforce the findings from the semistructured interviews. The Quality of Work Program was time-consuming and expensive and managers were not sure of the benefits in relation to the excessive costs. Managers who were closest to the process seemed to recognize the long-term implications of the process whereas those who were more distant responded to what they could see. Problems of inequity and resentment brought out earlier were also recognized by the managers. Reactions to the QWC were mixed; some managers were quite sympathetic to the difficulty of their task while others were critical of the way the QWC conducted its business. There were allusions to problems with Branch Chiefs on the committee. This issue will be addressed specifically in the next chapter.

SUMMARY AND CONCLUSIONS

In this chapter, the results of the TVA quality of work experiment have been presented. Multiple methods were used to determine the impact of the intervention on individuals in TPE. The global assessment results provided evidence that TPE employees' perceptions of personal influence and organizational climate increased when compared with employees at the comparison site (DED). The intervention had a lesser impact on individual outcomes in the form of attitudes and rewards, with the exception of intrinsic rewards associated with performance. Most change occurred during the first eighteen months of the experiment and remained constant during the subsequent eighteen months. Perceptions of union effectiveness remained unchanged during the experiment and reactions to the QWC were mixed.

The second analysis demonstrated that those employees participating more directly in the change program experienced rather dramatic increases in influence, organizational perceptions, and personal outcomes compared to indirect participants. Participation was seen as a major effect of the entire program, forming the foundation of other intervention strategies.

Finally, qualitative interview data were explored to gain more understanding about the nature of the change program and employee and management reactions. Results were again, mixed, indicating different vantage points. The adjusted time schedule, the merit awards, and the employee profile were considered the most obvious changes in the division. The experiment was seen as time-consuming and costly. Direct benefits were elusive and not overly visible. These results complemented the quantitative analyses, suggesting that those individuals more directly involved in the change process evaluated it more from a process point of view than more distant employees who thought more in terms of tangible outcomes.

The Quality of Work Program was seen as a device to begin solving deep-seated problems in TPE that seemed to defy short-term solutions. It is evident from the data that initial expectations of the division members were very high and that individuals more closely aligned with the program began to view progress in a more realistic way. The results make it apparent that the program was not an unqualified "success" as perceptions of basic problems remained near the end of the experimental period. However, there is some evidence that TPE was seen as a better place to work and that many employees were influencing key decisions that affected their work and lives.

9 PROCESS ISSUES

One of the benefits of assessing an organizational change program over a period of time is the opportunity for the assessor to "live with" the organization and to appreciate more fully its culture, traditions, and social interactions. Qualitative research is rare in organizational settings; researchers and practitioners are usually interested in "results" that can be quantitatively documented as was done in the previous chapter. Qualitative investigators, according to Van Maanen (1979, p. 520), are more interested in the "unfolding of social processes rather than the social structures that are often the focus of quantitative researchers." He also points out that "qualitative methods represent a mixture of the rational, serendipitous, and intuitive in which the personal experiences of the organizational researcher are often key events to be understood and analyzed as data."

Results of a quality of work life experiment are much more meaningful when viewed in the context of the social processes in which the program is immersed. The various interventions and structures known collectively as the TVA Quality of Work Program occurred in a network of human interactions that affected, and were in turn affected by, the events of the experiment. The purpose of this chapter is to bring to light these emergent processes by examining data collected by informal interviews with key figures and the direct observation of events. The focus is on such social phenomena as interactions, influence, power, and interpersonal relationships. A map of process relationships in TVA is developed from which major themes can be discussed.

EXAMINING POWER RELATIONSHIPS

The focus of this study is on participation in organizational change. The entire national Quality of Work Program was based on the premise of employee-management collaboration, and structures were established in each experimental site to promote the participation of employees in decision making around change issues. The results presented in the previous chapter demonstrated that participation indeed was a major intervention at TVA, producing positive effects on a number of variables. Participation was engendered through the formal procedures of the QWC and task forces assisted by the external consultants. As a result of this process, new programs were implemented such as the adjusted work schedule and employee profile. These programs were the products of this collaborative process rather than typical administrative action, although management was clearly part of the decision-making process.

The study of participation requires an examination of power relationships since participation implies the exercise of power and influence. These relationships give life to a QWL experiment by shedding light on how participation works in reality. Because power is such a pervasive concept, the processes of a QWL program strike issues that are vital to the essential functioning of the organization. The idea of "power centers" surfaced early in the TVA experiment and became the central set of issues as the project matured.

Although power is perhaps the most ubiquitous issue throughout organizations, it remains one of the most misunderstood and under-researched areas of study. Gaining access to the internal life of an organization is a difficult and time-consuming task. Understanding the nature of relationships requires careful observation and probing from which inferences can be made. As was the case at TVA, these relationships may not become apparent until the experiment is well along. Often these patterns of behavior are more visible in retrospect. The TVA experiment provides a rich opportunity to trace the development of power relationships and learn about their interweaving with the events of the project.

Understanding Power

Before undertaking the task of exploring power relationships in the TVA experiment, it is first necessary to understand power as a concept. A few definitions are, therefore, in order. The abundance of definitions of power impedes the development of a precise meaning of the term. Power, like participation and QWL, is a label that has been attached to numerous phenomena. Pfeffer (1981, pp. 2-3), recognizing the all-encompassing nature of the concept of power, distilled prevailing definitions of the term to include the following core attributes:

1. Power characterizes relationships among social actors and is relationship or context specific. A person or unit is powerful only in relation to others.
2. Although power is context specific, it is not necessarily limited to certain decisions or issues.
3. At the heart of most definitions is the idea that "power" is the capability of one social actor to overcome resistance in achieving a desired objective or result."

When power is legitimized according to accepted practices and values in the organization, it becomes known as <u>authority</u>. Related to these terms is the similar concept of <u>organizational politics</u>, defined by Pfeffer (1981, p. 7) as: "those activities taken within organizations to acquire, develop, and use power and other resources to obtain one's preferred outcomes in a situation in which there is uncertainty or dissension about choice."

Political activity is distinguished from decision making through rational bureaucratic procedures and depends more on the exercise of informal influence. Since uncertainty was a condition throughout the change program at TVA, the development and implementation of change was by definition a political process. In examining process issues at TVA which imply the use of social power, an attempt will be made to distinguish between events arising from political maneuvering and more typical administrative action or rational bureaucratic procedures.

Identifying Social Actors

There were numerous social forces at work within the TVA QWL project. The development of the experimental program in TPE resulted in new relationships in addition to those among traditional units. The major relationships in TVA are depicted schematically in Figure 9.1. The diagram identifies the social actors interacting within the QWL program. The TPE division is shown in its hierarchical position in TVA as a subunit of the Office of Power which reported to TVA top management. The two union bodies, the Salary Policy Employee Panel and the Trades and Labor Council represented white and blue collar unionized employees in the Authority. The Central Joint Cooperative Conference was the TVA-wide vehicle for the cooperative conference program. Within TPE was the existing organizational hier-

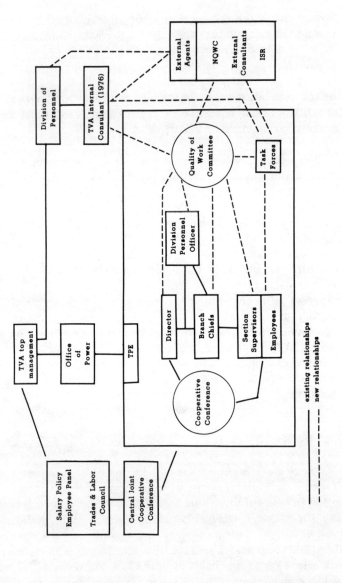

FIGURE 9.1. Relationships Among Social Actors Within QWL Program

existing relationships

new relationships

140

archy consisting of the Director and his staff, including the Personnel Officer, the five Branch Chiefs, the section supervisors, and employees. The cooperative conference is shown as the preexisting representative union-management committee. New relationships as a function of the QWL Program are depicted by dashed lines. The QWC, along with its task forces, were the central forces in the change program. The diagram also reveals relationships that involved outside parties to both TVA and TPE. These "external agents" included the National Quality of Work Center, the external consultants, and the independent assessors (ISR), all of whom interacted with each other. The TVA internal consultant, who entered the project in 1976, is also included as a party external to TPE. Each of these individuals and units is a major actor in the experiment, exercising his unique role and power at various times.

Context of the Experiment

To more fully comprehend the inner workings of the TVA project, one must first consider some larger contextual issues. First, TVA was an unusual organization. It began as one of the largest federal programs of the New Deal and was historically considered to be a major social experiment. Therefore, as an organization, TVA was unduplicated in the United States. Its mission included not only the production of energy, but also a responsibility for the welfare of the surrounding region.

As a government agency, TVA was not affected by the usual profit motive, meaning that there was little pressure to produce on the part of employees. This was frustrating for consultants accustomed to the more typical production-oriented company. As one consultant put it:

> You don't have any competition. You don't have the outside dynamic. You're not up against a competitor that you're losing market share to. You're not pricing yourself out of business necessarily.

As a result, the impetus for change had to come from within a system that was characterized by complacency and, in some views, stagnation. TVA was steeped in tradition, a kind of "that's the way it's been" attitude. One of the consultants characterized it as "everyone running around in quicksand." This lack of urgency was reinforced by the fact that the TPE was considered to be in a slow production period during the time of the experiment. One must also consider that the labor-management relationship in TVA was more harmonious than that which is usually found in organizations.

In summary, one receives a picture of the larger system, TVA, as a large, tradition-bound organization that was by nature resistant to change. In other words, TVA was similar to other large government bureaucracies. These contextual considerations affected the organization's readiness for change and had a definite impact upon the inner life of the Quality of Work Program.

Process Themes Within TPE

In reviewing the intricate pattern of relationships among the various parties to the TVA Quality of Work Program, several themes emerge that are ripe for analysis. The first issue concerns the role of the QWC as the instrument of organizational change. There were persistent questions throughout the entire program about where the QWC "fit" into the TPE decision-making system. The second theme involves the internal functioning of the QWC. As a committee, the QWC was subject to all of the dynamics that affect working groups. There were also concerns arising from previous analyses about how well the QWC performed its function as a representative group. The third and final set of issues revolves around the impact of external forces to TPE such as the consultants, NQWC, ISR, and the TVA internal consultant. Each of these themes will be discussed in terms of power relationships drawing upon data generated from interviews and observation.

THE ROLE OF THE QUALITY OF WORK COMMITTEE

A unifying factor of all of the quality of work life experimental sites was the establishment of a joint representative committee as the central agent of change. Although it took on slightly varying forms, the committee provided a means by which employees could have influence on change events through their elected or appointed representatives. At TVA and other sites, the Quality of Work Committee was the vehicle for management-employee interaction about problems and issues and the means of ownership over the change program. The QWC concept was a less radical approach to change in TVA because of the longstanding cooperative conference system. Yet, because the QWC was capable of addressing issues that were considered negotiable, and therefore vital to the organization, it was vested with considerable power.

The QWC also had the unique role of client to the external consultants. It was the QWC that interviewed candidates, finally settling on the consultants of their choice. The consultants worked with the

Committee, often finding this unique arrangement a frustrating experience. Their attempt to shift the role of client to the Director was met with hostile rejection, thus reinforcing the preeminence of the QWC. Even though the QWC was clearly the focal point of the experiment, the issue of where it fit into the system was one that would plague its functioning throughout the experimental period. Was the QWC an advisory group or did it have the authority to implement decisions on its own?

Opinions varied on this issue. The committee began operating as a discussion group prior to the arrival of consultants. The task force method of developing programs after the initial workshop seemed to give the QWC the authority to approach problem areas by appointing a task force, receiving and modifying task force reports, and finally implementing new programs such as the adjusted work schedule. One original QWC member described the original procedure as follows:

> Well, you might say the [the QWC] were the leaders.
> These were the people where all of the ideas from all
> the employees and management funnelled into this group
> and they decided whether or not it was worth looking into
> and whether or not a task force ought to be assigned to
> look into it. Then, after they made a report they made
> the decision whether to drop it or go on. In other words,
> they had all of the power.

However, what looked good as a model on paper was often not the way the procedure actually worked. Another QWC member explained:

> We had the guidelines that we ran a few things through
> at the first workshop on implementation and task force
> work and everything from the bringing of the problem to
> the Committee to getting it implemented. That was all
> written down in sequence on a piece of paper. We adhered
> to that very closely but each time there was something
> to be implemented and we got into this thing about who
> this, how do we do it, you don't have any business, you
> don't have . . . all the arguments, pros and cons, writing
> the minority papers and sending them on and all this kind
> of stuff, that just got to be a hassle.

The actual role of the QWC was never made clear either to QWC members or to the rest of the division. In the early days, marked by great expenditures of energy and the momentum of all-day meetings, the QWC seemed to exercise more discretion than in the second half of the experiment. There were many problems to discuss and the task forces were set in motion. As the experiment matured, the issues became more global, i.e., organization structure, and the committee bogged down. One member proclaimed:

> Oh, it [the QWC] started out with a lot of vigor to sincerely look at a number of problems. It made some progress and it gradually lost its momentum because it realized it wasn't an action group.

Another member noted the shift in focus, stating that the original QWC concept was like an "umbrella," that is, the QWC would "review innovative ways of accomplishing something. Now, they come up with ideas and dump them in the Director's lap."

There was considerable confusion about who was ultimately responsible for implementing change in the division. The QWC was perceived as having multiple roles. One employee explained the roles as follows:

> I think it had numerous roles. One role comes to mind immediately is chief complaint processor. I think that was very evident from the things that the employees brought in, personal or small group gripes. I think they saw a lot of that. I think the people that were a little more farsighted, and this includes some of the management and some of the employee people, felt like it was a different approach to getting things done—a worthwhile approach to try to get things done. I think some of the management people felt like it was an attempt by employees to wrest the power from their hands. I think there were a lot of different, maybe 380, different roles, depending on which person you happened to talk to.

Another QWC member did not see the QWC as having final authority:

> I always figured that it was no more than just an airing of the pros and cons to the problems, getting your feelings and your concerns out at the proper level and then hope that you could sell the individual who had to institute that particular action, sell them on the importance of it. That's all I figured that you could do. You can't make the decisions for the Director.

Most individuals saw the Director as having the final say. But the issue was not that simple. The relationship between the QWC and

the Director was complicated by the fact that the Director was a full
member of the committee. Even though many people perceived the
committee as a problem-solving group that made recommendations
to the Director, the Director was also part of the deliberations. It
would have been extremely difficult for the Director to reject an idea
that he helped develop, especially if it was an idea that had the full
backing of committee consensus. As one person put it, the Director
swapped his role from "one of authority to one of influence." He could
not fall back on his authority and simply state that he did not want
something to happen. Several comments reinforce this dilemma:

> I will hasten to say that both of the Directors of the divi-
> sion through the entire proceedings were very prone to
> be influenced by the QWC. Now I don't know of anything
> that the QWC recommended to them that was not carried
> out or it was pushed along as far as the Director could
> push it along.

> I think that their [QWC] recommendation carried very
> much weight with the Division Director. In other words,
> I think that he almost felt like he had a mandate to im-
> plement any decision that came out of the QWC.

The second Director summed up the issue as follows:

> It probably depends to some degree on the attitude of the
> Division Director and his relation to and his commitment
> to the concept. But to me it was always just a little bit
> fuzzy to have the Director participating in the committee
> and then having to put on another hat and accept or reject
> its decisions. I'm going to have the same thing in the
> [new] cooperative conference.

When asked about the authority of the QWC, the Director responded:

> Well, in my opinion, it really never had much authority.
> That was this question that we always seemed to get hung
> up on. I think its authority was primarily through its abil-
> ity to make recommendations. Perhaps that's an authority
> of sorts. I think that's power. It has the power of recom-
> mendations with the backing of a number of influential
> people in the division which no director in his right mind
> can ignore. But I think it was power rather than authority
> that the committee possessed.

The relationship between the Director and the QWC, then, was symbiotic. The presence of the Director on the committee gave the committee the necessary stature to bring about change. QWC members had instant access to the Director and could interact with him directly. At the same time, the Director could participate in problem solving with a highly knowledgeable and visible group that represented the division. In effect, the QWC served as another highly competent staff to the Director. While this relationship was mutually beneficial, it also limited each of the parties in fully carrying out their roles.

The presence of the Director at times inhibited the deliberations of the QWC. It was hard for employees to disagree with top management sitting directly across from them. Conversely, the Director sometimes downplayed his role in order not to overly influence decisions. This aspect was particularly frustrating for the consultants who wanted the first Director to assert his role more authoritatively. According to one of the consultants, the QWC needed someone to direct their energies toward, in effect; to say "Aren't we doing good? Hey, boss, what do you think?" This lack of leadership, exacerbated by the conspicuous absence of the first Director from several QWC meetings, was, according to the consultants, deleterious to the progress of the program. Employees perceived that the Director was not interested in the program and did not consider it a high priority. The key role of the Director is brought out by the following recollection of the observer-facilitator:

> . . . there was a meeting going forward with a very lively debate, the Director was called out of the room, and the debate ceased. It was as though the queen bee had been killed in a hive—a fairly dramatic exhibition, I think.

The change of Directors midway through the program certainly slowed the work of the QWC, mainly because the new Director was not "brought up" in the program. By this time, however, the consultants were no longer present, the Branch Chiefs were members of the QWC, and a more advisory role of the committee was becoming accepted both by the QWC and others in the division. The new Director was not as crucial to the program as his predecessor who was among its progenitors, but his commitment to the quality of work concept increased during the latter parts of the experiment, eventually becoming his most central concern.

Relationships with Branch Chiefs

Perhaps the greatest implicit power struggle in the Quality of Work Program occurred between the QWC and the Branch Chiefs.

When the QWC was first formed, only one Branch Chief was a member. Another original member eventually became the head of the new Siting and Clearance Staff and assumed a role that was the equivalent of a Branch Chief. Other senior management positions on the QWC were occupied by three Assistant Branch Chiefs. This arrangement caused some early friction attributable to the fact that Branch Chiefs traditionally had a large amount of power in the Division. References were constantly made to the fact that the branches were like islands or "empires" that did not communicate across boundaries. The Director was perceived as having minimal influence over branch decisions. According to one of the external consultants, one of the "peculiar characteristics of the TVA culture . . . has to do with [the fact] that there are no sanctions in the traditional way over the Branch Chiefs. . . . About the only thing that the Division Director can use to influence the behavior of the Branch Chiefs is an appeal to their pride in the organization as a whole which is not a trivial thing."

The absence of the Branch Chiefs from the QWC during its first eighteen months removed them from the change process. This distance, coupled with the Branch Chiefs' divergent opinions concerning the overall value of the change program, was a significant issue for the entire project. According to one QWC member,

> I think each Branch Chief saw this differently. I think at least one or more of them saw it as a direct threat to their authority and they were not committed to the Program. I think one or more of them saw it as a very good thing. Then the rest of them sort of fell somewhere in between.

Another QWC member reinforced this assessment,

> [The QWC] had to go back to the Branch Chiefs and suddenly they found out that the assistant had agreed to something that the Branch Chief wouldn't buy. This made for a sticky situation, especially as far as the Director was concerned. Because here sits the Branch Chief, out on a limb by himself. The man above him and the man below him agree to something that he doesn't like. So he's in a sticky situation. Yes, it created some real problems and I think ultimately, that's why the Branch Chiefs were brought on board.

To alleviate these problems, the Branch Chiefs were included in the second workshop and thereafter became QWC members. There were differing opinions about the efficacy of this move. Some people, including the consultants, thought the Branch Chiefs should have been members from the beginning. Others, however, expressed the feeling that the Branch Chiefs' resistance would have precluded the program from ever getting started had they been members from the start.

The advent of the Branch Chiefs, in retrospect, came at a precarious time. The second workshop left many people disillusioned, the consultants ceased their work with the division, and there was a change in Directors. The QWC came to a virtual standstill. One Branch Chief described the task of adapting to being a member.

> When I did get there, I had to start where the other people had already started a year ago. I was at a very much of a disadvantage from that standpoint. In working with groups that way, you build up confidence as you work with them and you find that we can discuss things and so forth. If you're not used to working in that type of a group you might have questions in your mind . . . how much do you say and so forth . . . can you really lay it on the line . . . or what are you supposed to do. It takes a while to learn where you are and how you're going to operate. I went through all that. It was quite an experience in view of that fact that everybody else in the room had already done this for a year, a year-and-a-half.

Additionally, bringing the Branch Chief onto the QWC did not quell their resistance, although most agreed that their stances mellowed somewhat. This was particularly true with one Branch Chief who was known for his early staunch resistance, referring to the program as something akin to a "communist plot." As he became more involved, he softened his stance, yet remained an enigma to some and a barrier to others. In fact, according to some observers in the division, the interest in division reorganization was kindled by the hopes of some employees that the second workshop would provide a means to topple this Branch Chief from his position. He already viewed the development of the new Siting and Clearance Staff as a loss of part of his domain. The reorganization never occurred, the Branch Chief retained his post, and remained a significant factor for the rest of the program.

As was the case with the Director, the membership of the Branch Chiefs on the QWC had both positive and negative effects. While the Branch Chiefs were more active and informed about the program, their presence altered how the QWC went about its business. Attributable partly to the timing of the move, the Branch Chiefs' coming on to the committee slowed its progress considerably as everyone had to adjust to new people and new roles. Meetings became shorter and more frustrating for some veteran members accustomed to more open problem solving. Branch Chiefs complained of the large time investment and were more accustomed to leaving the details of a job to others. As a result, they often came to meetings unprepared to fully discuss issues. One QWC member summed up the experience of having the Branch Chiefs on the QWC:

> It's like we started all over again. A lot of the problems, I think, stemmed (I'm talking about previous problems now) from a lack of trust of upper management. I'm talking specifically about Branch Chiefs and Directors. When the Program first got underway, the Assistant Branch Chief, of course, represented the Branch Chief so you had some of this between employees and Branch Chiefs. There wasn't a lot of mutual trust. I think that sort of thing was built during the first 18 months until, at the end of it, I'd say there was a great deal of trust. More so than any place I've been, between the parts. When the Branch Chiefs came aboard, it was just like startin' all over again. There was not that trust, or that bond that had been built up. I think, consequently, the first 6 months were feeling each other out all over again. Even though we were a lot further down the road toward accomplishing things, . . . that trust wasn't there. I don't feel like the trust ever grew in the second group the way it did in the first group. The first group was just really hard to beat.

Relationships Between the QWC and Task Forces

The Quality of Work Committee was formed as a representative body for the division. All constituencies, including management, both unions, each branch, and minorities were clearly represented on the committee. In its weekly meetings, the QWC pursued division problems first by open discussion, formation of a subcommittee which prepared a charge, and then selection of a task force to work on the problem and report its recommendations back to the QWC. Task forces were also representative groups comprised of individuals who were considered knowledgeable about a particular area. This formal procedure, initiated with the help of the consultants at the first workshop, was generally regarded as an ideal way to address the problems of the division.

While the procedure worked for the most part, there were still problems concerning how well the QWC carried out its role as a representative group. There was tension between the QWC and its task forces. Since most of the problems identified by the QWC were general, e.g., rewards and recognition, career development, many of the charges given to a task force were unclear. In some cases, task forces did not have a sufficient idea of what it was supposed to do. One observer noted:

> Those task forces which did the best work I guess from
> observation, were those who had the clearest charge,
> who knew where they, what they were to be about, and
> who had the best reporting back relationship, in the sense
> that they could go about the task assigned, and felt com-
> fortable in coming back and dealing with the Quality of
> Work Committee on the issue. The broader, the more
> ill-defined the task, the less effective.

Although lack of task clarity was a problem, the major source of difficulty was how the QWC interacted with a task force once its work was under way. Task forces become disillusioned when their work of several months was brought to the QWC only to have the group question their assumptions and rationale. Often, the QWC could not keep from becoming involved in the task force's work, a practice that was considered "meddling" by some task forces. One QWC member commented:

> I think that there was a little bit too much hesitancy on
> the part of the QWC to accept face value, the work that
> the task forces had done. They invariably wanted to
> kind of get in and get right down to the nitty gritty, al-
> most to the point of redoing everything that the task
> force had done before they were willing really to say
> this is a part of our work.

A similar thought was expressed by a union member of the QWC:

> Yeah, I think most of our task forces got a little disturbed
> with the Quality of Work Committee because we kept them
> on the spot too much it seems like. We had some good task
> forces and I think they did some good work, but I think we
> disturbed them with the amount of time that they had to sit
> and justify their recommendations to the total Quality of
> Work Committee. I think that's the place where we maybe
> lost the respect of some of the task forces. I think some
> of them decided, "If I've got to put up with this trash, I
> don't even want to be involved with this thing." I believe
> that was the attitude some of them got.

Part of the problem was that task force members were generally more knowledgeable about an area than QWC members. The implicit issue of "Who is in charge?" was consistently revealed by excessive attention to trivial details on the part of the QWC. One disappointed QWC member explained this phenomenon as follows:

> . . . I think the task forces were treated rather badly by the Committee. You select a group of people and in essence what you're saying is, "Okay, you fellas represent the cream of the division as far as this particular problem's concerned," and I think people were very carefully selected. I don't recall any cases where you just drug up anybody you could think of. Normally these were very qualified people on these task forces. You send them out and they beat their heads against the wall for 3 months or whatever. They come up with a solution and then the question is never asked, how can we implement it? The question is always turned into a nit-picking session. "We don't like this word and we don't like that paragraph." I was real disappointed.

Another QWC member reaffirmed the problem:

> Yeah, what we're trying to do, I believe, was look at the problem and decide who in the division was best able to deal with that problem, who had the most knowledge to bring to bear on the problem. Then we would appoint these folks to study the problem and write a recommendation. This worked fine except that it brought the recommendation back to the people who may have had the least knowledge about the thing, you see—the committee itself. As I said earlier, we had some folks—maybe one or two—who were quite familiar with the problem—maybe three sometimes. But generally speaking, the total committee was not knowledgeable about what some of these folks were working on. And yet, they were sitting there trying to make decisions about, in their own mind, whether or not this ought to be recommended to the division as a direction we ought to be heading. It made it very difficult, in my opinion. So, the task force method of solving problems is still good. I think it ought to be used. I think it's as good or maybe the best way to solve some of our problems.

The uncomfortable and sometimes adversarial relationship between the QWC and task forces reflects several continuing themes.

The QWC was not trained in the skills that were necessary to maintain effective relationships with its own offspring. Unsure of its own role as an implementing group, the QWC exerted its authority by assuming the role of evaluators of task force reports. The task forces resented this unnecessary intrusion into their work which they regarded as the best they could do given the inherent ambiguity of their charge. The often excessive nit-picking by the QWC was partly an outward indication of their self-doubt and partly the result of a natural tendency for engineers to get involved in nitty-gritty details. The same complaint was made by employees whose supervisors could not keep from trying to do their work for them. Nevertheless, the problem persisted and remained a source of strain throughout the program.

Relationships Between the QWC and the Division

Unencumbered by the contractual constraints that limited the cooperative conference, the QWC was a beacon of hope for many employees in the division. The QWC was something new and experimental, had high visibility and status, including the support of the Director and the attention of outsiders, and was given free rein in examining any problem in the division. With the aid of its selected consultants, the QWC began its task with the high spirit of organizational renewal. As the program moved along, however, people in the division began to complain about a lack of knowledge about what the QWC was doing. There was a gap between the QWC representatives and their constituents that would have a pervasive effect on how the experimental program was perceived by those outside the inner circle.

The reasons for this "communication problem" were varied, depending on one's point of view. One member of the committee took the time each week to summarize the events of the meeting and distribute a one-page newsletter to every employee in the division. Employees were made aware of what task forces were doing and which changes were in the process of being implemented. There were also a few division-wide meetings. The intensive data feedback sessions following the Time 2 measurement were also an attempt by the QWC to communicate its outcomes to the division at large. Several members of the QWC thought this was quite enough and that it was up to the employees of the division to take the responsibility for keeping informed:

Well, this is one of the things which I frankly feel like that there was adequate communication. I think, I know that there were people who complained that they don't know what's going on and so forth. As far as I'm con-

cerned, any time that you have to work through committees, you've got this problem. The only way you can keep
all 378 people in the division completely up to date is to
have a meeting with all 378 people. You can't have your
grass roots committee go back and tell each man, woman
and child in the 378 member division every single thing
that was said at the QWC or any other committee. If
you're going to work through committees, you've got to
have and trust the representatives to carry on the work
and bring you back the important things that happened.
But to keep you up to date on everything that Joe said
when Tom said this and so forth is impossible. I feel
like that a lot of the complaints that we had here was
because people didn't read what was put out.

Between the Committee and the division, we put out so
much material, employees just got to where they didn't
read it and keep up with it. It's like taking a math course,
once you get behind in it, you can't catch up. So, I think
that's what happened. We just put out so much material,
mostly employees just quit reading it and got behind and
disinterested so the communication broke down.

But I never have seen the Quality of Work Committee's
efforts in communication with the division lacking. I have
seen the efforts of the division in listening to the Quality
of Work Committee lacking. I saw that from the beginning
and in retrospect, I still see that. You know, I can write
you a hundred memos, and if you don't read one of them,
you're not going to know a damned thing of what I've
written in there.

Yeah, my position here is probably going to be a lot different from that of the rest of the division. I think the
Quality of Work Committee made an honest and sufficient
effort to communicate with the rest of the division. I've
always felt that; I've never felt the communication problem
was the Quality of Work Committee's fault.

There was confusion about who was responsible for initiating
interactions. Some QWC members clearly believed that employees
should have let their representatives know their concerns, as demonstrated by the following remark:

I personally feel like if there had been some more . . .
problems that they could identify more with on a larger
scale, like the Professional and Career Development and

> well, for one thing, I don't feel like the division as a
> whole lived up to its responsibilities in relationship to
> the QWC members. Simply because it is impossible, you
> don't know, as a committee member, what a particular
> person might be interested in. And you don't really have
> that much time to mingle and try to talk to people on an
> individual basis or even in group situations a lot of times.
> More sessions like that would have been helpful.

In keeping with this last thought, other QWC members believed that
the committee did not do an adequate job of keeping people informed:

> I don't think the people on the committee took time to
> represent the people they were representing. I don't
> think they took time to go around and talk and let peo-
> ple know what was going on. All they did was pass
> around a bunch of papers, and that's not as good as
> ad hoc contact or talking.

While some QWC members took issue with this assessment,
there was little face to face interaction between representatives and
their respective Branch employees. As a result, employees knew an
event that was taking place, but not the thinking that went on behind
it. Their focus was on outcomes and not process. As a result, there
was a growing suspicion among division members that the QWC was
accomplishing very little.

Obviously, the communications gap was not the fault of any one
party. One QWC member drew the following insight:

> I think it rests on both, and certainly they [employees]
> can't claim that they didn't receive information about
> the QWC. God knows they got tons of information. I
> think a lot of times it was not what they wanted to hear.
> A lot of times they just weren't interested in it. At first
> maybe, until something stirred their interest. You know,
> after a decision was made, suddenly their interest got
> stirred and it was too late to input into it then.

Moreover, the problem was rooted in the more complex issues of
where the QWC fit into the division and the internal dynamics of the
committee itself. The initial resentment of the Branch Chiefs that
some would say carried over into their committee membership affected how the QWC was received by the division. A veteran QWC
member explained the underlying distrust:

But really, the problem we had with communications all
along was the fact that the management attitude was so
negative toward the thing and, the Branch Chiefs promoted
that with the section chiefs and the section chiefs in turn
promoted that with the employees in their sections and,
employees kept hollering that there's a communications
problem. I don't think there ever was really . . . it
wasn't a communications problem, it was a trust/attitude
problem of management.

If one does not believe in the concept, it is unlikely that he will work
to ensure adequate understanding of others. This problem was exacerbated by the natural tendency for the QWC to develop as a group,
thereby becoming separate from the division. The observer-facilitator
noted:

It became very closed, boundaries became very much
closed, overbounded . . . a feeling of camaraderie which
existed within the Quality of Work committee which gave
elitist concepts, which made them less accessible to the
division, at least the perception of the division was: it
had become an elitist, overbounded group—which I'm
sure at various times came as a shock, surprise to many
of the members of the Quality of Work Committee who
perceived themselves as being out in front and out in
the organization.

Dachler and Wilpert (1978), in their theoretical assessment of
participation, brought out the issue of elitism as a potential problem
with representative forms of participation. The QWC was a special
group. The members worked together weekly, participated in intensive
workshops, and received the attention of high level consultants for
over a year. The QWC's sense of common purpose and importance in
the division, which allowed it to operate the way it did, also created
barriers that were difficult to overcome. The early resistance by
some Branch Chiefs heightened feelings of competition and drew the
committee closer to each other. By the time the Branch Chiefs became
members, the patterns were well established. The presence of a higher
level of management on the committee removed the committee even
further from the division. Employees' early hopes were dashed by the
inherent slowness of the change process, and they tended to become
less interested in the committee's work and more worried about the
large time investment. There was also a feeling among employees
that the employee members of the QWC were looking and acting more
like managers. As the Director commented at the end of the program:

I think there was a tendency, on the part of the employees
particularly, to lose confidence in the Quality of Work Committee representatives. They just sort of assumed that
they'd gone over to management while they were sitting on
the Quality of Work Committee. We never seemed to learn
the secret of how to keep them properly informed and involved. . . . The relationship wasn't like you have at a
union bargaining table at all. I think I made the remark
once in observing the Quality of Work Committee operate
for the first time, if I hadn't known the people, it would
have been tough for me to tell who's the management and
who's the employees. But I don't see anything wrong with
that—I think it's great. I'm not sure all the employees feel
that way about it.

INTERNAL LIFE OF THE QWC

As a well identified group, the QWC was subject to the dynamics
that typically characterize working groups. Beginning in June 1974,
the QWC met every Thursday for three and one-half years (a total of
163 meetings). In addition to its tasks performed during this time,
the group developed its own internal life consisting of interaction patterns, differentiation and subgrouping, norms, leadership, conflict,
and adaptation to changes.

These patterns were influenced very heavily during the first
year of the experiment by the presence of the consultants. Although
the QWC had been meeting for three months prior to their arrival at
TPE, it was generally recognized that the consultants focused the
work of the group and gave them their framework of operation. The
first workshop launched the problem-solving method and the single
issue task forces, ideas that would remain throughout the QWC's lifetime. The consultants kept the committee on track as they dealt with
a very full agenda of issues derived from the consultants' initial observations. Within a few months, nine task forces were in various
stages of their assigned tasks. There was a feeling expressed by
some original members that perhaps the QWC took on too much at the
beginning. They were going off in so many directions, they could not
keep up and eventually became overwhelmed and then tired. There
were others who believed that the excitement and energy generated
by this initial level of activity was difficult to maintain over the long
term. One member explained:

I think that we were trying to get our money's worth out
of the consultants to the extent that we were working ourselves to death. I think we went at it too fast and too furi-

ous. I just feel like for months on end, we met all day
long, 8 hours every week. Now that gets to be pretty
pressing on you if you've got a few other things to do
which most of us have. I think that did get to be a very
tiring situation.

The initial excitement also raised expectations throughout the
division that major changes would be occurring in rapid succession
when, in fact, the process of change was a much slower, deliberate
process. An original employee member of the QWC was philosophical
as he commented:

Ramada II. I think everybody was at a low ebb and ready
to give the whole thing up because they felt like they had
been jilted. And there wasn't anything coming out of it.
It was just spending a lot of money for nothing and we
were losing a lot of production. But that wasn't true, because from then on [the QWC] kind of motivated and went
back into where we were. But that was the low point, I
believe, for the Quality of Work Program.

The committee, which had taken many of its initial cues from
the consultants, became known as a "debating society." Unsure of its
actual decision-making authority, the QWC often became mired in its
own attempts to reach consensus on issues arising from task force
reports. In fact, some QWC members believed that they spent too
much time discussing the task force reports, a process that often
turned into quibbling over wording. These tendencies were only made
worse when the committee had to adjust to the combination of personnel changes which unfortunately came at a crucial time in the life of
the QWC. There were new faces at the table, some of them very
threatening to existing members. The meetings, which were typically
lively exchanges, became more formal. People commented that the
meetings seemed more like staff meetings with the primary objective
of finishing by lunch time. Whether this change in tone was attributable to the presence of the Branch Chiefs is unknown, but the QWC
was clearly different and was looked upon as being less effective.
Some observations highlight how the committee operated during
its final eighteen months. The Branch Chiefs often dominated the discussions while employee members sat back and watched. An employee
member's influence was enhanced when occupying the role of chair.
When Branch Chiefs chaired a meeting, they usually sat at the head
of the table, creating a more formal atmosphere whereas employee
chairs remained in their usual spot. Four of the Branch Chiefs usually
sat together at meetings, sometimes on the other side of the table

from employees. The original Branch Chief member of the QWC varied his seating and often sat with employees. The Branch Chief who was characterized as being most resistant to the program occasionally sat away from the table, particularly during the last year. Resistance to ideas was expressed as passive aggression, i.e., withdrawing, throwing up hands, quibbling over wording. By early 1977, some clear coalitions were evident among three veteran employee members and between at least two of the Branch Chiefs. The impact of the Branch Chiefs on the Committee was revealed rather dramatically when all of them were absent from one of the meetings. The exchanges among the remaining employee and management members were much freer and more relaxed at this meeting.

Individual member reactions to the manner in which the QWC operated were mixed as the following comments suggest:

> Okay, it was . . . I was trying to think of what decisions were really made. They were basically made by an airing of the problem, discussion and agreement on the severity of the problem, and then it ended up by the decision on what to do being made purely with the director weighing those pros and cons and doing whatever he thought fit to do, with . . . and there's one thing that I never liked about this and it got worse as the program grew to an end, and that was the fact that every decision that was coming out of there was not really a decision. It always went to the director with a minority report. What kind of a decision is a group making when you've got almost every individual in that group writing their separate thoughts, instead of coming to agreement together and coming up with something we can all buy?

> I don't know, there's just something about the spirit of the thing that led people to do more work than they were getting paid for. The meeting with the Assistant Branch Chiefs and the Director was sort of a new thing to everybody, and you know, sort of a personal basis. More personal than the cooperative conference had been. I think this caused everybody to put a little more into it. And we were new and we didn't have . . . I think we did gain some skills during the lifetime of the Program which we didn't have earlier on. But I think we were struggling but I think we were headed in the right direction. The last 18 months, I think the Committee began to become more stuffy.

> We had some breakdowns in the way we approached different issues. A lot of times, people would be out, certain

meetings, then they'd be in the next meeting when you'd discuss the same issue and you'd have to bring them up to date and everything. In other words, they didn't keep up with the newsletter, what was discussed. You'd have a change in chairmanship. Just little things like this, you know, really disrupted an issue when you're trying to solve it and get it out and implement it.

Well, it was mostly a consensus type decision making thing. One of the big problems I had with it was the fact that I think that we didn't have enough expertise in how to conduct the meetings and start at a point and get to it in a logical manner. There's an awful lot of wheel spinning. I think this was because we really didn't know how to handle it ourselves. Some training along the line would've helped us out. I know personally, I found it very difficult and I think it is in any type of meeting, if you're not really trained to do it, to keep the meeting on track and get to a point without getting off on a lot of tangents.

The first eighteen months I envisioned us as being a young committee, still in the learning process, and maybe heading off in several directions at the same time, trying to find the optimum solution to some problems— in a learning phase, I guess you'd say. I believe the last eighteen months was a more seasoned approach to some of the problems, a slower approach admittedly, because we had so many things going that we had to keep our fingers on the pulse of, plus trying to add all these new things to it. I think people saw themselves in a different light and that was one of . . . instead of taking off, let's sit down and think this thing through before we start and see where we're going to go, and then plot us out a course of action that will get us there instead of taking all these false starts. I think we took some false starts early on in; we took less of those in the last eighteen months. We've moved a little slower in the last eighteen months, which I don't think was all that bad.

One fact that begins to emerge from member comments is that often the group lacked some essential skills in problem solving. Most members seemed to agree that the QWC meetings became less productive and therefore more frustrating since members did not know how to interact with each other effectively. Outward displays of conflict were seen as going against the prevailing norms of politeness in the organization although there was considerable conflict beneath the

surface. With the absence of the external consultants to keep the meetings on track and to raise issues, the QWC floundered during the last
eighteen months. The numerous membership changes only made matters worse as the QWC struggled to maintain equilibrium. Meetings
became shorter, more formal, and less effective.

To elucidate how the QWC actually functioned, the following
case study is presented as an example. The case involves a major
decision that was addressed by the committee early in 1977, its final
year of existence. The decision concerned how the work of the QWC
and the entire experiment would continue beyond the formal experimental period (see Chapter 6). Although the case is a snapshot of
events that occurred during a very critical time, it serves to uncover
the general nature of the internal interactions of QWC members and
the difficulties the committee encountered in making decisions.

CASE STUDY—THE DECISION TO CONSOLIDATE: ANATOMY OF A DECISION THAT WASN'T

Background

During the last year of the TVA experiment, the QWC approached
the idea of how to institutionalize the experiment and make the process
of the committee a permanent part of TPE. Chapter 6 documented the
foundation of the consolidation of power centers task force which developed plans to eventually combine the QWC and cooperative conference into a single group after the formal end of the experiment in
December 1977. It was apparent that the various membership changes
on the QWC and the change in leadership in the division during 1976
slowed the committee's progress considerably. Also, some veteran
QWC members were becoming weary of the entire process.

As the consolidation task force struggled along, the internal
consultant, the former personnel officer and observer/facilitator who
was promoted out of the division began to take a more active role in
accelerating the process of the transition. The internal consultant
suggested that the Division Director attend organizational development
seminars at the University of Michigan so that he might more adequately deal with the issues of organizational change that he inherited.
In February 1977, the internal consultant prepared a four-page memo
to the Director outlining suggestions for future consulting needs for
the QWC. Among his suggestions were revitalization of the QWC, a
strategy of transition to extend the QWC concept beyond 1977, training
in facilitation skills for QWC members, and general improvement in
communications between the QWC and task forces as well as the rest
of the division. These concerns were widely considered as areas in

which the Quality of Work Program was falling short. The Director agreed on these needs and presented the memo to the QWC on February 24. The QWC recommended that a task force of the Director, the internal consultant, and an employee representative to the QWC develop a set of recommendations from the memo and present them to the QWC. The Director underscored his commitment to the issues in the memo by formally addressing the QWC about his Michigan training experience, ending with the charge, "We need to move on." Reactions to the Director's speech were favorable. He had stressed the ideas of training and more involvement of first line supervisors and assured the committee of his support of the QWC concept that had evolved over two years.

The deliberations of the QWC over the course of two meetings provide some of the richest examples of the internal workings of the committee. The meetings are recounted in narrative form to capture the flavor of the events and the complexity of the discussions that occurred concerning if and how a transition to something permanent would take place.

Meeting I—March 31, 1977

The QWC meeting began at its usual time of 9:00 A.M. on Thursday, March 31. The issue of the memo was last on the agenda and, therefore, was not addressed until after a short break around mid-morning. The meeting was chaired by an original management member of the QWC. Present as guests at the meeting were the former Division Personnel Officer (DPO), the internal consultant, and an ISR observer. One original employee member was absent.

The first part of this section of the meeting was devoted to a presentation by the task force commissioned to work with the memo. The spokesperson for the task force was an employee representative to the QWC and one of the quieter members of the committee. He opened his remarks by stating, "People usually begin presentations by saying, 'Unaccustomed as I am to public speaking.' I'll begin by saying 'Unaccustomed as I am to speaking at all.'" He presented three major strategies for the QWC to consider:

1. Internal Consulting Only: The program would continue without the aid of external consultants until October 1 at which time the QWC would decide whether more work was needed.
2. Internal and External Consulting: Retain the former Division Personnel Officer (DPO) as observer-facilitator as of April 1. An external consultant would be selected by the QWC and the cooperative conference by May 15 immediately followed by implementation.

3. Underline{External Consulting Only}: This strategy would be identical to #2 without the DPO as facilitator.

The task force recommended the second strategy to the QWC, a combination of internal and external consulting. The former DPO was seen as a vital resource, and his role had been missed since his recent promotion.

The Director then gave a formal presentation to the QWC, outlining the major issues he envisioned for the future. These issues included transition (i.e., making the QWC permanent by combining with the cooperative conference), communications, transfer of the QWC style to the rest of the division, and the issue of the morale of the division. The issues were enlargements of what originally appeared in the internal consultant's memo. The cost for additional consulting was estimated at about $50,000 over an 18 to 24 month period. After a few questions for clarification, a discussion ensued. The following is a reconstruction of that discussion based on observations of the meetings. When possible, direct quotes are used to capture the tone of the exchanges. Otherwise, ideas are paraphrased and summarized.

Branch Chief 1: "The QWC may get caught between a rock and a hard place." He stated that it would be more than a year before the final evaluation of the project from ISR would be ready. "We really don't know whether to combine or to continue the process or not."

Branch Chief 2: "The consultant actually trains us. It's up to us, not him—he will just lend guidance."

Branch Chief 1: In response, he stated that he doesn't want to "reinvent the wheel."

Internal Consultant: The consultant could request help from experts if necessary. It is better to start with a generalist. The former personnel officer could assist on a short-term basis.

Branch Chief 3: Perhaps the consultant could be put on salary for a few weeks at a time.

Internal Consultant: Using himself as an example, he stated that there would not be enough money to have a consultant on board full time.

Employee 1: It is better to use someone outside TVA.

Director: Relating his recent Michigan experience, he stated that internal consultants have to worry more about pleasing the one who directs them.

Branch Chief 2: The present QWC knows more about transition than anyone else. With proper guidance, they would be perfectly capable of carrying it out.

Employee 1: Asks specific questions about what would go on between June and October.

DPO: (Interrupting) "One of my problems as observer-facilitator was being so closely tied into the QWC." He made reference to his conflicting roles, stating that there needs to be objectivity or detachment from day-to-day activities. Also, the QWC becomes a kind of breeding ground for internal consultants (i.e., the members of the QWC develop consulting skills for other areas of TVA). He reiterated the importance of having an observer-facilitator at every meeting.

Branch Chief 1: Objects to "having a facilitator at every meeting from now to eternity."

Director: Pointed out the need for the DPO's skills.

Chairman: (Changing the subject) He stated that he felt rather presumptuous receiving training if he was not going to be in the new group.

Branch Chief 1: Restated that he does not see the need for starting all over. They just need help in some specific areas. A new consultant would "reinvent the wheel" and there would be no way to do it by the projected date of October 1.

Internal Consultant: Challenged Branch Chief, stating that the consolidation of power centers task force identified the plan and now they are ironing out the specifics.

Director: Supports the idea, saying, "We're not suggesting the plan was put up there because the Quality of Work Program was considered a failure. We simply, through the process, identified some specific needs that need attention."

Internal Consultant: (To Director) "Do you feel that your role would have been better if you would have had training before coming on to the QWC?"

Director: Agreed wholeheartedly. He said he "didn't know what his role was at first and his recent training experience at Michigan helped a great deal."

Employee 1: Brought up another idea saying that the Quality of Work Program is something that is different from the normal way of doing things in the division, i.e., "employees meddling in management's business. This new process requires training and in-indoctrination. There are still employees who do not feel comfortable talking with people above them. That's the new approach."

Branch Chief 2: "What action do we take now?"

Branch Chief 4: "Is the consulting going to be a one-shot deal or is it going to continue and continue?"

Director: Responded that "We hope to be on our own although we may require some help later on."

Branch Chief 1: Stated that he wanted a definite goal and a definite cutoff date.

Branch Chief 3: "Have we agreed to continue the Quality of Work concept beyond December 31, 1977 in a combined manner? Maybe the cooperative conference should be brought into these decisions."

Branch Chief 1: The Quality of Work Committee has not been evaluated yet.

Internal Consultant: "Can you really evaluate the QWC yes or no? The intervention wasn't pure."

Branch Chief 1: "Employees need a stake in it, too."

Employee 2: "Use the Quality of Work [Program] feedback sessions."

Branch Chief 2: "The QWC should have an idea of its own success."

Branch Chief 1: "Engineers want black and white answers."

Internal Consultant: "The QWC or not, the issues on the checklist will have to be dealt with anyway."

Employee 1: "We [the QWC] missed in a lot of areas. The issues listed here give the experiment a fair shake."

Branch Chief 1: "This group is making a judgment that we've failed in these areas."

Internal Consultant: "It's not a question of failure or success, black or white. These issues are needed."

Branch Chief 2: "If we have agreed that the QWC and the cooperative conference will merge, then there will be a transition."

Director: Brought out the point that the "sense of ownership" has not been developed in the division by the QWC.

Employee 2: "We need the support of employees."

Internal Consultant: "Well, maybe you could consider putting off the Quality of Work feedback sessions [which were scheduled for May] and introduce the consultant at that point. I'm reserved about using the feedback to evaluate the program since employees have not been keyed in on the QWC process."

Director: Suggested that maybe they present the ideas to the cooperative conference. Branch Chief 5 agreed.

Branch Chief 1: Stated that these things could be done without a program. The Director could unilaterally hire a consultant. [This idea was rejected by the Director, indicating that he thought the process was important.]

DPO: "Decide yourself first. Give the plan some validity before presenting it to the cooperative conference."

Branch Chief 3: (Standing) "Even before a plan is developed, do we want to continue the Quality of Work concept in some form? That is the major question! Give the cooperative conference all the options."

Director: "Why can't we make a recommendation to the cooperative conference?"

Branch Chief 4: Said he wants to see the feedback before making a recommendation. "Have we done good or bad? Maybe we want to hang it up if the feedback looks bad."

Branch Chief 3: (Makes a motion) "Let's agree to call a joint QWC-cooperative conference meeting, present the task force recommendations to both groups with the understanding that this presentation does not commit us to continue the QWC or the concept after December 31, 1977 in some form." The motion was seconded by Employee 3.

Director: "If we wait until after the feedback sessions, we won't make the schedule of the plan."

Employee 1: "Why did we work on consolidation of power centers if it was not going to be?"

DPO: "You have to decide yourself in order to make a recommendation."

Employee 2: "Doesn't the fact that we are considering the plan indicate that the merger between the QWC and the cooperative conference will be done?"

Employee 4: (A member of the task force who made the original presentation to the QWC) "Can't the QWC decide which strategy out of the three they want to take now?"

DPO: "Is this a strategy that the QWC wants to propose?"

The motion was called again and it was passed unanimously. The task force was to present the options to both groups the following week. The meeting ended abruptly as it was 12:30 and people were anxious to get to lunch. People were confused about what had happened at the meeting. The QWC never endorsed the task force's recommendation to hire an external consultant and retain the DPO as observer-facilitator.

Discussion

It is obvious that the QWC became confused and avoided the central issue of whether they would merge with the cooperative conference, thereby institutionalizing the "Quality of Work" concept in a permanent form. The meeting also made apparent several power struggles underlying the issues. The Director, heavily influenced by the internal consultant and former DPO, was firmly committed to the continuation of the concept. He and the internal consultant were on the task force that developed the alternatives and recommendation to seek external consulting. The presentation to the QWC, however, was done by the employee member who until that time was the most silent member of the committee. Resistance to these ideas came mainly from one

Branch Chief (1) who historically was considered a barrier to the program. He clearly dominated the meeting by getting the QWC off on tangents and challenging the ideas of the task force.

Another Branch Chief (4) was also negative and suggested using the Time 2 feedback data as a deciding factor. This would provide a convenient "out" if the feedback was not positive. The Branch Chief who stood to make his point (notably the first time anyone on the QWC rose to address the membership) was trying to steer the committee back on course. It was his motion that finally passed. Yet, the motion was to provide alternatives to the cooperative conference without the recommendation of the QWC or the task force. Both the internal consultant and DPO were actively pushing the QWC to commit itself, but the QWC backed off. With the exception of the Chair and one vocal employee member, the meeting was completely controlled by four of the Branch Chiefs and the external people. One Branch Chief remained silent.

The Second Meeting

Because of the confusion emanating from the March 31st meeting, the joint meeting was postponed until April 12 so that the QWC could continue discussing the issues at its April 7 meeting. This move was orchestrated by the Director and the ISR study director. There were important differences noted at this second meeting. The Chair was a female member of OPEIU and a less vocal member of the QWC. Branch Chief 1 was absent for the greater part of the meeting, entering during the last hour of discussion. The former DPO also was not present at this meeting. Again, the discussion took place after other less important matters were taken care of. The discussion concerned what was to happen at the upcoming joint meeting of the QWC and cooperative conference.

In the opening moments, there was still confusion about whether a consolidation would take place, what the new group would be called, and whether it was appropriate for the QWC to make a recommendation to the cooperative conference. A key moment came when Branch Chief 5, silent for the most part the previous week, asked, "We are a child of the cooperative conference. Are we telling our 'pappy' what to do?" The QWC proceeded to avoid this issue by grappling with semantics. The Director explained what he thought would happen at the joint meeting. He would make a formal presentation and provide the three options. He then asked the QWC, "Are we making a recommendation from this group?" There was no answer. Instead, the committee discussed the nature of a new group. Would it work the same as the old cooperative conference? Would it be called the cooperative conference or something new? Employee 1 stated, "I thought the consolidation was going to be a new animal, not the QWC or the cooperative conference, but something new with some features of both—a new 'child.'" After some deliberation, the QWC was assured by the Director and the new DPO (and former union member) that a cooperative conference could legally do anything the QWC currently could do. Branch Chief 5 stated, "It's not the name, it's the people."

Finally, Employee 3, a QWC veteran, stated that he wanted to see a decision on one of the options, whereupon the Director restated the options and the task force recommendation to combine and hire a consultant. A vote was not taken as the committee dealt with the issue of what a cooperative conference was. There were also concerns about how often a new group would meet. Seeing that a resolution was not forthcoming, management member 1 (who chaired last week's meeting) suggested that they go around the table, soliciting each person's opinion. Each person in one way or the other expressed a desire to adapt the QWC's methods to the cooperative conference, although there was some confusion about how it would be done. Several members expressed a desire for consulting assistance. Employee 1 emphatically supported the task force recommendation.

At this point, Branch Chief 1 entered the meeting. After some additional confusion, the internal consultant, who was silent up to this point, interjected that he thought the QWC was having difficulty reaching a decision or even understanding what the decision was about. He proceeded to make a formal presentation to the QWC about the differences between the QWC and the cooperative conference. The major difference, in his view, was expediency (i.e , the cooperative conference was slower than the QWC). He continued to clarify the issues in the memo and focused on consulting, stating, "The recommendation is to get a consultant on board." Branch Chief 1 tried to bring up the issue of getting employee feedback, but was squelched by the internal consultant who said that in viewing feedback employees would be judging the past and not the future potential of the program. After hearing this, Employee 3 stated, "I'm willing to buy in on this and am ready to go!" He quickly received support from Employee 1. The internal consultant, realizing he now had support, pushed further as he said, "The cooperative conference has not been exposed to these issues, and the QWC is in a much better position to make such a recommendation." The internal consultant asked the QWC to agree on hiring a consultant. Once this was accomplished, the consolidation would inevitably occur. The QWC finally endorsed the task force recommendation with a unanimous "yes" vote. The recommendation was presented to the cooperative conference on April 12 where it was readily accepted.

Discussion

 Much of the confusion from the first meeting was carried over
into the second meeting. This time, however, there were some important differences. Branch Chief 1, a major force in the first meeting, was present only at the end of the second meeting and could not
exert as much influence. The former DPO was also absent, precluding
the two of them from engaging in their previous conflict.
 The issues of the second meeting focused on the meaning of the
new group. The new personnel officer, previously a strong union
member of the QWC, made it clear that a cooperative conference
could have the same contractual authority while adapting the skills
and process of the QWC. The most active participants in the second
meeting were veteran employee members who wanted the work of the
QWC to continue. References were made to producing a "new child,"
an offspring of the parent groups that would carry on the collaborative
tradition. The weary members of the QWC could find a sense of vitality
and hope in this "birth." The internal consultant remained silent until
a crucial moment and from that time on took complete control of the
meeting, steering the QWC to its eventual decision. Essentially, the
internal consultant did what the Division Director would not do, and
that was push the committee to decide on a recommendation.
 The two meetings typify rather graphically the difficulties the
QWC faced in making decisions, particularly in its latter phases.
Most of its work was accomplished and members were looking to an
uncertain future. There were clearly conflicting hidden agendas that
caused the QWC to bog down in peripheral issues. Members who
brought up the central issues for a vote were sidetracked as those in
opposition to the whole concept clashed with the forces of continued
change. The committee itself found it difficult to consider its future
mainly because it was unsure of its present identity, or for that matter, its past accomplishments. They became overly concerned with
feedback as a device to provide them with a sense of who they were.
Were they a success or failure? Good or bad? The feedback that was
based on the Time 2 or "during" measures could not really provide
them with those answers. The opposing members, sensing that the
feedback might be negative, could perhaps use this as a basis to put
the whole program to rest and get back to business as usual.
 The QWC was also very uncomfortable about making a recommendation to the cooperative conference. The reference to the conference as their "pappy" highlighted the QWC's feelings of being young
upstarts in the eyes of the elder and more legitimate institution. It
was only when the QWC realized that, in effect, they could also be
considered a cooperative conference under the union contractual agreement that they were more sanguine about creating a new group. At
least they felt less presumptuous.

Finally, the political movements behind the scenes must be noted. It was clearly through the influence of the internal consultant that these meetings came about. Teaming up with the former DPO and getting the commitment of the Director were crucial aspects for the continuation of the program. The internal consultant's memo to the Director and the Director's Michigan training experience were catalysts for moving forward. The internal consultant was at the forefront of the discussion, fending off attacks by the opposition, and finally steering the QWC to the decision that both he and the Director wanted. The ISR study director became involved, although more distantly, by persuading the Director to postpone the joint meeting. This allowed another discussion to occur wherein the internal consultant could have more influence. In the long run, the decision was a crucial one. The QWC became focused on a clear objective—hiring a consultant and the eventual transition to a permanent part of TVA. These matters were to remain the central focus of the QWC for the remainder of the experiment.

Conclusions about the QWC

It is clear from the preceding case and comments from participants that the QWC was not as effective as it could have been. Although it was considered fruitful in generating ideas in a relatively open format and spinning off the task forces, the process of the committee was lacking in several respects. Although it was often denigrated as a debating society, the debates were often around trivial issues while the real issues remained submerged. The QWC was most effective in the presence of the consultants whose process skills kept the committee on track and productive. As the experiment wore on and the consultants departed, these skills were missed by the QWC. Skills such as communicating clearly, listening, and appropriately expressing feelings which were definitely present were not developed within the membership of the committee. The former DPO tried to fill in this skills gap but was limited because of his dual role. His recognition of the need for skills is revealed in the following remarks:

> Skill building is an essential part of process to make it work. The group came together without the necessary skills to deal in group situations. They were still finding out their boundaries, their identities, and all the rest. They did need skills in even going about those basic issues, skills which they didn't have. I sort of avoided, I suppose, the other part of that, and that's the specific skill, the observer-facilitator role, which is observing

process rather than content, more concerned with the
actual continuing flow of the activity. I think that is a
specialized skill, a specialized need, that this process
has to have to make it effective. But that's not the only,
I'm not saying that that particular and specific skill is
the only one. Certainly the participants themselves need
to be aware of their own needs, own skills, how to become more effective in group work. But having said
that, it's difficult to convince a group, I think, from my
own experience, that they lack these skills they have
been needing in a variety of situations most of their
careers. They may feel that those meetings have not
been as effective as they might have been, and a host
of other concerns about meeting and effectiveness. The
admission that the individual is the problem and needs
skills to function in that environment, in my experience
is a difficult one to get across. And I might add that the
longer the group operates together, the less likely they
are to recognize their need for additional skills, because
they become comfortable, they're anticipating each other,
to a point that there can at least be a warm feeling of,
well, we've got a nice thing going here, let's not mess
it up. But I think the longer you go without that, the more
difficult it is to get those skills added to the group and yet
the dilemma is that people who come together in groups
the first few times, don't recognize a need for skills!
An interesting dilemma, I think.

The QWC, formed prior to the arrival of the consultants, had
already developed "appropriate" ways to interact. These interactions,
influenced largely by previous experience, the historical model of the
cooperative conference, and what was learned as generally acceptable
behavior within TVA, were difficult to change. The continuous adaptation to membership changes only added to the difficulty. However,
some skills training on how to be an effective group was clearly
needed. This, of course, was a matter of the style and choices made
by the consultants and the general readiness of the QWC to receive
such training.

THE IMPACT OF EXTERNAL AGENTS

In addition to its interactions within the division, the QWC was
also influenced by several parties external to the division. These external agents included the consultants, the TVA employee development

specialist who acted as an internal consultant, the ISR assessors, and the National Quality of Work Center. The following discussion will concentrate on the ways in which these outside social actors influenced the events of the experiment.

The External Consultants

The consultants' role in QWL projects such as the TVA experiment is a delicate balancing act. Since unions and management are considered equal parties and joint owners of the project, the consultants must not be seen as aligning themselves with either party. Although joint ownership is a necessary condition for effective collaboration, it places considerable limits on consultants accustomed to working for a single client. The consultants at TVA were certainly affected by these constraints but seemed to handle the situation well, especially during the first contract period. However, they ran into problems when they began rotating their visits to the site and when they attempted to change the client from the QWC to the Director.

While opinions about the impact of external consultants varied, most people involved in the TVA project agreed that they were extremely helpful in getting the program started, focusing the energies of TPE employees, and generating the necessary momentum to keep the program going. The consultants were considered to be the forces for change without whom the project would never have survived. One original QWC member summarized their impact as follows:

> They caused the people on the Quality of Work Committee
> and the division management to look back over its shoulder
> at what is going on in the division and maybe we found
> some things we didn't know about—total. You know in the
> first 170 cards or so that we went through over there,
> that's what I'm talking about. That might have been OK.
> They helped us recognize some of the things about the
> division that maybe we didn't recognize because we were
> too close to it. So that may have been causal from that
> point of view. And then, they did an excellent job facili-
> tating our review in these things and boiling our thoughts
> down to about an eight-point program that was gone into.

The three primary consultants exerted influence in a gentle manner. They were seen as expert facilitators, collecting much data, assembling the information and helping the QWC and others develop ways of approaching the problems. The consultants did not impose their own solutions, and when they did make suggestions, they were made from their more distant perspective. This style was deemed extremely effective at the first workshop. The observer-facilitator recalled the first workshop:

> I think the cliché which is fairly current is that Ramada I was [the consultants'] finest hour, that sort of thing. They began a skill-building program, they brought people together in an intense way, they had done good data gathering, they had gained the confidence, if not the confidence, certainly the attention, of the people that they interviewed/interfaced with, in the organization, and had built up some credibility in the organization for themselves and for the process. And that you know came to full flower at Ramada I when people began leaving with group process and problem identification and the various skills that were laid out for them by [the consultants]. That was a significant impact.

An employee confirmed this perception:

> Okay, I think that just the mere fact that there was acceptance by the management people on the committee to discuss freely and really operate along with the employees was something that the consultants did for us. That was the most essential part of the experiment anyway. The fact that you could come together and sit down in a good, clean atmosphere and discuss things. I feel like the consultants really facilitated in that manner. They made it easy in that first workshop for people to let their hair down and just be a person.

However, others on the QWC thought the consultants may have been too removed in their relationship. A Branch Chief commented:

> I think you'd have to give them credit for initiating the methods and the approach to this thing. I think an observer would have to come to the conclusion that it was a very gentle type of guidance you might say there and this was brought to the attention at some point along the way there at different places that there was a feeling that there was not enough specific guidance and choices of solutions given by the consultants, whereby he more or less attempted to just throw you out there and just let you decide everything. Some were expecting him to come up with suggestions and so forth to choose from. It was a very loose guidance and possibly too so.

Another comment suggests that the role of the consultants was simply to set things up while the QWC actually did the work:

> Now, I believe our own little system that we worked out over there didn't have a thing to do with the consultants. I think we figured that out in a room by ourselves, after they got out of the way. You see what I mean? Of course, their guidance in their discussion with us maybe put our minds to dwelling on this kind of thing. But I think they sure did facilitate our looking at these problems.

Yet, the consultants were seen as generating the enthusiasm that made the first workshop such a success. An employee recalled:

> [Not having the consultants] would be like a plane that needed a jet-assisted takeoff trying to take off without one. Maybe we would've made it without assistance but then again maybe we wouldn't have. Some people think that we would've done better. But they gave us, gave me personally, and a few others on the Committee a real boost by their knowledge and their enthusiasm and their, "We can do it" attitude, that which later on sort of fizzled out.

The "fizzling out" perception had several potential sources. There was a natural erosion of the initial excitement generated by the first workshop. Once the workshop was over and the QWC and task forces settled down to their jobs, the initial fervent pace settled into a more normal routine. The fact that the consultants began to rotate their visits was disruptive to some members of the QWC. Even though the rotation was done to save travel costs, the consultants broke the continuity of their presence.

Each member of the consultant group had different skills and styles. One had an engineering background while the principal consultant was seen by some as a "silver-tongued Yankee." Their attempt to change the client before the second contract and the perceived failure of the second workshop significantly lessened the credibility of the consultants. Many people in TPE believed that the consultants were extremely expensive and had far outlived their effectiveness:

> Well, in the beginning I think they taught us how to lay out progress, a method of implementing things. Progress and development. But to me, the first few months with the consultants was the best month that we got. The second workshop, I think it was just a waste of money.

I feel like they did not give us all that they could have and
what the reason for that was, I don't know but I kind of felt
like it might have been so that there would always be some
work here. We'll make them [TPE] dependent to a certain
degree.

Toward the end of my association with them, they seemed
to have lost a lot of that real enthusiasm. They seemed to
have been looking for a lost ball in tall weeds. They didn't
quite admit that they had, they and we, had sort of bombed
out but you could tell that their enthusiasm was falling off
and they were more anxious maybe to get on to other projects.

. . . the biggest weakness I saw of the whole program they
had down here, they did not train and tell us, "Look, you've
got to be able to live by yourselves." They did not give us
the ability to live by ourselves.

These last comments highlight some of the ambivalence expressed toward the consultants. While people wanted more from the
consultants, they also felt that they had left the QWC overly dependent
on their expertise. There is a sense of feeling "used" underlying these
sentiments. After the consultants left the scene early in 1976, further
attempts to call on them for guidance were looked upon with considerable skepticism and distrust.

The Second Consultant

While his role was certainly not as central to the project as the
first group of consultants, the second consultant highly influenced the
transition from experimental program to institutionalized change.
His major impact was the development of the philosophy statement
and guidelines (see Chapter 6) that defined the new cooperative conference. The second consultant's exposure was mostly confined to the
combined memberships of the QWC and cooperative conference and he
worked with the division for about six months. Although less visible
than his predecessors, his major impact was rejuvenating the project
at a crucial time. He was also seen as focusing the change process
more toward management as the final voice in decisions. Consequently,
the boundaries of the program became more clearly defined. The only
criticisms of the new consultant were around his tendency to over-
theorize about sociotechnical systems to a group more interested in
action. He was generally seen as successful in carrying out what he
intended to do.

The Internal Consultant

The internal consultant was an employee development specialist in the Division of Personnel. Widely regarded as a bright and aggressive young man and well skilled in the area of organizational development and evaluation (he had prior experience as a consultant in industry), the internal consultant was sent to TPE in 1976 to monitor and assist the project. His initial work was with the Evaluation Subcommittee, helping them to prepare for the second survey by ISR. He served as an advocate of data and other evaluation issues. It was the contention of the internal consultant that TPE should benefit from the data generated from the surveys. Consequently, he had considerable influence over the scope and nature of the Time 2 survey. Since the QWC and division members were inexperienced with social research, the services of the consultant were greatly appreciated.

As his sphere of influence increased in the division, the internal consultant became more directly involved in the change effort. He worked most intensively with the Field Survey section of the Civil Engineering Branch and was particularly instrumental in the success of their specific interventions, i.e., four-day week, equipment, and per diem changes. Within a year, the internal consultant was considered a major resource. He began to attend QWC meetings and at times provided facilitation skills that were lacking in the committee. His style was direct and, at times, provocative, a form of behavior that contrasted with the polite and reticent interactions in TPE and TVA in general. As a result, some people did not fully understand or accept him while others found his approach a refreshing change. Here is an assortment of reactions:

> To me, he had quite an impact. [He] said what he felt he should say. A lot of people, I think, couldn't accept that. They thought he was too bold. To me that was his greatest asset, telling the people the way it was.

> [The internal consultant] is an interesting figure in my mind. He helped us and he hurt us both. [He] did keep us thinking. Some of [his] suggestions, I thought, were not too good. But the fact is that he had a lot of ideas that he kept throwing out that I think, overall, were beneficial. I personally took a lot of [his] ideas with a grain of salt. I didn't at first. At first I accepted his ideas. Then, as I began to get experience, I sort of began to look each one over.

> He doesn't really play around. He doesn't mince words, he just throws it out and there it is and he kind of calls

it like he sees it. [He] hasn't been with TVA all that long and consequently, there's a big difference from TVA and the historic background of TVA and the things that people within TVA hold so dear in the outside world. There's a big difference. [He] had worked in some places where, this place looked like a joke and so whenever he had that opportunity, he would zero in on it and you either bought it or you didn't.

I think [the internal consultant] was one of the best assets we had in the whole Program. [He] and I became good friends. I guess anybody on the Committee would consider him a friend. We did a lot of hard work together. We went out to meet with the survey people several times. Although I was surprised to learn something [the Director] wrote one time about [him]. That [he] did all this work and really didn't think much of the Quality of Work Program. In spite of that, he did a good job so I guess that says a lot for him. He's given a job to do and he did it even though he wasn't all that in favor of it. I think one of [the internal consultant's] weaknesses, if I could point out one, which is the only one that comes to mind, is that he tends to think that his way is right. He's a hard person to argue with. He's going to win in the end.

[The internal consultant] had a significant impact on the Quality of Work Program. I guess in order of priority, I guess [he] introduced, onsite, a lot of behavioral science skills which were, sounded like his own training and his own background, who he represented, what he represented in the way of skills. And how he interpreted those in the day-to-day activity of the Quality of Work Program was his significant impact. I don't know whether the handling of the data, good/bad/indifferent, a much more professional approach to the data analysis would have been possible without [his] participation. His involvement in the feedback design and so forth, also, was a significant impact. Plus his tremendous energy as an individual, being everywhere at the same time, was sort of phenomenal, in fact, in itself.

Yes, I think he did fill a role, a vacuum in fact, that was present. Here again, we're back to the skills question again, he represented a fairly high degree of sophistication in his background.

From these comments one receives the impression of the internal consultant as a highly influential actor in the program attributable largely to his expertise and style. He started with a relatively limited set of responsibilities and gradually became a major resource who in many ways filled the vacuum created when the external consultants departed. A major aspect of his success was his accessibility to the site. He became a ubiquitous figure and exercised considerable power. He was highly instrumental in the promotion of the Division Personnel Officer to a position where he could more readily employ his facilitation skills to organizational change in TVA. It was also the internal consultant who wrote the memo to the Director, assessing the Quality of Work Program, making concrete suggestions for its revival, and finally steering the QWC to the decision leading to the new consultant and the new cooperative conference.

The Assessors

In accordance with the intent of NQWC and the contractual agreements with TVA, the Institute for Social Research (ISR) was a neutral third party assessor of the experimental program. In maintaining neutrality, the role is both a blessing in the sense that one does not become immersed in the program and a curse for precisely the same reason. The power associated with the assessment role resides in access to information that is not known to all parties. Because of this knowledge and special expertise in evaluation, the role has great potential for abuse. It is also a role that at times puts the assessor in direct conflict with other parties who want to use the data collected.

Although several emissaries from ISR visited TPE to set up the assessment procedures and collect data, the assessment role belonged primarily to the study director and was later shared by his assistant. The study director was a very familiar face to the employees of TPE and in many cases was better known than any of the outside parties, including the external consultants. In fact, as third party assessor, the study director employed many of the same personal skills as a consultant would use in building trust and in finding out what is going on at a particular time in the division. Thus, by being such a presence at the site, the assessors, no matter how neutral their role, constituted an intervention that cannot be ignored. By operating strictly as a recipient of information, the assessor can be instrumental in the development of ideas and the raising of issues that would not have otherwise occurred. The observer/facilitator noted:

> I felt that saying [the assessors] were a completely neutral
> third party is going beyond the power of management, and

you in fact did represent an intervention on occasion into
the actual project, just by your presence if nothing else.
But neutrality, I think, you did maintain.

By and large, ISR was perceived as successful in the third party
role. Some members of the QWC even criticized the assessors for
being "too neutral" which reinforces the idea that mere presence can
raise the expectations of those being observed. Having the benefit of
the overall picture creates a certain desire within individuals in the
experimental unit for the assessors to "do something," i.e., to exercise their power. One QWC member commented,

> As a matter of fact, I used to get a little irritated because
> I kept feeling like, somehow or another, y'all knew some
> things about measuring productivity that we didn't know.
> "And, by God, you ought to tell us." Looking back on it,
> I'm glad you didn't. I'm glad you took the stance that you
> have. Being as impartial as you have been, I think you're
> very credible, as far as what's going on here. I don't
> think anyone would question that.

On occasion, the study director did drop the pure assessment
role. He served as a resource person for the task force working on
productivity measures. At other times, the study director was a con-
fidant to individual managers and employees. It was very clear that
he would not stand by and allow something to happen that would be detrimental to the program. This occasionally resulted in some maneuvering behind the scenes to avert danger. He was instrumental in
arranging the meetings when the external consultants attempted to
change the client. He also persuaded the Director to postpone the
joint QWC-cooperative conference meeting when it was apparent that
the QWC was struggling with the decision of whether to consolidate
and hire a new consultant. In several instances, the study director
was informed of events before they occurred, including many of the
personnel changes.
Given his more activist and nonclinical stance, the study director
was extremely cautious about the release and use of survey data. However, conflicts over data occurred mostly with the division rather than
among the external consultants as might be expected. The consultants
largely respected the boundaries of the mutual roles. Conflicts between the study director and those in the division arose when requests
were made for data that the study director believed would endanger
confidentiality. An example of this was when a Branch Chief wanted
to see the survey results for his Branch. The study director would
not release such data unless all Branch Chiefs would agree separately
in writing. When this condition was not met, the request was denied.

Conflicts such as this point to the difficulty in maintaining the boundaries of the third party role. These boundaries were usually challenged by the internal consultant who had considerable evaluation experience and became the advocate of the QWC. Although the relationship between the study director and the internal consultant was strained at first, they later became allies during the transition period of the QWC. After the formal experiment ended and the new cooperative conference and branch conferences were operating, the study director assumed a formal consulting role, assisting the division in interpreting the survey results and suggesting future action plans.

Relationships with the National Quality of Work Center

The most distant external relationship occurred between the division and the National Quality of Work Center. NQWC was the catalyst of the Quality of Work Program as it was at other sites. It was responsible for identifying the site, generating excitement and interest, and then stepping aside while the consultants and the assessors pursued their tasks. After the program was under way, NQWC exerted little influence over events at TVA except for monitoring the project from a distance. The only time that NQWC was directly involved was when the consultants attempted to change the client. The Director of NQWC was highly influential in his opposition to this move. At other times, NQWC sent a representative to visit TPE and attend a QWC meeting. In 1976, the QWC was informed of the change in title to the American Center for Quality of Work Life. The Center, previously linked with ISR, operated more autonomously from that point on.

Because of the distance of the relationship, the QWC was rather leery of the Center and its intentions. The Director of NQWC, a national media figure, was looked upon as a "super salesman" by members of the more reserved TPE organization. They resisted attempts by NQWC to use the TVA project as a showcase. The QWC was reluctant to participate in conferences and other forms of national exposure unless they believed that TPE would directly benefit from their participation. Some members of the QWC did appear on QWL panels, most notably the Academy of Management Meetings in 1977. Several QWC members presented papers at a special symposium that included representatives from other QWL sites and members of the academic community. Other than those few occasions, the QWC was more concerned with their own program and did not readily accept the role of promoting the interests of NQWC.

SUMMARY AND CONCLUSIONS:
THE INTERACTION OF PROCESS ISSUES

The process themes explored in the previous sections were in-
terrelated phenomena. Figure 9.2 illustrates the mutual interactions
among the three major themes, the role of the QWC in the division,
relationships between the QWC and external parties, and the internal
dynamics of the QWC. The latent issue pervading these themes and
linking them together is the concept of social power. The questions
of who was responsible for change, who influenced whom, and who
actually made decisions were never fully resolved during the experiment and this uncertainty was at the heart of the problems experienced
in the project.

FIGURE 9.2. Interaction of Process Issues

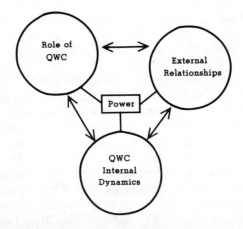

Throughout the experimental period, the QWC was the most
powerful unit in TPE. The addition of three Branch Chiefs to the committee only increased the powerful role of the QWC. The implicit
power struggle between Branch Chiefs and the QWC was perhaps the
most important dynamic occurring during the experiment. In fact, the
underlying tension between the Branch Chiefs and the QWC may have
provided the necessary leverage that kept the experiment alive. The
Branch Chiefs, historically the most powerful actors in the division,
provided the necessary resistance for the forces for change to act
upon. This situation certainly affected the internal interactions of the
QWC as was clearly demonstrated in the decision to consolidate the
QWC and the cooperative conference.

Despite its inherent power, the QWC was lacking in specific

goals and direction other than to make the division a better place to work and revitalize the cooperative conference. Without an explicit mission, the opportunity for more subtle hidden agendas to be played out was increased. This was evident when those opposed to the QWC concept pushed for using the survey data to determine whether the QWC approach was "successful" and should continue beyond the experiment. Also, several people on the QWC clearly wanted to dilute the power of the Branch Chiefs.

Because the QWC was unsure of its role vis-à-vis the Director with regard to decision making and since the Director was a regular committee member, there was a leadership vacuum within the QWC. The external consultants provided the necessary focus during the early phases, the QWC's "finest hour" by most accounts, but the facilitative role of the consultants was weakened when their attendance became more intermittent. The Division Personnel Officer provided some guidance but he was limited because of his dual role. When he was finally promoted out of the division, his influence on the QWC lessened rather than increased. The combined effects of the departure of the consultants, the loss of the Director and DPO, and the replacement of members left the QWC in limbo. As the TVA internal consultant was introduced, his role and power gradually increased as he possessed skills that the QWC vitally needed. He was a major influence during the latter phases of the experiment and served as a counterforce to the Branch Chiefs that was not expressed on the committee.

These phenomena bring to light some of the unintended consequences of participation via committees that have been suggested by Mulder (1977) and more recently by Kanter (1982). Mulder hypothesized and subsequently demonstrated that participation in representative groups, usually seen as a means to reduce power discrepancies, may actually increase them. This likely outcome is based on the fact that more powerful individuals on the committee have an increased opportunity to demonstrate their expertise and skills in the presence of less knowledgeable members. According to Kanter (1982, p. 15), " . . . the less knowledgeable may not only be 'shown up' for their lack of knowledge, thus losing power, but they may also be forced to endorse, de facto, the decisions they supposedly helped make. Their right to complain is later lost." When all of the Branch Chiefs were members of the committee, some of their resistance was reduced. However, the distance between employee members and Branch Chiefs increased largely because the issues discussed were more familiar to higher management, e.g., cost accountability and workload predictions. The historical tensions between the two groups increased this polarization, which was evident in the seating arrangements and the general flow of information during meetings. It was here when the veteran members of the QWC looked to the internal consultant for support. It was his memo that mobilized the Director into a more activist role and shaped the events of the transition to a permanent group.

The internal functioning of the QWC also had an impact on relationships with other constituencies within TPE. As the QWC meetings increasingly became shorter and, to some observers, more like staff meetings, the QWC became more insulated from the rest of the division. There were strained relationships between the QWC and the task forces and especially between the QWC members and their constituents. Internal politics notwithstanding, the QWC developed a strong identity and continued to have high status. Employee members learned a considerable amount about the division and, because of their direct association with Branch Chiefs and the Director, became equated with management in the eyes of their peers. The resentment engendered by the QWC's special status was exacerbated by the difficulty QWC members had in communicating with the rest of the division. Although both parties must share some blame for this gap in communications, it was a circumstance that ultimately reduced the effectiveness of the QWC. The representation skills necessary for the smooth traversing of boundaries were never developed. Nevertheless, these processes point out a basic irony about representative groups in which representatives grow further apart from their constituencies as their internal identity increases (Kanter 1982). The development of the branch level conferences after the experiment was devised in direct response to this communication problem.

The preceding analysis makes it very clear that an examination of process issues is vital to understanding organizational change programs. While quantitative analysis is useful for demonstrating the effects of interventions on specified variables, the qualitative approach lends insight into how the interventions came about and why particular effects were present. It is also evident that power and politics are central themes in QWL type programs where participation is the main intervention (Beer 1980; Cobb and Margulies 1983). By identifying the major social actors and their relationships and influence patterns, a deeper understanding of organizational change as a myriad of complex human forces emerges.

10   LEARNING FROM TVA

The TVA experiment was the culmination of a participatory process aimed at the global objective of improving the quality of work life of the TPE division. It is difficult, if not impossible, to place a stamp of ultimate "success" or "failure" on the project because programs of this sort cannot be examined in such absolute terms. It is possible, however, to explore the major findings and implications from a relatively objective standpoint and determine what can be learned about organizational change that might be of use to both researchers and practitioners. As will be seen, some of the implications are not as simple and straightforward as one might initially expect. This chapter summarizes the major findings—what appeared to be successful, what fell short of expectations, and what remains unknown. Participation as a mechanism for change will be analyzed according to its effects and implications. From these findings and implications suggestions will be made for implementing quality of work life programs.

MAJOR OUTCOMES OF THE EXPERIMENT

In reviewing the results of both the quantitative and qualitative analyses in Chapters 8 and 9, several major findings emerge. Because of its systemic approach, the TVA experiment touched virtually every area of the division in some way. The following outcomes capture the major "successes" of the program.

Successes

1. Participation was the single most important intervention of the experiment. The participatory process of the QWC and the task force method of problem solving and change initiation were successful means for harnessing a considerable amount of talent and creative energy directed toward improving the division. The participatory process made all other changes possible and had a positive impact on individual perceptions and attitudes. In this sense, the gains of the change process were more intangible than tangible. Employees, particularly those most directly involved, perceived a greater voice in decision making and generally saw the division as having a more human orientation by the end of the experiment.

2. Several important technical and structural problems were resolved. One task force eliminated duplication of work with another division of TVA. Equipment improvements, changes in per diem allowances, and the four-day work week were highly successful interventions for the field workers. The reorganization of one branch and the creation of the new environmental staff improved coordination in the division and streamlined the workflow.

3. The division began to explore longer term issues. By creating new task forces to examine methods for workload predictions and develop measures of cost accountability, the division began to project further into the future.

4. Management was viewed by employees as being more open and responsive to new ideas. There was a greater recognition of the fact that employees in lower levels could have valuable ideas and that some traditional hierarchical barriers were dismantled. Employees perceived that those higher in the division were receptive to their ideas by the end of the experiment.

5. The cooperative conference was revitalized and the experiment was institutionalized. Long considered an atrophied organ of the division, the cooperative conference became the legitimate vehicle for carrying the change process forward. The QWC and the division cooperative conference were actually competing entities during the experimental period. While the conference continued to carry out its admittedly mundane tasks (e.g., blood drives, picnics) during this time, the QWC was given carte blanche in approaching issues formerly limited by union contract restrictions. This latitude greatly increased the power of the QWC as it now could influence major decisions. The combining of the two collaborative bodies at the end of the experiment was perhaps the most significant outgrowth of the project since the work of the QWC could be carried forth with minimal disruption.

The above outcomes make it clear that the TVA project was, in

large measure, successful. However, the experiment was also
plagued by shortcomings which also provide the basis for considerable learning. These inadequacies are discussed below.

Shortcomings

    1. <u>A clear statement of goals and objectives was never devel-
oped by either the consultants or the QWC</u>. The lack of direction created several undesirable consequences. Since it was unclear what was
to be accomplished, expectations among division employees varied
considerably. Unrealistically high initial expectations were tempered
by participation as more direct participants learned that change is a
slow and sometimes cumbersome process. Those employees who were
less involved retained their high expectations and began to see the
QWC as ineffective since they could not see anything tangible being
accomplished.
    2. <u>An implicit power struggle between some of the Branch Chiefs
and others on the QWC became a shadow issue</u>. The absence of the
Branch Chiefs on the original QWC alienated and heightened the resistance of the most powerful members of the division. While there
is some question as to whether or not the program would have ever
gotten off the ground had the Branch Chiefs been involved initially,
bringing them in later brought the change process to a screeching
halt. When all of the Branch Chiefs finally joined the QWC early in
1976, the consultants were leaving, original committee members
were growing weary, and the potentially useful conflict was never
directly addressed.
    3. <u>Communications between the QWC and task forces and the
division as a whole were inadequate</u>. Although survey data indicated
that communications in the entire division improved as a result of the
experiment, the effectiveness of the QWC was marred by its inability
to interact effectively with its constituency. This was partly attributable to structural barriers and largely a result of a lack of appropriate representation skills on the part of QWC members. The consultants recognized early that there was a need to somehow link the QWC
with the division. They suggested developing smaller branch level
groups, however, the idea was lost during the process of putting the
Branch Chiefs on the QWC. Since the consultants left the division soon
thereafter, the idea did not surface again until the end of the experiment. To add to the difficulty, the members of the QWC and task
forces were not trained to carry out their representative roles. As
a result, the QWC remained very much an island that was very powerful, yet removed from the division at large.
    4. <u>A problem of inequity between people in different salary lev-</u>

els who performed comparable work was addressed but never resolved. The task force working in this area suggested several remedies including additional training, professional development, and various forms of recognition, but the problem was larger than these remedies suggest. The pay issue was addressed without examining the actual work performed. The original statements from the consultants' observations indicated that many engineers felt underutilized and that they desired more variety and challenge in their work. It is puzzling why some form of job redesign was not considered as part of the interventions, since the problem may have been rooted more in the nature of the work itself than in the pay system. Also, attempts to recognize high performers were ill conceived. A merit award program failed after one year because it was not seen as being connected to performance. Rather, it was viewed as a political award and the resulting resentment and envy were at the root of its demise.

5. The project apparently had minimal effects on the unions. This outcome cannot be considered a failure as such since survey data suggested that the experiment neither enhanced nor adversely affected union member attitudes. Yet, union leaders expressed some dismay that the unions were not perceived as stronger at the end of the program. The unusually high level of union-management harmony prior to and during the experiment suggests that the project reinforced the status quo with regard to union-management relations.

6. An accurate measure of productivity was never developed, therefore, the actual impact of the experiment on productivity could not be assessed. Because of the type of work carried out by the division, productivity was difficult, if not impossible, to quantify. As a result, an accurate cost-benefit analysis could not be carried out. Data from interviews indicated that productivity did not increase or decrease appreciably. However, it was recognized that the experiment occurred during a slow production period. It is clear that despite the substantial time investment (i.e., approximately $450,000 in manhours, representing 2 to 3 percent of the division's manpower budget over the experimental period) the project did not detract from work output. Even so, some managers expressed concern that the project was too costly and time consuming in relation to the perceived benefits.

7. Although the program became a permanent part of the division, the change process was not diffused to other divisions in TVA. Early proponents of the program expressed hope that other divisions in TVA would emulate the experimental division and adopt the "quality of work" process. However, the project was not seen as a rousing success by others in TVA. The mixed visible results and large time investment did not create a mandate to develop similar programs in other divisions. The lack of commitment by middle management and

the varying attitudes of the Branch Chiefs also dampened efforts at widespread diffusion. Perhaps the key factor was the absence of opinion leaders from the division who could assist in transferring appropriate change ideas and skills to other sites (Macy 1978).

The shortcomings of the experiment reflect ambiguities in both anticipated results and in new relationships engendered by the participatory process. While the limitations are each serious concerns, they represent some of the inevitable complexities inherent in trying to implement system-wide change. The next section examines these complexities in greater detail.

IMPLICATIONS: THE PARADOX OF PARTICIPATION

Participation has traditionally been considered as a linear variable by organizational researchers. It is usually introduced into a system as a new procedure with the implicit assumption that the more participation the better. Data are then collected to determine whether or not participation "works." In reality, participation takes on varying forms and qualities (Lowin 1968; Sashkin 1976; Hespe and Wall 1976) and applying the general label is not very useful for empirical analysis or conceptual clarity (Seashore 1977; Dachler and Wilpert 1978).

The TVA project implies some lessons about how participation in organizational change works in reality. An analysis of the events at TVA reveals that some of the conclusions about the process of participation seem to defy more common notions about how organizational change occurs. Such contradictory ideas reflect the complex nature of participation and, although managing the process becomes more of a dilemma, perhaps the issues are made more clear. Participation, then, is viewed as a paradoxical process rather than a panacea. To stimulate thinking about participation as a change process, three paradoxes will be explored concerning 1) the initiation of change, 2) the nature of leadership and boundaries, and 3) the balance between formal and informal processes. The discussion is based on interviews with key figures in the experiment and direct observation of events.

The Paradox of Change

The more favorable the conditions for participatory change seem, the more difficult it is to create change. The long history of labor-management cooperation, the existence of the cooperative conference, and a general democratic value system with ideological roots in the New Deal made TVA an ideal site for a participatory quality of work life program. Many of the barriers that caused difficulties at other sites such as intense adversarial relationships between unions and management and widespread employee and management skepticism about the value of the collaborative process were not present at TVA in 1973. In many ways the germ of the QWL process seemed already in place; it simply had to be rejuvenated. The process, quite obviously, was not that easy.

In keeping with its heritage and the norms of the region, TVA was a very "polite" organization. Conflict and other emotions were not overtly expressed even though they were present. There was also a well entrenched feeling of traditional practice pervading the Authority. The stability and longevity of the work force contributed to a widely understood status quo.

The external consultants and many QWC members saw this status quo as a barrier to change. One employee humorously characterized the creation of change in TVA as trying to change the course of a moving train, implying that one first has to stop the train. As Lewin (1951, p. 229) stated in describing the process of "unfreezing": "To break open the shell of complacency and self-righteousness it is sometimes necessary to bring about deliberately an emotional stir-up." Since there was so little tension within TVA, finding the appropriate leverage for change was a source of frustration to action-oriented consultants.

The primary source of useful tension within the division was the immediate resistance of some of the Branch Chiefs to the program. Since they were not included on the original Quality of Work Committee (with one exception), they felt bypassed and their subtle opposition increased. They were finally included on the committee at a very inopportune time. At this point the QWC was too far along and the conflict was not productive, much to the detriment of the QWC which floundered for a considerable period of time. Even the existing cooperative conference created a barrier to change as the Quality of Work Committee was reluctant to overstep their territory.

The conflict between the forces favoring and opposing change became more productive during the latter phase of the experiment when the decision was made to combine the QWC and the cooperative conference. By this time, new coalitions had formed within the QWC which were enhanced by the new consultant to counter the forces of resistance. From this tension the new cooperative conference was founded along with a formal philosophy statement and the experiment was made permanent.

From these events, it becomes evident that too little tension in the system can be just as detrimental to change as too much. Finding the right "friction point" becomes the task of skilled consultants who may need to create the necessary tension for effective participation to come about. Since informal cooptation or the absorption of opposing forces was historically such a part of TVA's larger social fabric (Selznick 1949), it could have been a most useful process during the early stages of the TVA project. The tension created by including the Branch Chiefs early on may have slowed the change process, but the results may have been more meaningful.

The Paradox of Leadership

   In order for employees to exert more power, the leader must also assume a powerful role. Concerned that their own inherent power might interfere with the change process and preclude employees from expressing themselves, well-intentioned managers often assume a lesser role in participatory programs. This was clearly the case at TVA in several instances. The first Director of the division was a strong figure in the early phases of the experiment. However, the fact that he did not provide a focal point as the experiment matured was a source of considerable frustration for the QWC and the external consultants.

   Part of the problem was the fact that the Director historically had little power over the Branch Chiefs. This characteristic of the role coupled with the rather noncommittal style of the first Director resulted in vague boundaries that were the heart of the problems experienced in the program. As one of the consultants explained:

   . . . we wanted [the Director] to realize that he has a
   key role to play out in that organization. Not just vis-à-
   vis the Quality of Work Committee, but vis-à-vis [the
   division] and unless he were willing to play that out,
   people were really very uncomfortable in moving in any
   direction. They could come up with some recommendations, but they weren't really sure whether or not they
   had the power to move ahead.

The consultants wanted the Director to assume the executive role, receiving the recommendations from the QWC and then assigning proper task responsibilities. Since the Director was a regular member of the QWC, the distinction between member and leader was blurred. The succeeding Director was plagued by the same authority issues.

   A difficulty lies in the assumption that strong leadership and participation are at opposite ends of a power continuum. Yet, it appears that strong leadership must be present in order for participation to work effectively. This is a rather disconcerting thought to those who believe that increasing participation somehow shifts the balance of power toward employees and away from management. This conceptual problem was addressed some time ago by Tannenbaum (1968) who suggested that rather than viewing influence as a fixed quantity to be apportioned to various parties, one can envision the total amount of influence in an organization as an expanding sphere. In other words, for effective participation, management's influence must increase along with that of employees.

If appropriate boundaries and authority relationships are not well defined at the beginning of a participatory program, the participants will waste productive time and energy trying to create them for themselves. The QWC devoted much attention to what their appropriate role was, a process that often resulted in "wheel-spinning" and internal power struggles. Having the Director as a regular member and rotating the chair position monthly satisfied their egalitarian desires but removed any sense that anyone was in charge. As Kanter (1982, p. 11) aptly expressed:

> Erich Fromm's classic book title, Escape From Freedom, was intended to convey the ways in which people slide into neurotic behavior when they are given freedoms they cannot handle. True 'freedom' is not the absence of structure— letting the employees go off and do whatever they want—but rather a clear structure that enables people to work within established boundaries in an autonomous and creative way.

The leader role, in participatory programs becomes one of empowering, of establishing what can and cannot be decided by the collaborative group, how they will report their findings, and how their ideas will be implemented. To add to the paradox, Kanter further stated that a leader's close monitoring of the participatory process is a signal to the employees that he cares about what they are doing. The frequent absences of the first Division Director and his distance from the QWC resulted in the perception that their work was of little importance to him and they continued to flounder. The consultants attempted to resolve this problem prior to the second workshop by attempting to make the Director the client, instead of the QWC, thereby forcing him to be the focal point. However, their ill-timed attempt was seen as usurping the QWC and undermining the collaborative theme of the project. They withdrew the suggestion under intense pressure.

The structure of the new cooperative conference was clearly superior to the experimental program as it clearly defined authority relationships and established committees at a lower organizational

level (i.e., Branches). The new and permanent program also more
clearly delineated the role of Director as having the ultimate authority
to implement programs.

The Paradox of Process

As structures for participation become more formalized, more
attention must be devoted to informal process issues. Creating new
structures such as collaborative committees and task forces means
more interacting parties, a situation that requires greater attention
to process issues. Even the existence of a joint committee does not
always mean that the group will act in accordance with its collaborative
mission. There are inevitably conflicting agendas that most often remain hidden, creating a highly politicized atmosphere.

Social scientists have studied groups for years and have documented situations in which groups become mired in their own internal
dynamics. Janis (1972) presented the "groupthink" hypothesis whereby
groups develop illusions of consensus and invulnerability based on an
inherent desire to remain cohesive, leading to an inability to engage
in critical discussions. Rather than express dissent, the group relies
on rationalization, self-censorship and what Kanter (1982, p. 17) re-
fers to as the "benign 'tyranny' of peers" to guide their interactions.
There is the additional problem of the more powerful members of the
group banding together and forcing ideas on others, turning an out-
wardly "democratic" committee into an oligarchy dominated by a few
powerful members (Mulder 1977).

Such forces were clearly at work within the Quality of Work
Committee, especially after the Branch Chiefs became members.
There was a reluctance on the part of less influential members to
disagree with prevailing ideas based on the illusory notion that these
were accepted by the QWC as a whole. There were often feelings of
"Why open a can of worms when we can arrive at a decision?" Unfortunately, many meetings remained at an implicit stalemate as real
issues such as conflicts between employee members and the Branch
Chiefs were dealt with only at a superficial level, for example, quibbling over the wording of a proposal. As the QWC solidified as a group
and came under attack from the division for their lack of progress,
they tightened their boundaries only to make these matters worse.
Clearly, there was a need for skills, particularly representation
skills. Kanter (1982, p. 17) suggests:

> Cooperation and reduced politicking are more likely to
> occur when team members are participating in the group
> as individuals rather than as representatives, because

they can make individual deals free from the pressures
of a 'shadow group' symbolically looking over their
shoulders.

Thus, committee members need to simultaneously strive for a
strong sense of team and individual identity. QWC members must provide an outlet for information from their peers, yet retain enough individual integrity to speak their minds within the committee. When
they go too far in identifying with the group there is the danger of
elitism, resulting in a detachment from the organization, eventually
leading to an over concern with cohesion and the preservation of the
group.

SUGGESTIONS FOR MANAGING
PARTICIPATORY CHANGE PROGRAMS

In their recent and highly celebrated book, In Search of Excellence, Peters and Waterman (1982) stated that one of the major characteristics of successful organizations is the ability to manage paradox and to appreciate the inherent contradictions of human nature.
Researchers and practitioners who seek to apply participation as a
change device could benefit from examining the paradoxes inherent
in the process.
    The TVA project demonstrates that participation and organiza-
tional change are political phenomena, rife with uncertainty, and subject to dynamic relationships among human beings who are not always
rational in their approaches to problems. The willingness and ability
to tolerate the ambiguities raised by the interactions engendered by
participation are necessary ingredients for a successful change effort.
Concurrently, the models and methods employed to study and assess
organizational change must incorporate a more dynamic and evolutionary viewpoint as Van Maanen (1979) and other proponents of qualitative
research strategies have suggested.
    Furthermore, the outcomes and implications of the TVA project
reify some significant issues in managing and maintaining participatory
Quality of Work Life programs. The lessons are synthesized as six
needs underlying organizational change efforts:

1. The need for well-defined boundaries: Since participants in
an organizational change program are dealing with each other in an
atmosphere of uncertainty, appropriate structures and boundaries are
needed to define an environment that facilitates their interactions.
This means not only establishing the appropriate committees, but also
developing explicit goals, authority and working relationships, time

constraints, and, if possible, measures of effectiveness. Without such controls, the participants will expend much energy creating them for themselves, often at the expense of more productive activity.

The lack of clear-cut boundaries at TVA, especially in regard to authority relationships, was definitely at the root of many of the problems faced by the QWC. Participants need a sense that they are working within an acceptable framework that defines what they can and cannot do so that their knowledge and creative talents can be used effectively. From the experience at TVA, it seems desirable to develop very clear working rules that carefully define how decisions to implement new programs are made.

The development of a steering committee comprised of top management and union leaders can provide the vehicle for monitoring boundaries and structures. Such a committee was not formed at TVA. However, the initiators of programs at other QWL experimental sites have created a hierarchical committee structure that closely parallels the structure of the organization (Drexler and Lawler 1977). The steering committee's function is to monitor change events. The QWC in TVA attempted to create and monitor change, causing confusion about its proper role and reducing its effectiveness.

2. The need for salient issues: Obviously, in order to participate, employees must perceive a set of issues and problems that they consider vital and want to improve. Identifying the need for change and generating data about existing problems are crucial prerequisites for a participatory program. The issues must be real and expressed in terms of specific, attainable goals. Significant areas for improvement include the nature of the work itself and the evaluation and reward systems. Lawler (1981) suggested that pay can be a useful leverage point for organizational change. By focusing on pay and reward issues, the organization demonstrates its commitment to meaningful change. While this was attempted at TVA, the pay equity issues were intricately tied to the work performed by different salary levels, making the problem more complex than the recommended solutions.

One of the most effective aspects of the TVA project was the careful manner by which problem areas were identified by the QWC with aid from the consultants. It is far more desirable for the participants themselves to identify the issues to be addressed. The observations of the consultants at TVA were verified and categorized by the QWC to form the agenda for change but were not translated into concrete goals. Once the issues are identified, a meaningful set of explicit goals related to the overall philosophy are necessary to guide the program and provide realistic expectations for participants.

3. The need for involvement of all key parties: A major problem at TVA was the fact that the most powerful actors in the division, the Branch Chiefs, were left out of the change process at the beginning.

Their introduction to the QWC later was a difficult transition that created power issues that were never fully resolved. The crucial stakeholders in a program, especially managers who often feel left out or caught in the middle of the process, must be actively and genuinely involved. The absence of such involvement will only increase resistance to a point where it is dysfunctional to change. The disenfranchised parties often try to block or thwart proposals, not because they dislike the ideas, but rather because they resent how the ideas came about. Such dynamics were certainly present during many QWC meetings, resulting in stalemates and quibbling over minor issues. Identification of these crucial parties and finding ways to gain their early involvement saves dealing with hidden and destructive power struggles later on.

To prevent a participatory committee from becoming tired and ritualistic, the membership should be changed periodically. How this is accomplished, however, can have serious implications for the functioning of the group. The introduction of a new member changes the interaction pattern of the group as the new member becomes socialized and the veteran members adapt. Too many membership changes break the continuity while too few can result in entrenched ideas or overly comfortable relationships that suppress creativity. Replacing members ensures that more people have the opportunity to participate and that new ideas get introduced into the group. Careful attention to the timing of replacements minimizes disruption of the work of the committee and makes the transition less stressful.

4. The need for training: The difference between real participation and the illusion of participation is the degree of human skill employed by participants. Having representatives sit around the conference table and "discuss" issues is clearly not enough and runs the risk of a collaborative group degenerating into a "debating society," a criticism often directed at the QWC. Skills in problem solving and decision making are developed by training the participants early in a change effort. Knowledge of how groups function, the role of a representative, conflict resolution, and running effective meetings are all crucial to effective participation.

The training, however, should not be merely a series of presentations that are isolated from the change program. Care must be given to selecting consultants who can integrate the skills into the daily life of a QWC or task force. Such training can also enhance the possibility that the participants can serve as catalysts for the eventual diffusion of changes so that the process is transferred along with the new ideas.

5. The need for strong leadership: Leadership is not anathema to participation. As was described above, the exercise of leadership, in fact, is a requirement for participation. A sense of backing off or noncommitment of a leader perceived by participants, as was the case

at TVA, sends messages that their participation is not important and
gives a sense that the process is merely a formality. Top management
provides role models and is the focal point for the efforts of employees. Although management may fear that their role inhibits open employee involvement, the lack of the role is far more damaging. Although it is not necessary for top management to be present on committees, employees must feel that their ideas are being received and
acted upon by those who have the formal authority to do so. In essence,
management must remain powerful to free others to participate. One
of the main functions of the leader is to legitimize participation by
espousing a philosophy of shared values. Walton (1983, p. 152) stated:

> Where I have observed participative systems work effec-
> tively, there has been a high level of consciousness at all
> levels of the organization about goals and ideals and an
> understanding of the philosophical rationale for design
> elements.

By providing this sense of shared values, the leader imparts meaning
to events created by participants.

    6. The need for rewards: Some participants at TVA were chided
because they spent so much time at meetings, thus they were subtly
punished for their involvement. The rewards for participation can be
many, including the intrinsic rewards of engaging in lively discussions,
feelings of accomplishment in helping the organization, and a sense of
ownership of the changes. Participants need to feel that their efforts
are encouraged and rewarded.

    In TVA, task force and QWC members experienced greatly ex-
panded jobs because of their additional roles. Given the intrinsic value
of participation for many employees, there is a concern that extrinsic
rewards also be provided. If participation is seen as part of one's total
performance, then it should be rewarded as such. If the organization
benefits financially from a change effort, there must be ways to distribute the gains so that employees see a connection between organizational improvement and their well-being as organization members.
If such rewards are not forthcoming, employees will cease to see
involvement as an attractive activity and the potential for continued
participation is lowered along with the value of the process.

THE FUTURE: WHITHER QWL?

    After more than a decade of thought and experimentation about
the "quality of work life," the era of urgency and excitement about
QWL programs seems to be waning. One of the reasons for this tend-

ency is the fact that considerable progress has been made in introducing new structures and methods into U.S. workplaces. Many major corporations have begun QWL type programs and participatory mechanisms such as quality circles have become quite commonplace. The rise of foreign competition and the concern with productivity and the development of an industrial policy have resulted in a fascination with alternative management techniques, such as those of the Japanese, which have served to legitimize experimenting with different management styles in this country.

Although many successful QWL efforts have occurred, the concept of QWL unfortunately has fallen victim to the fadism propagated by short-sighted consultants and managers in search of panaceas. Nadler and Lawler (1983) refer to this type of thinking as a "QWL equals everything" phenomenon. Any organizational development or effectiveness attempt is labeled QWL and the meaning of the concept is diminished while expectations are raised far beyond realistic levels. The danger, according to Nadler and Lawler (1983), is that because these expectations cannot be fully met, overzealous proponents turn away from the concept and search for another magic cure. The result is that ultimately "QWL equals nothing" (Nadler and Lawler 1983, p. 24) and joins MBO, job enrichment, and organizational development, gathering dust in the minds of managers and change agents. This outcome is lamentable because the ideas underlying these terms, that is, improving the nature of jobs and human relationships, remain valid.

The desire to improve life at work is neither new nor revolutionary. One might even argue that Frederick Taylor, the ideological antagonist of humanistic change agents, wanted to improve the quality of work life by making work less burdensome to the average pig-iron worker (Taylor 1911). Organized labor fought for years to improve "working conditions" in addition to gaining economic rewards. Ironically, unionists resisted much of the humanistic approach to change because of their fears about management increasing job responsibility without commensurate rewards, or using work improvement programs as a union-busting tool.

The human relations movement with roots in the Hawthorne Studies introduced the notion that interpersonal relations and social interaction patterns were important components of work. The focus of organizational development practitioners in the 1950s and 1960s was to improve these relationships through sensitivity training, team building, and the like. Drawing upon the self-actualization theories of Abraham Maslow and Frederick Herzberg and the individual human potential movement of the 1960s and early 1970s, change agents turned their attention to the work itself and attempted to "enrich" jobs by increasing such attributes as skill variety, autonomy, and challenge (Hackman and Oldham 1980). Management by objectives arose as both a motivation/control device via the establishment of specific goals and a developmental performance appraisal process between a superior and subordinates.

Advocates of the QWL approach rejected the piecemeal application of these organizational change attempts and pushed for multiple intervention strategies based on an underlying mechanism for participation in change decisions. Consequently, over the years the scope of organizational change interventions has expanded beyond jobs to include whole systems. Yet, despite such systemic approaches, the grand experiments, such as those at Rushton Mine, Harman International (Bolivar), and TVA have a restrictive quality about them in the sense that the model for change is imported from outside the company and superimposed upon the existing structure. While these experiments have been necessary and scientifically valuable in discovering how change occurs, there is the danger of becoming overconcerned with the ultimate success or failure of QWL methods rather than concentrating on what was learned. QWL becomes another in a succession of tools that organizations can import. When "success" is not clear, as is most often the case, the label is discarded along with potentially valuable ideas.

QWL AND ORGANIZATIONAL CULTURE

The QWL idea is transcending into current thinking about organizational culture defined by Sathe (1983, p. 6) as "the set of important understandings (often unstated) that members of a community share in common." There is a renewed interest in the implicit assumptions, beliefs, and values underlying organizational behavior and change. A considerable body of literature is developing which is laying a new foundation of thought about organizations (e.g., Jelinek, Smircich, and Hirsch 1983) and providing a set of themes fusing such diverse areas as anthropology and organization theory. Some of these themes include corporate culture, organizational cognition, organizational symbolism, and unconscious processes (Smircich 1983).

The QWL approach, with its strong value base emphasizing participation and collaboration in problem solving, implies cultural change. Indeed, one of the most striking aspects of the TVA project was the underlying grass roots ideology. The second external consultant at TVA helped to redefine these values with the QWC and cooperative conference resulting in the Philosophy Statement that set the stage for the institutionalization of the QWL program. This effort was a prime example of blending cultural change with behavioral change. Both Peters and Waterman (1982) and Sathe (1983) highlight the ongoing psychological debate concerning whether attitudes, beliefs, and values (i.e., components of culture) precede behavioral change or vice versa. While it is clear that culture influences behavior, Peters and Waterman (1982) stress the importance of acting, of trying many experiments, and building a supportive culture around the new behaviors. It is here once again that the role of the leader is crucial. Earlier it was stated that participants look to the leader to legitimize their participatory efforts. From the standpoint of culture, the task of the leader is to provide meaning to new behaviors or what Peters and Waterman (1982, p. 74) refer to as the "management of the after-the-act labeling process—in other words, publicly and ceaselessly lauding the small wins along the way." In essence, this is what Lewin (1951) meant by "refreezing."

SUMMARY AND CONCLUSIONS

The results of the TVA experiment have cast participation not only in the light of a moderately successful intervention, but as a paradoxical concept implying simultaneously: tension and stability, freedom and well managed boundaries, and attention to formal structures and informal processes. In addition to supporting the hypothesis that participation leads to positive outcomes for the individual, this study has enabled one to appreciate some of the underlying political realities or the nonrational components of organizational change. These processes, explored through the analysis of qualitative data, provide added meaning to the quantitative results.

The quality of work life ultimately is a long-term evolutionary change process embedded in the culture of organizations. It is much more than an experimental program with a definite end point. Viewing QWL efforts in "bottom-line" terms increases the risk of creating short-lived programs that are bound to disappoint managers and employees looking for an answer to all problems. Rather, improving work life requires many experiments, both large and small, grounded and reinforced by the values and beliefs that provide meaning to the work lives of organization members. The TVA project provides hope that the search for meaning continues.

EPILOGUE:
THE END OF COOPERATION

The TVA quality of work life experiment was fully dependent upon the existence of the cooperative conference, the manifestation of TVA's spirit of cooperation between unions and management for almost forty years. Once the official experiment ended it was fused into the newly constituted cooperative conference of TPE where the ideas and programs of the experiment joined the less fervent day-to-day life of the division.

Most of the activity of the New Cooperative Conference (NCC) occurred at the branch level carried out by six branch conferences, including the Director's office. Although the pace was slower than the QWC, and items such as the division picnic, the savings bond campaign, and the health and safety program appeared on the agenda along with other action programs, considerable progress had been made. By mid-1980, the conference was considering flextime beginning at 7 a.m., an experimental 4-day week in the Civil Engineering Branch, interbranch training, and merit pay raises. The NCC was reorganized and cut from 23 to 13 members, consisting of one employee and one manager from each branch plus the Director. The recommendation/ charge committees were eliminated and more discretion and responsibility were allocated to the branches.

The 1980s, which were to bring a changing political climate to the nation, also began to leave their mark on TVA. The Reagan administration demoted the chairman of TVA, an appointee of Jimmy Carter, to one of the Authority's three directors. The progress of the New Cooperative Conference was subsumed by several larger forces including union-management strife brought about in 1981 by a new "hard line" management attitude in relation to the white collar unions. A new contract lowered wages for some employees, based promotions on merit rather than seniority, and held annual increases for thousands of employees to 3 percent for the next two years (Business Week, 1981). Management claimed that dramatic increases in electricity rates had angered the public accustomed to low rates. Also, TVA salaries were considered high for the southeastern region. Although the unions considered a possible strike, their threat was immediately disarmed by President Reagan's firing of the striking air traffic controllers, also a white collar government union. The unions in TVA including OPEIU, which are prohibited by law from striking, had no choice but to accept the contract with considerable bitterness. In retaliation, the unions canceled the cooperative conference program,

199

signaling a new era of adversarial relations between labor and management, something quite out of the ordinary for TVA. Although management insisted that they would continue the cooperative program by going directly to employees, a union official was quoted as saying "Cooperation is by the boards," (Business Week, 1981, p. 32).

By this time, the experimental division no longer existed as such because of a reorganization that merged TPE with a much larger construction division. Many of the most active members of the Quality of Work Committee either had retired or left the division prior to the merger. Ironically, in the same issue of Business Week (September 21, 1981, p. 32) which reported the demise of labor-management cooperation at TVA, an article appeared several pages later titled "Quality of Work Life: Catching On."

APPENDIXES

APPENDIX A: FUNCTIONAL DESCRIPTION OF TPE

Office of the Director[1]

The Director administered the work of the division along with
the Assistant Director and several other assistants. These assistants
performed tasks such as representing the division in conferences and
discussions, coordinating and clarifying work programs, providing
recommendations to the Director about problems, coordinating the
work of the division staff, and carrying out special technical assignments and studies. Three units reporting to the Director were:

The Administrative Services Staff advised and assisted the Director by interpreting and applying administrative policies and procedures, preparing cost records, administrative reports, and the
division's budget, administering the division's records management
program, and provided payroll services for the division.

Personnel Services, headed by the Division Personnel Officer
(DPO), advised and assisted the Director in planning and carrying out
personnel administration for the Division within established policies
and standards. It maintained close relations with Personnel and Information Services in the Office of the Manager of Power and with the
Division of Personnel in coordinating personnel activities.

Environmental and Design Services reviewed existing transmission, substation and communication facilities and developed modifica-
tions designed to enhance their appearance in order to make them
more compatible with the surrounding environment. This service
staff also provided drafting services and prepared diagrams, maps,
and other drawings of TVA's and its distributors' electric power facilities for such purposes as operation, maintenance, project proposals, and specifications. It also provided training for draftsmen
and coordinated training for engineers.

Transmission System Planning Branch

The Transmission System Planning Branch made engineering
studies and economic analyses for planning the development of TVA's
power transmission system. It conceived and developed plans and
recommendations for additions or changes in the power transmission
system in order to ensure system stability and reliability of service

---

[1]Functional descriptions are adapted from an undated internal
TVA document.

to load centers. System planning also developed budget recommendations for changes and additions to the transmission system. In addition, this branch made continuing longrange studies of the performance of the transmission system, using the results as a basis for future planning. It advised and assisted other organizations concerned with problems of power transmission where the application of specialized mathematical analysis and specialized computer programs was required. Finally, the branch conceived and developed coordinated relay protective plans and selected equipment required for the control and protection of TVA's power transmission facilities, and provided engineering advice to other divisions on relays and control devices for the transmission system.

Electrical Engineering and Design Branch

The Electrical Engineering and Design Branch performed electrical engineering and related services involved in planning and designing substations and switching stations for the TVA power system, including the rehabilitation or expansion of these facilities. The branch prepared final designs, specifications, and estimates of costs for new and existing substations, requisitioned materials and equipment, analyzed bids, and made recommendations for awards on such items being purchased for approved projects. Electrical Engineering made economic studies for selection of sites for major substations or switching stations and recommended the sites. It studied new materials and developments for adapting them to the practical application in substation designs and layouts. The branch also provided engineering advice to other divisions on technical matters involving physical and electrical design of substations and switching stations, and it prepared, along with other divisions, equipment specifications for transformers, and other items of equipment.

Civil Engineering and Design Branch

The Civil Engineering and Design Branch had as its major function civil engineering and related services involved in planning and designing structures and transmission lines for the TVA power transmission and communication facilities, including rehabilitation or improvement of existing transmission lines or related facilities. In carrying out this task, the branch developed and prepared final designs, specifications, and estimated costs and requisitions for material and equipment. It analyzed bids and prepared recommendations for awards of contracts on such items being purchased for approved projects and scheduled such additions or revisions to the existing transmission network to meet system operating requirements.

Civil Engineering selected routes and made terrain surveys for transmission lines considering maximum future land use, environmental impact, and economics, and performed structural design and related engineering work for power transmission structures and for foundations for buildings and equipment. It worked with the Land Branch in acquiring rights of way for transmission lines. It made investigations and surveys and prepared property maps of lands needed for transmission lines and substation projects or for other power facilities provided by the Office of Power. It performed special studies and investigations of new developments in conductor and tower designs, transmission accessories, substation and microwave structures, and buildings and foundations. The branch also provided engineering advice to other divisions on technical matters involving civil and mechanical features of structures, foundations and heavy equipment. It also worked with other TVA divisions, government agencies, manufacturers, and neighboring utilities on all civil engineering matters related to the TVA system.

Communication Engineering and Design Branch

The function of the Communication Engineering and Design Branch was to perform planning and economic analyses for overall development of the power communication system. It developed budget recommendations for changes and additions to the communication system. It made engineering investigations of new or advanced communication technology, evaluating its possible use, and making recommendations for its application to the communication system. The branch planned all communication facilities for the power system and performed engineering and design of the facilities, except at generating plants.

Communication Engineering prepared final designs, specifications, estimates of cost, and requisitions for material and equipment, analyzed bids and recommended awards of contracts on items being purchased for approved projects, and scheduled additions or revisions to the existing communication network. The branch also provided engineering advice to other divisions on technical matters pertaining to transmission of intelligence by electrical and electronic devices. The branch also interacted with other divisions, power users, government agencies, manufacturers, neighboring utilities, and railroads on communication engineering matters related to TVA.

Sex	N	Percent
Female	50	13.0
Male	294	77.0
Missing	38	

Marital Status	N	Percent
Married	281	73.6
Not married	61	16.0
Missing	41	

Age	N	Percent
Under 20 years	5	1.3
21-25 years	25	6.5
26-30 years	72	18.8
31-35 years	55	14.4
36-40 years	35	9.2
41-45 years	37	9.7
46-55 years	92	24.1
56 years or older	21	5.5
Missing	40	

Education	N	Percent
Some elementary school (grades 1-7)	0	0
Completed elementary school (grades 1-7)	0	0
Some high school (1-3 years)	2	0.5
Graduated from high school	45	11.8
Some college (1-3 years)	110	28.8
Graduated from college (B.A., B.S., or other Bachelors degree)	124	32.5
Some graduate school	36	9.4
Graduate degree (Masters, Ph.D., M.D., etc.)	14	3.7
Missing	51	

Race	N	Percent
Black	17	4.5
Oriental	2	0.5

Race	N	Percent
American Indian	2	0.5
Spanish Surnamed	0	0
None of the above	318	83.2
Missing	43	

Primary Income Earner	N	Percent
Yes	298	78.0
No	42	11.0
Missing	42	

Community Size—Past	N	Percent
On a farm or ranch	53	13.9
In a rural area, not on a farm or ranch	64	16.8
A suburban town near a city	47	12.3
A small city (less than 100,000 people)	74	19.4
A large city (more than 100,000 people)	104	27.2
Missing	40	

Past Yearly Income	N	Percent
Under $4,000	5	1.3
$4,000 to $5,999	5	1.3
$6,000 to $7,999	17	4.5
$8,000 to $9,999	32	8.4
$10,000 to $12,999	70	18.4
$13,000 to $15,999	74	19.4
$16,000 to $19,999	48	12.6
$20,000 to $24,999	70	18.4
$25,000 or more	21	5.5
Missing	40	

Employment Tenure	N	Percent
Less than 30 days	2	0.5
1–3 months	9	2.4
4–11 months	10	2.6
1–3 years	36	9.4
4–5 years	36	9.4
6–10 years	81	21.2
11 years or more	169	44.2
Missing		

Current Job Tenure	N	Percent
Less than 30 days	3	0.8
1-3 months	13	3.4
4-11 months	34	8.9
1-3 years	65	17.0
4-5 years	47	12.3
6-10 years	79	20.7
11 years or more	101	26.4
Missing	40	

Hours Worked Per Week	N	Percent
30-34 hours	3	0.8
35-39 hours	14	3.7
40-44 hours	317	83.0
45-49 hours	4	1.0
50-54 hours	3	0.8
55-59 hours	0	0
60-64 hours	1	0.3
65 hours or more	0	0
Missing		

Overtime	N	Percent
Time and one-half	197	51.6
Straight time	79	20.7
Not paid	47	12.3
Missing	59	

Work Unit—Branch	N	Percent
Transmission System Planning	51	13.4
Civil Engineering and Design	104	27.2
Electrical Engineering and Design	99	25.9
Communication Engineering and Design	51	13.4
Director's Office	44	11.5
Missing	33	

APPENDIX C: FUNCTIONAL DESCRIPTION OF DED

Office of the Director

The Director of Engineering Design was responsible to the Manager of Engineering Design and Construction for technical and administrative planning and served as the director of all activities of the division. He was assisted by three Assistant Directors, an assistant to the Director and other staff groups as follows:

The Assistant Director (Thermal Power Engineering) assisted the Director in the overall executive management of the division. He had specific responsibility for coordinating the activities among the Mechanical Engineering, Electrical Engineering, and Civil Engineering Branches.

The Assistant Director (Thermal Power Engineering Design) assisted the Director in the overall executive management of the division. He had specific responsibility for coordinating the activities among all major thermal design projects and the Plant Additions Design Project.

The Assistant Director (Architectural, Hydro, and Special Projects Engineering and Design) assisted the Director in the overall executive management of the division. He had specific responsibility for coordinating the activities of the Architectural Design, Civil Engineering and Design, Electrical Engineering and Design, and the Mechanical Engineering and Design Branches.

Administrative Services was responsible for the functions of the Quality Assurance, Procedures Control, Project Control, and Engineering Services Staffs, each with several sections.

The Personnel Services Staff provided general administrative services for the division, including personnel, organization, training, and stenographic services.

Civil Engineering and Design Branch

The Civil Engineering and Design Branch developed the final general layout and prepared designs, drawings, and specifications for the construction of civil engineering structures and facilities for all hydro and nonpower-related projects, including bridges. For all projects, it prepared the designs, drawings and specifications, and handled other procurement activities for highways, railroads, and bridges. For thermal power projects, it normally prepared the designs, drawings, and specifications for all civil features of facilities. It executed an inspection and maintenance program for all TVA-owned dams, bridges, and related hydro facilities to keep them in a safe and satisfactory condition. It also was responsible for reconnaissance, location, and design for highway, railroad, and bridge relocations and the negotiation of contracts with federal, state and county agencies, and railways for all projects. It conducted research and development work related to design of civil engineering features within its assigned scope of work.

Electrical Engineering and Design Branch

The Electrical Engineering and Design Branch prepared designs, drawings, and specifications for electrical systems for hydro and non-power-related projects, and normally for electrical features of facilities. For all projects, it prepared designs, drawings, and specifications, and handled other procurement activities for communications facilities. It conducted research and investigative work of a developmental nature with manufacturers of communications equipment and established testing procedures. It was also responsible for the coordination and handling of electrical suborders, including preparation of estimates, designs, drawings, and specifications.

APPENDIX D: DEMOGRAPHIC PROFILE: DED

Sex	N	Percent
Female	25	7.6
Male	301	92.0
Missing	1	

Marital Status	N	Percent
Married	267	81.7
Widowed	3	0.9
Separated	1	0.3
Divorced	17	5.2
Never Married	37	11.3
Missing	2	

Age	N	Percent
Under 20 years	4	1.2
21-25 years	62	19.0
26-30 years	87	26.6
31-35 years	51	15.6
36-40 years	37	11.3
41-45 years	35	10.7
46-55 years	39	11.9
56 years or older	12	3.7
Missing	0	

Education	N	Percent
Some elementary school (grades 1-7)	0	0
Completed elementary school (8 grades)	0	0
Some high school (1-3 years)	0	0
Graduated from high school	8	2.4
Some college (1-3 years)	118	36.1
Graduated from college (B.A., B.S., or other Bachelors degree)	109	33.4
Some graduate school	62	19.0
Graduate degree (Masters, Ph.D., M.D., etc.)	22	6.7
Missing	8	

Race	N	Percent
Black	18	5.5
Oriental	3	0.9
American Indian	0	0
Spanish Surname (American)	0	0
White	302	92.4
None of the above	1	0.3
Missing	3	

Primary Income Earner	N	Percent
Yes	295	90.2
No	31	9.5
Missing	1	

Community Size—Past	N	Percent
A farm ranch or home in the country (rural)	76	23.2
A small town in the country (rural area)	64	19.6
A suburban town near a city	34	10.4
A small city (less than 100,000 people)	64	19.6
A large city (more than 100,000 people)	88	26.9
Missing	1	

Past Yearly Income	N	Percent
Under $4,000	6	1.8
$4,000 to $5,999	4	1.2
$6,000 to $7,999	33	10.1
$8,000 to $9,999	23	7.0
$10,000 to $12,999	43	13.1
$13,000 to $15,999	78	23.8
$16,000 to $19,999	55	16.8
$20,000 to $24,999	54	16.5
$25,000 or more	31	9.5
Missing	0	

Employment Tenure	N	Percent
Less than 30 days	2	0.6
1-3 months	3	0.9
4-11 months	37	11.3
1-3 years	108	33.0
4-5 years	60	18.3

Employment Tenure	N	Percent
6–10 years	38	20.8
11–19 years	47	14.4
20 years or more	32	9.8
Missing	0	

Current Job Tenure	N	Percent
Less than 30 days	5	1.5
1–3 months	10	3.1
4–11 months	57	17.4
1–3 years	134	41.0
4–5 years	61	18.7
6–10 years	33	10.1
11–19 years	21	6.4
20 years or more	5	1.5
Missing	1	

Hours Worked Per Week	N	Percent
30–34 hours	1	0.3
35–39 hours	3	0.9
40–44 hours	188	57.5
45–49 hours	116	35.5
50–54 hours	15	4.6
55–59 hours	2	0.6
60–64 hours	0	0
65 hours or more	0	0
Missing	2	

Overtime	N	Percent
Time and one-half	176	46.1
Straight time	38	11.6
Not paid	8	2.4
Between straight time and time and one-half	103	31.5
Missing	2	

Work Unit Branch	N	Percent
Architectural Design	1	0.3
Civil Engineering and Design	136	41.6
Electrical Engineering and Design	151	46.2
Mechanical Engineering	1	0.3
Plant Additions Design Project	1	0.3
Director's Office	27	8.3
Missing	10	

APPENDIX E: SCALES AND COMPONENT ITEMS

Scale	Items		Reliability			Correlation	
			T_1	T_2	T_3	r_{1-2}	r_{2-3}
	Perceived Personal Influence						
Influence over resources	1. Decisions about hiring people. How much say do you <u>actually</u> have in making these decisions?	C K	0.84 0.76	0.85 0.75	0.90 0.81	0.78	0.77
	2. Decisions about pay raises. How much say do you actually have in making these decisions?						
	3. Decisions about promoting people. How much say do you <u>actually</u> have in making these decisions?						
Influence over work activities	1. Decisions about changing work procedures. How much say do you <u>actually</u> have in making these decisions?	C K	0.85	0.87 0.83	0.84 0.82	0.61	0.71

C = Chattanooga
K = Knoxville
R = Reversed Scale

(continued)

213

Appendix E, continued

Scale	Items	Reliability			Correlation	
		T_1	T_2	T_3	r_{1-2}	r_{2-3}
Perceived Personal Influence						
	2. Decisions about work will be performed, the methods used, etc. How much say do you <u>actually</u> have in making these <u>decisions</u>?					
	3. Decisions about scheduling work activities. How much say do you <u>actually</u> have in making these <u>decisions</u>?					
Influence over coordination activities	1. Decisions about how work related problems are solved. How much say do you <u>actually</u> have in making these <u>decisions</u>?	C 0.83 K 0.74	0.84 0.78	0.84 0.79	0.66	0.75
	2. Decisions about how to settle disagreements between people in your branch or section. How much say do you <u>actually</u> have in making these <u>decisions</u>?					

214

3. Decisions about how work tasks will be divided up among people. How much say do you <u>actually</u> have in making these decisions?

Influence over work hours
1. Decisions about when the work day will begin and end. How much say do you <u>actually</u> have in making these decisions?

Perceived Organizational Climate

		T_1	T_2	T_3	r_{1-2}	r_{2-3}
Clarity of decision-making						
1. Deciding how you coordinate your activities with others.	C	0.72	0.74	0.80	0.60	0.53
	K	0.63	0.64	0.61		
2. Deciding whether you are promoted.						
3. Deciding to spend anything more than small amounts of money.						
Trust						
1. When management of this division says something, you can really believe that it's true.	C	0.85	0.86	0.87	0.74	0.74
	K	0.79	0.82	0.82		
2. People in this division will do anything behind your back. (R)						
3. I feel I can trust the people in this division.						

(continued)

Appendix E, continued

Scale	Items	Reliability			Correlation	
		T_1	T_2	T_3	r_{1-2}	r_{2-3}
	Perceived Organizational Climate					
	4. This division will take advantage of you if you give it a chance. (R)					
Human orientation	1. In this division, I am treated as an individual.	C 0.65	0.71	0.67	0.60	0.71
		K 0.57	0.52	0.58		
	2. This division cares more about schedules and costs than people. (R)					
Quality of communication	1. People in this division don't really talk to each other. (R)	C 0.57	0.59	0.67	0.53	0.51
		K 0.66	0.62	0.69		
	2. Communication in this organization is really good.					
Acceptance of lower level influence	1. I feel free to tell people higher up what I really think.	C 0.77	0.77	0.82	0.67	0.70
		K 0.74	0.70	0.74		
	2. Decisions are made around here without ever asking the people who have to live with them. (R)					

		T_1	T_2	T_3	r_{1-2}	r_{2-3}
3. It is hard to get people higher up in this division to listen to people at my level. (R)						
Supervisory encouragement of Participation						
1. My supervisor encourages subordinates to participate in important decisions.	C	0.82	0.82	0.81	0.52	0.67
2. My supervisor encourages people to speak up when they disagree with a decision.	K	0.78	0.75	0.77		
Perceived Effectiveness of the Quality of Work Committee						
How effective has the QWC been in:		T_1	T_2	T_3	r_{1-2}	r_{2-3}
Relationship between QWC and employees						
1. Listening to views of individuals.	C	0.80	0.82	0.83	0.31	0.73
2. Gathering information about current conditions.						
3. Keeping employees informed about the activities of the committee.						
4. To what extent (do) (did) you feel able to have your own concerns considered by the Quality of Work Committee?						
Representation of QWC						
1. Listening to the views of unions?	C	0.61	0.66	0.67	0.23	0.58

(continued)

217

Appendix E, continued

Scale	Items		Reliability			Correlation	
			T_1	T_2	T_3	r_{1-2}	r_{2-3}
Perceived Effectiveness of the Quality of Work Committee	How effective has the QWC been in:						
	2. Listening to the views of management?						
	3. Representing the interests of all groups within the division?						
Impact on Organization	1. Improving working conditions in the division?	C	0.99	0.93	0.94	0.36	0.61
	2. Improving the effectiveness of the division?						
Power of the QWC	1. Influencing important decisions in the division?	C	0.78	0.84	0.85	0.30	0.73
	2. Dealing with important rather than trivial issues?						
	3. How much power does (did) the QWC have in the division?						

	Perceived Union Effectiveness		T_1	T_2	T_3	r_{1-2}	r_{2-3}
Member Evaluation of Union	1. How satisfied are you with the success your union has in bargaining wage issues?	C	0.91	0.92	0.90	0.70	0.62
		K	0.90	0.93	0.88		

2. How satisfied are you with the amount of communication between your union and its members?

3. How satisfied are you with the success your union has in bargaining non-wage issues?

4. How satisfied are you with the union's leadership?

5. How satisfied are you with your ability to influence union decisions?

6. All in all I am very satisfied with the union.

7. Participation in union activities is worthwhile.

Union Processes

	C	K
1. Members of my union are afraid to express their real views in union meetings. (R)	0.64	0.59
2. Decisions are made in the union without ever asking the people who have to live with them. (R)	0.76	0.73
3. In the Union, everyone's opinion gets listened to.	0.84	0.75
4. In general, I like the way the union handles things.	0.59	0.65

(continued)

Appendix E, continued

Scale	Items	Reliability			Correlation	
		T_1	T_2	T_3	r_{1-2}	r_{2-3}
Union Procedures	Perceived Union Effectiveness					
	1. How satisfied are you with the way your union handles grievances?	C 0.66	0.78	0.76	0.61	0.59
		K 0.76	0.82	0.76		
	2. How satisfied are you with the way union officers are chosen?					
	3. How satisfied are you with the way issues are selected for collective bargaining?					
General Attitudes toward Unions	1. Unions protect against favoritism on the job.	C 0.67	0.64	0.73	0.57	0.53
		K 0.65	0.67	0.65		
	2. Unions improve wages and working conditions.					
	3. Unions make sure that employees are treated fairly by supervisors.					
	4. Unions interfere with good relations between employers and employees. (R)					

220

Dependent Variables		T_1	T_2	T_3	r_{1-2}	r_{2-3}
Job Satisfaction						
1. All in all, I am satisfied with my job.	C	0.69	0.77	0.76	0.56	0.59
2. In general, I like working here.	K	0.80	0.79	0.76		
Job Involvement						
1. I am very much personally involved in my work.	C	0.63	0.70	0.68	0.64	0.73
2. I live, eat, and breathe my job.	K	0.59	0.65	0.56		
3. The most important things which happen to me involve my job.						
Intention to Turnover						
1. How likely is it that you will actively look for a new job in the next year?	C	0.80	0.72	0.76	0.66	0.60
2. I often think about quitting.	K	0.80	0.76	0.77		
Internal Work Motivation						
1. I feel bad when I do a poor job.	C	0.60	0.65	0.76	0.54	0.59
2. I get a feeling of personal satisfaction from doing my job well.	K	0.62	0.63	0.55		
3. When I do my job well, I feel I've done something worthwhile.						

(continued)

221

Appendix E, continued

Scale	Items		Reliability			Correlation	
	Dependent Variables		T_1	T_2	T_3	r_{1-2}	r_{2-3}
Self-rated Performance	1. In general, do you do quite large quantities of work?	C	0.56	0.73	0.67	0.59	0.57
	2. In general, do you do quite high-quality work?	K	0.36	0.41	0.48		
Organizational Involvement	1. I don't care what happens to this division as long as I get a paycheck. (R)	C	0.71	0.74	0.82	0.57	0.66
	2. What happens to this division is really important to me.	K	0.80	0.71	0.81		
Intrinsic Reward Satisfaction (1) Personal Accomplishment	1. The chances you have to learn new things.	C	0.92	0.93	0.92	0.57	0.66
	2. The chances you have to accomplish something worthwhile.	K	0.88	0.90	0.90		

Intrinsic Reward Satisfaction (2)—Performance and Advancement

3. The chances you have to do something that makes you feel good about your-self as a person.

C	0.76	0.76	0.73	0.70	0.70
K	0.74	0.74	0.74		

1. The chances you have to do the things you do best.
2. The opportunity to develop your skills and activities.
3. Your job performance.
4. Your chances for getting a better job.

Extrinsic Reward Satisfaction

C	0.40	0.49	0.57	0.64	0.66
K	0.54	0.57	0.65		

1. Your pay.
2. Your fringe benefits.

C = Chattanooga
K = Knoxville
R = Reversed Scale

BIBLIOGRAPHY

Appley, D. G. and A. E. Winder. 1977. "An Evolving Definition of
Collaboration and Some Implications for the World of Work."
Journal of Applied Behavioral Science, 13 (3), 279-91.

Argyris, C. 1957. Personality and Organization. New York: Harper.

Bedeian, A. G., A. A. Armenakis and R. W. Gibson. 1980. "The
Measurement and Control of Beta Change." Academy of Management Review, 5, 561-66.

Beer, M. 1976. "The Technology of Organization Development." In
Dunnette, M., Handbook of Industrial and Organizational Psychology. Chicago: Rand McNally.

Beer, M. 1983. "The Politics of OD." In W. L. French, C. H. Bell,
and R. A. Zawacki, Organization Development. Plano, TX:
Business Publications, Inc.

Bowditch, J. and A. F. Buono. 1982. Quality of Work Life Assessment: A Survey-based Approach. Boston: Auburn House.

Brookshire, M. L. 1975. Collective Bargaining in the Tennessee
Valley Authority. The Salary Policy Employee Experience.
Doctoral dissertation, University of Tennessee.

Bullock, R. J., B. A. Macy and P. Mirvis. 1983. "Assessing Unions
and Union-Management Collaboration in Organizational Change."
In Seashore, S. E., E. E. Lawler, P. H. Mirvis and C.
Cammann, (eds.), Assessing Organizational Change. New
York: Wiley-Interscience.

Burns, T. and G. M. Stalker. 1961. The Management of Innovation.
London: Tavistock.

Cammann, C., M. Fichmann, G. D. Jenkins and J. Klesh. 1983.
"Assessing the Attitudes and Perceptions of Organizational
Members." In Seashore, S. E., E. E. Lawler, P. H. Mirvis
and C. Cammann, (eds.), Assessing Organizational Change.
New York: Wiley-Interscience.

Campbell, D. T. and J. C. Stanley. 1966. Experimental and Quasi-Experimental Designs for Research. Chicago: Rand McNally.

Cobb, A. J. and N. Margulies. 1983. "Organization Development: A Political Perspective. In French, W. L., C. W. Bell, and R. A. Zawacki, Organization Development. Plano, TX: Business Publications, Inc.

Coch, L. and J. R. P. French. 1948. "Overcoming Resistance to Change." Human Relations, 1, 512-32.

Cohen, J. and P. Cohen. 1975. Applied Multiple Regression/Correlation Analysis for the Behavioral Sciences. Hillside, N.J.: Lawrence Erlbaum Associates.

Cook, T. D. and D. T. Campbell. 1976. "The Design and Conduct of Quasi-Experiments and True Experiments in Field Settings." In Dunnette, M. D. (ed.), Handbook of Industrial and Organizational Psychology. Chicago: Rand McNally.

Dachler, H. P. and B. Wilpert. 1978. "Conceptual Dimensions and Boundaries of Participation in Organizations: A Critical Evaluation." Administrative Science Quarterly, 23, 1, 1-39.

Drexler, J. and E. Lawler. 1977. "A Union-Management Cooperative Project to Improve the Quality of Work Life." Journal of Applied Behavioral Science, 13, 3, 373-87.

Duckles, M. M., R. Duckles and M. Maccoby. 1977. "The Process of Change at Bolivar." Journal of Applied Behavioral Science, 13, 387-99.

Feather, J. 1978. Integrating Individuals and Structure in Organizational Research. Doctoral dissertation, University of Michigan.

French, J. R. P., J. Israel and D. As. 1960. "An Experiment on Participation in a Norwegian Factory." Human Relations, 13, 3-20.

Friedberg, J. J. 1982. "Elephants, Uranium, and The Energy Crisis." Tennessee Law Review, 49, 885-918.

Golembiewski, R. T., K Billingsley and S. Yeager. 1976. "Measuring Change and Persistence in Human Affairs: Types of Change Generated by OD Designs." Journal of Applied Behavioral Science, 12, 133-57.

Goodman, P. S. 1979. Assessing Organizational Change: The Rushton Quality of Work Experiment. New York: Wiley-Interscience.

Gordon, M. E., J. W. Philpot, R. Burt, C. A. Thompson and W. E. Spiller. 1980. "Commitment to the Union: Development of a Measure and an Examination of its Correlates." Journal of Applied Psychology, 65 (Monograph).

Guest, R. H. 1979. "Quality of Work Life: Learning from Tarrytown." Harvard Business Review, 57 (4), 76-87.

Hackman, J. R. and G. R. Oldham. 1980. Work Redesign. Reading, MA: Addison-Wesley.

Herrick, N. Q. and M. Maccoby. 1975. "Humanizing Work: Priority Goal of the 1970's." In Davis, L. E. and A. B. Cherns (eds.), The Quality of Working Life, Vol. 1, New York: The Free Press.

Hespe, G. and T. Wall. 1976. "The Demand for Participation Among Employees." Human Relations, 29, 411-28.

James, L. R. and A. P. Jones. 1974. "Organizational Climate: A Review of Theory and Research." Psychological Bulletin, 81, 1096-1112.

Janis, I. 1972. Victims of Groupthink. Boston: Houghton Mifflin.

Jelinek, M., L. Smircich and P. Hirsch. 1983. "Introduction: A Code of Many Colors." Administrative Science Quarterly, 28, 3, 331-38.

Kanter, R. M. 1982. "Dilemmas of Managing Participation." Organizational Dynamics, 11, 1, 5-27.

Katz, D. and R. L. Kahn. 1978. The Social Psychology of Organizations (2nd edition). New York: Wiley.

Kotter, J. 1980. "An Integrative Model of Organizational Dynamics." In Lawler, E. E., D. A. Nadler and C. Cammann, Organizational Assessment. New York: Wiley-Interscience.

Lawler, E. E. 1981. Pay and Organizational Development. Reading, MA: Addison-Wesley.

_____ 1980. "Adaptive Experiments." In, Lawler, E. E. III, Nadler,

D. A. and Cammann, C. (eds.), Organizational Assessment: Perspectives on the Measurement of Organizational Behavior and the Quality of Work Life. New York: Wiley-Interscience.

Lawler, E. E. III and G. E. Ledford, Jr. 1982. "Productivity and the Quality of Work Life." National Productivity Review, 1 (1), 23-36.

Lawler, E. E., D. A. Nadler and P. H. Mirvis. 1983. "Organizational Change and the Conduct of Assessment Research." In Seashore, S. E., E. E. Lawler, P. H. Mirvis and C. Cammann (eds.), Assessing Organizational Change. New York: Wiley-Interscience.

Lewin, K. 1951. Field Theory in Social Science. New York: Harper & Row.

Likert, R. 1967. The Human Organization. New York: McGraw-Hill.

____. 1961. New Patterns of Management. New York: McGraw-Hill.

Lilienthal, D. E. 1953. TVA: Democracy on the March. New York: Harper.

Linn, R. L. and J. A. Slinde. 1977. "The Determination of the Significance of Change Between Pre and Post-testing Periods." Review of Educational Research, 47, 121-50.

Lippitt, G. L. 1969. Organization Renewal. New York: Appleton-Century-Crofts.

Locke, E. A. and D. M. Schweiger. 1979. "Participation in Decision-making: One More Look." In Staw, B. M. (ed.), Research in Organizational Behavior. Greenwich, Conn.: JAI Press.

Lord, F. N. 1963. "Elementary Models for Measuring Change." In Harris, C. W. (ed.), Problems in Measuring Change. Madison: University of Wisconsin Press.

Lowin, A. 1968. "Participative Decision-making: A Model, Literature, Critique, and Prescriptions for Research." Organizational Behavior and Human Performance, 8, 68-106.

Macy, B. A. 1978. "Forces Favoring and Opposing Organizational Change: Two Case Studies." Paper presented at the American Psychological Association annual convention, Toronto, Canada.

Macy, B. A. and A. J. Nurick. 1977. "The Tennessee Valley Authority Quality of Working Life Experiment." Paper presented at Academy of Management annual meeting, Kissimmee, Florida.

Macy, B. A. and M. Peterson. 1983. "Evaluating Attitudinal Change in a Longitudinal Quality of Work Life Intervention." In Seashore, S. E., E. E. Lawler, P. H. Mirvis and C. Cammann (eds.), Assessing Organizational Change. New York: Wiley-Interscience.

Mann, F. C. and F. W. Neff. 1961. Managing Major Change in Organizations. Ann Arbor: The Foundation for Research on Human Behavior.

Marrow, A. J., D. G. Bowers and S. E. Seashore. 1967. Management by Participation. New York: Harper and Row.

McGregor, D. 1960. The Human Side of Enterprise. New York: McGraw-Hill.

Mills, T. 1975. "Human Resources—Why the New Concern?" Harvard Business Review. March/April, 127-34.

Mirvis, P. H. and S. E. Seashore. 1979. "Being Ethical in Organizational Research." American Psychologist, 34 (9), 766-80.

Moch, M., C. Cammann and R. A. Cooke. 1983. "Organizational Structure: Measuring the Distribution of Influence." In Seashore, S. E., E. E. Lawler, P. H. Mirvis and C. Cammann (eds.), Assessing Organizational Change. New York, Wiley-Interscience.

Moch, M., J. Feather and D. Fitzgibbons. 1983. "Conceptualizing and Measuring the Relational Structure in Organizations." In Seashore, S. E., E. E. Lawler, P. H. Mirvis and C. Cammann (eds.), Assessing Organizational Change. New York: Wiley-Interscience.

Morse, N. C. and E. Reimer. 1956. "The Experimental Change of a Major Organizational Variable." Journal of Abnormal and Social Psychology, 52, 120-29.

Mulder, Mauk. 1977. The Daily Power Game. Leiden: Martinus Nijhoff Social Sciences Division.

Nadler, D. A. 1980. "Role of Models in Organizational Assessment."

In Lawler, E. E., D. A. Nadler and C. Cammann (eds.), Organizational Assessment. New York: Wiley-Interscience.

Nadler, D. A. and E. E. Lawler. 1983. "Quality of Work Life: Perspectives and Directions." Organizational Dynamics, 11, 20-30.

National Center for Productivity and Quality of Work Life. 1976. Recent Initiatives in Labor-Management Cooperation. Washington.

Neuse, S. M. 1983. "TVA at Age Fifty: Reflections and Retrospect." Public Administration Review, November/December, 491-99.

Nunally, J. C. 1967. Psychometric Theory. New York: McGraw-Hill.

Nurick, A. J. 1978. The Effects of Formal Participation in Organizational Change on Individual Perceptions and Attitudes: A Longitudinal Field Study. Doctoral Dissertation, University of Tennessee.

____. 1982. "Participation in Organizational Change: A Longitudinal Field Study." Human Relations, 35, 413-30.

Owen, M. 1973. The Tennessee Valley Authority. New York: Praeger.

Patchen, M. 1970. Participation, Achievement, and Involvement on the Job. Englewood Cliffs, N.J.: Prentice-Hall.

____. 1965. "Labor-Management Consultation at TVA: Its Impact on Employees." Administrative Science Quarterly, 10, 149-74.

Perkins, D., V. Nieva and E. E. Lawler. 1983. Managing Creation: The Challenge of Building a New Organization. New York: Wiley-Interscience.

Peters, T. J. and R. H. Waterman. 1982. In Search of Excellence. New York: Harper and Row.

Pfeffer, J. 1981. Power in Organizations. Marshfield, MA: Pitman.

Powell, R. M. and J. Schlacter. 1971. "Participative Management: A Panacea?" Academy of Management Journal, 14, 165-73.

Pritchett, C. H. 1943. The Tennessee Valley Authority. Chapel Hill: University of North Carolina Press.

Rogers, M. D. 1973. Collective Bargaining in the Tennessee Valley Authority: The Trades and Labor Experience. Doctoral dissertation, University of Tennessee.

Sashkin, M. 1976. "Changing Towards Participative Approaches: A Model and Methods." Academy of Management Review, 7, 75-86.

Sathe, V. 1983. "Some Action Implications of Corporate Culture: A Manager's Guide to Action." Organizational Dynamics, 12, 4-23.

Scheflen, K., E. E. Lawler and J. R. Hackman. 1971. "Long-term Impact of Employee Participation in the Development of Pay Incentive Plans: A Field Experiment Revisited." Journal of Applied Psychology, 55, 182-86.

Schrank, R. 1983. Industrial Democracy at Sea. Cambridge, MA: MIT Press.

Seashore, S. E. 1983. "Issues in Assessing Organizational Change." In Seashore, S. E., E. E. Lawler, P. Mirvis and C. Cammann (eds.), Assessing Organizational Change. New York: Wiley.

____. 1977. "Participation in Decision-making: Some Issues of Conception, Measurement, and Interaction." Paper presented at 37th Annual Meeting, Academy of Management, Kissimmee, Florida.

Seashore, S. E., E. E. Lawler, P. Mirvis and C. Cammann (eds.). 1983. Assessing Organizational Change. New York: Wiley-Interscience.

Seashore, S. E. and P. H. Mirvis. 1983. "Doing Independent Research." In Seashore, S. E., E. E. Lawler, P. H. Mirvis and C. Cammann (eds.), Assessing Organizational Change. New York: Wiley-Interscience.

Selznick, P. 1949. TVA and the Grass Roots. Berkeley: University of California Press.

Siegel, A. L. and R. A. Ruh. 1973. "Job Involvement, Participation in Decision-making, Personal Background and Job Behavior." Organizational Behavior and Human Performance, 9, 318-27.

Smircich, L. 1983. "Concepts of Culture and Organizational Analysis." Administrative Science Quarterly, 28, 339-58.

Tannenbaum, A. S. 1968. Control in Organizations. New York: McGraw-Hill.

Taylor, F. W. 1911. The Principles of Scientific Management. New York: Harper.

Tennessee Valley Authority. 1976. The Quality of Work Program and the TVA Experiment: Vol. 1.

"The New Industrial Relations." 1981. Business Week, May 11, 85-98.

Trist, Eric. 1977. "Collaboration in Work Settings: A Personal Perspective." Journal of Applied Behavioral Science, 13 (3), 268-78.

"TVA's hard line ends years of labor peace." 1981. Business Week, September 21, 31-32.

Van de Ven, A. H. and M. A. Morgan. 1980. "A Revised Framework for Organizational Assessment." In Lawler, E. E., D. A. Nadler, and C. Cammann (eds.), Organizational Assessment. New York: Wiley-Interscience.

Van Maanen, J. 1979. "Reclaiming Qualitative Methods for Organizational Research: A Preface." Administrative Science Quarterly, 24, 4, 520-26.

Walton, R. 1983. "Critique of the Hoegh Mallard Work System." In Schrank, R., Industrial Democracy at Sea. Cambridge, MA: MIT Press.

INDEX

adaptive experiments: in field research, 93; and organizational change, 8; researchers' role in, 8

American Center of Quality of Work Life, 1, 30

American Federation of Labor (AFL), 31

assessors, impact on TVA experiment, 177-179

Association of Professional Chemists and Chemical Engineers, 31

attitude measurements, 95

authority, and power, 139

behavioral data, in TVA experiment, 96, 98

Bolivar project, 4. See also Michigan program

Branch Chiefs, QWC relationships, 146-149

Brown's Ferry, nuclear plant, 17

Business Week, 199, 200

career development, 57

Carter, J., 199

cash awards, 67

change program: adapting to unplanned changes, 70-74; chronology of, 54-57; consultants in, 46-47; feedback phase, 48-51; formal process, 51-52; implementation phase, 52-53; internal evaluation of, 74-76; phases

of, 47-48; reconnaissance phase, 48; in TVA experiment, 46-54

client, attempt to change, 60-61

collaboration: defined, 4; premise of, 3-4

collective bargaining, 31; and cooperative program, 33

committees: collaborative, 6-7; multi-tier structure, 5; success of, 6. See also Quality of Work committee

communications: quality of, 105, 216; shortcoming of, 185

consultants: departure of, 74; external, 171-174; funding of, 43; influence of, 174; objectives and philosophy, 46-47; reactions to, 85; selection of, 43, 81-83; strategies of, 161-162

control group, nonequivalent, 93

co-optation, defined, 19

cooperative conferences: guidelines for, 87; importance of, 32-34; as power centers, 78-79; revitalization of, 99-100; success of, 184

Council of Office, Technical and Service Employees Unions, 31

decision-making: clarity of, 104, 215; employee participation in, 99; in TVA experiment, 53

dependent variables: in employee participation, 124; in global

ABOUT THE AUTHOR

AARON J. NURICK (Ph. D. , University of Tennessee). With a background in Industrial/Organizational Psychology, Dr. Nurick has devoted his teaching and scholarly career to the application of behavioral science to work situations. He teaches graduate and undergraduate courses in organizational behavior, interpersonal relations, and performance appraisal, with particular emphasis on developing interpersonal competence. Dr. Nurick's research is focused on the area of organizational change. This book is the product of his association with the Quality of Work Program, a national research effort of the Institute of Social Research, University of Michigan.

His articles have appeared in Human Relations, Psychological Bulletin, and Compensation Review. He is currently studying human problems in small, high tech organizations and the psychological effects of mergers. He has made presentations at national meetings of the Academy of Management and the Institute for Management Science/ Operations Research Society of America and has conducted interpersonal growth groups and training programs on supervisory skills and decision making for both students and practicing managers. He has been a member of the Management faculty at Bentley College, Waltham, Massachusetts since 1979.

DATE DUE

8-16-91			
MAY 11 1995			